Not One Less

Critical South

The publication of this series is supported by the International Consortium of Critical Theory Programs funded by the Andrew W. Mellon Foundation.

Series editors: Natalia Brizuela and Leticia Sabsay

Leonor Arfuch, *Memory and Autobiography*
Aimé Césaire, *Resolutely Black*
Bolívar Echeverría, *Modernity and "Whiteness"*
Celso Furtado, *The Myth of Economic Development*
Eduardo Grüner, *The Haitian Revolution*
María Pia López, *Not One Less*
Pablo Oyarzun, *Doing Justice*
Néstor Perlongher, *Plebeian Prose*
Nelly Richard, *Eruptions of Memory*
Silvia Rivera Cusicanqui, *Ch'ixinakax Utxiwa*
Tendayi Sithole, *The Black Register*

Not One Less

Mourning, Disobedience and Desire

María Pia López

Translated by Frances Riddle

polity

First published in 2020 by Polity Press

Polity Press
65 Bridge Street
Cambridge CB2 1UR, UK

Polity Press
101 Station Landing
Suite 300
Medford, MA 02155, USA

ISBN-13: 978-1-5095-3191-2 hardback
ISBN-13: 978-1-5095-3192-9 paperback

A catalogue record for this book is available from the British Library.

Library of Congress Cataloging-in-Publication Data
Names: López, María Pia, 1969- author. | Riddle, Frances, translator.
Title: Not one less : mourning, disobedience and desire / María Pia López
   ; translated by Frances Riddle.
Description: Cambridge ; Medford, MA : Polity Press, 2020. | Series:
   Critical south | Includes bibliographical references and index. |
   Summary: "A first-hand account of the internationally renowned movement
   protesting against femicide and violence against women"-- Provided by
   publisher.
Identifiers: LCCN 2019057554 (print) | LCCN 2019057555 (ebook) | ISBN
   9781509531912 (hardback) | ISBN 9781509531929 (paperback) | ISBN
   9781509531943 (epub)
Subjects: LCSH: Women--Crimes against--Argentina. | Protest
   movements--Argentina. | Feminism--Argentina.
Classification: LCC HV6250.4.W65 L665 2020 (print) | LCC HV6250.4.W65
   (ebook) | DDC 362.88082/0982--dc23
LC record available at https://lccn.loc.gov/2019057554
LC ebook record available at https://lccn.loc.gov/2019057555

Typeset in 10.5 on 12pt Sabon
by Fakenham Prepress Solutions, Fakenham, Norfolk NR21 8NL
Printed and bound in Great Britain by TJ International Limited

The publisher has used its best endeavours to ensure that the URLs for external websites referred to in this book are correct and active at the time of going to press. However, the publisher has no responsibility for the websites and can make no guarantee that a site will remain live or that the content is or will remain appropriate.

Every effort has been made to trace all copyright holders, but if any have been overlooked the publisher will be pleased to include any necessary credits in any subsequent reprint or edition.

For further information on Polity, visit our website:
politybooks.com

Contents

Foreword

Natalia Brizuela and Leticia Sabsay

Scholarly interest in women's social movements is timely, given the massive demonstrations led by women internationally in opposition to the rise of the Global Right, the feminist mobilizations against anti-"gender ideology" campaigns, and the performative afterlife of #MeToo, #TimesUp and other hashtag feminist initiatives traversing borders and cultural contexts. In Europe, the Polish "Black Protests" against abortion restriction laws since 2016, the huge rallies that accompanied Ireland's vote for the legalization of abortion in 2018, or the enormous demonstrations in Spain of 8 March, which since 2017 have accompanied the International Women's Strike, have made mainstream media headlines. In the US, hundreds of thousands of women led counter-inauguration rallies across the country on 20 January 2017 protesting against the blatant misogyny of the new president and the foreseeable attacks on already fragile reproductive rights. To this "lean in" feminism, an intersectional collective responded with a call to a "feminism for the 99 percent" on International Women's Day. These experiences, among others, have greatly contributed to a renewed receptivity to feminist topics and theories by non-specialized publishers and journals. In this context, authors writing about the contemporary forms in which feminist ideals and tropes have been captured and neutralized called attention to the challenges raised by the renewed appeal of feminism and re-encountered some new hopes as well.[1]

This growing feminist trend has also provided an opportunity for women's movements and feminisms from the Global South to acquire a new visibility and, to some extent, a long overdue acknowledgment of their contributions. Visibility is, however, a tricky business, since the terms in which it emerges are never entirely straightforward. More often than not, neither those social movements to which some visibility is granted nor their (often self-instituted) spokespersons are in an easy position to set the terms. The false notion that the transnational feminist movement is some brand-new phenomenon, dating back to the last three to five years, speaks to a temporal framing shaped by a blind (and in many cases irritatingly white!) English-speaking gaze from the Global North. Such temporality belongs to, and relies on, a politics of ignorance furthered by academia and publishers alike. To give but one example, Fraser's recent discovery of the potentiality of a popular feminist future sits in stark contrast to her sustained dismissal of decades of black, postcolonial and subaltern feminist work.[2]

The reframing of a social movement, rendering it more or less visible or intelligible, is often marked by the social conditions that obscured the movement in the first place. The fact that such a tension is inevitable does not mean that it is not productive or that it cannot be reworked in ways that disrupt dominant logics of knowledge production and hegemonic narratives. And this is precisely the kind of work done by María Pia López's book.

Not One Less: Mourning, Disobedience and Desire tells one of the possible stories of Not One Less – the Argentinean women's movement that emerged in 2015. To Latin American feminists and Spanish-language readers more broadly, López is recognized as one of the key activists and chroniclers at the heart of what quickly became a widespread movement. Through a first-person narrative, *Not One Less* offers an account of the formative years of that movement as experienced by the author. Through this first-person voice, López masters the embodied writing for which many feminists have advocated. The author embraces two distinct roles, crafting a *plural-singular voice*: on the one hand, the body acting as part of a collective in the heat of every battle and, on the other hand, the meditative scholarly voice of the intellectual.

Not One Less emerged in Argentina as a collective affirmation of life and bodily presence in the face of a rampant increase in brutal murders and gender violence. In late March 2015 a small group of feminist activists and writers, María Pia López among them, organized a reading marathon with the slogan "Not One Less" at the National Library in Buenos Aires. At that time López was the director of the National Library's Museo del Libro y de La Lengua (Museum of the Book and Language). This reading marathon was not the first public event that linked politics, performance and collective outrage. In April 2014 a reading marathon had been organized in support of the national campaign for free, legal and safe abortion. The 2015 event was called to make femicide and gender-based violence a matter of public concern, and the large crowd that gathered for the mourning of individual deaths through a collective performance set the stage for the years ahead and, more specifically, became ground zero for the call to take to the streets to protest the systemic war being raged against feminized bodies.

On 10 May 2015 a hashtag went viral: #NotOneLess. We want to be alive. 3 June, 5 pm. The message brought together, under a single slogan, a polyphonic multitude and a long anti-patriarchal, anti-colonial and anti-capitalist feminist genealogy. The collective scream of "Not One Less" was a reaction to the growing number of brutal murders and forced disappearances of cis and trans women that had risen exponentially to such dramatic proportions that, on average, by 2015 in Argentina, one woman was murdered every day. To the extent that femicide had become an epidemic ignored by the state, Not One Less began to articulate, on the one hand, a transversal fight against gender-based attacks and, on the other hand, a counter-hegemony against myriad forms of state-sponsored violence and neglect.[3] The 2015 hashtag has now become a collective with chapters throughout Argentina and beyond and has established alliances of solidarity with other collectives and labor unions relating gender-based violence to race, class and labor. These alliances have articulated a heterogeneous spectrum of demands. As an example, the second Not One Less march in June 2016 brought forth demands both for the decriminalization of abortion and an end to transphobia and for the rights of sex workers.

This heterogeneity is reflected in María Pia López's crafting of a *plural-singular voice*, where the sensory, the scholarly and the activist have merged through decades of writing as both a scholar and a public intellectual. Since the late 1990s she has authored academic texts as well as novels and essays. A professor, a researcher, a writer and a militant, López has been pushing the boundaries of academic writing for the last two decades. In *Not One Less*, her activist research structures the fluctuation between genres and authorial voices. As she asks in the Introduction:

> Can a person write as an activist and as a theorist and critic at the same time? Is agitation so as to question people's wills and organize antagonistic to the analysis of obstacles and limits? It would be considered conflictive from the traditional conception of knowledge, where supposed objectivity overlooks the practical, historic and political conditions in which the very questions being studied here emerged. On the other hand, exposing these conditions, situating the questions to be answered among an archipelago of mobilizations and practical dilemmas, shows us that our words are always dependent on others' words, our bodies and existences entwined with those of others.[4]

In fact, López's voice is more than her own; it depends on a plurality of voices with which hers is entangled. It is an assemblage, but no less singular for that reason.[5] Or, said otherwise, it can be singular precisely because it is an assemblage.

This book is not alone. It lives in company with the contemporary writings of feminist voices from Abya Yala to India, moving through Italy, Spain and France and back to Argentina.[6] It is also in conversation with other insufficiently acknowledged voices, such as when López discusses the feminist strike in dialogue with the nineteenth-century French-Peruvian feminist and socialist Flora Tristan – a figure somehow overshadowed by the canonical name of Mary Wollstonecraft.

Honoring the transversal and transnational soul and history of Not One Less, the movement for which it is named, *Not One Less* is in dialogue with, and contributes to the construction of, a collective "live memory, capable of continuing to produce unforeseeable meanings and territories," as Virginia Cano and Laura Fernández Cordero put it. As they rightly remark, depriving this feminist revolt of an account of the "minoritarian genealogy of women's, feminist and LGBTQI social movements," as well as the sedimented memory of other radical mobilizations for social justice (such as the movement that emerged in Argentina immediately after the 2001 financial crisis), not only diminishes the success of Not One Less but also devalues its significance. And it entails surrendering to a sustained patriarchal and neoliberal effort to erase these insurgencies, both materially and symbolically.[7] As López makes clear in this book, the transformative meanings opened up by Not One Less are possible to the extent that disobedience has a history – in fact many histories – and it is the performative afterlife of those disobediences that provides each iteration with an overdetermined and therefore incalculable strength. She states:

> The mobilizations of women are ceremonies of creation and transmission; they affirm belonging to an identity in construction, something new that would not have been possible in the past. They seek reaffirmation through ritual. No one was born into this community (as one is born into rites and liturgies of national identity), because the community is built through the very act of public appearance. Every action may live on as citation, as a ritual.[8]

Surely, the force of this community, ever in formation, carries, over the reverberations of symbolically charged public spheres, political words and claims such as "diss-appearance" and "the right to identity," as well as objects and rituals such the use of scarves, all practiced by historic and contemporary struggles. The May 2015 hashtag called for demonstrations in the major public squares and plazas in Argentina. Those in the city of Buenos Aires assembled in the Plaza del Congreso, where a set of demands were "delivered" to the state legislature, which had failed to address the disappearances properly. In April 1977, during the first years of the military dictatorship that ruled Argentina between 1976 and 1983, a group of fourteen women had come together in another highly symbolic public plaza in Buenos Aires, demanding the appearance of their forcibly disappeared children and grandchildren. The Mothers of Plaza de Mayo made their demand in public outside the federal government building, at the time a symbolic site of the suspension of democracy. As López reminds us in her account, both in their manifestos and in their public actions and performances, the women of Not One Less established a relationship with the Mothers of Plaza de Mayo as a gesture of alliance and solidarity against "dictating who may live and who must die," making evident the necropolitics at the heart of power.[9] Establishing a relationship between the disappearances under military rule and the disappearances under democratic government also made visible the relationships between state and market violence. The Mothers of Plaza de Mayo embroidered the names of their disappeared onto head scarves, alongside the demand "We want them back alive." Not One Less demanded: "We want ourselves alive." The demands and voices of the Mothers were reactivated as Not One Less recognized the long history of female-led struggles against government-sponsored violence.

Furthermore, as López suggests, the force of this emerging movement and its capacity for organization would probably have been unsustainable without the previous experience of many of their protagonists in popular, LGBT, HIV and cultural activism. Nor would its capacity to grow have been possible were it not thanks to the experience amassed by the feminist movement over decades of National Women's Assemblies and the National Campaign for the Right to Legal, Safe and Free Abortion.

Not One Less traces a genealogy that transcends national borders and insists on transnational solidarities because the structures that safeguard the long histories of violence against women's bodies are themselves transnational. The Argentine movement has produced its mobilizing calls by quoting Mexican activists, scholars and writers in particular. Its name is a Mexican slogan that had been crucial in what was probably the first femicide epidemic in the Americas under neoliberal rule. The slogan "Not one woman less, not one more death" had been written in 1995 by Susana Chávez Castillo, a Mexican poet and activist, as part of a poem that reflected on the femicides taking place in Ciudad Juárez, Chihuahua. As the NAFTA agreement between the US, Mexico and Canada strengthened neoliberal measures, a series of femicides broke out in the Mexican border town of Ciudad Juárez. The first faint news of the disappearance of fifty women dated to late 1993, as the first *maquilas* or sweatshops for US clothes companies were set up in Mexico in order to increase profits. By the end of the 1990s the number of disappearances had grown close to one thousand women. Even though the Mexican legal apparatus was put to work, the crimes were never resolved, and they remain largely unpunished. Susana Chávez Castillo was murdered in Juárez in 2011. The Argentine movement's name is an elegy to the memory of a prominent and fearless poet and activist and the identification of a political and economic problem as, at the very least, hemispheric.

The 2015 Not One Less strike also quoted the demand to the Mexican state that emerged after the disappearance of the forty-three students in Ayotzinapa in 2014. That slogan read "The government is responsible," to which Not One Less added "We want ourselves alive." Months before, in July 2014, the Mexican feminist collective Mujeres Grabando Resistencias (Women Carving Resistance) began an international graphic campaign through their webpage around the hashtag #WeWantOurselvesAlive. They created seventeen artworks, which they distributed via Facebook and feminist organizations throughout Mexico, Latin America and Europe, to be printed and used for political activities in public spaces. In February 2015 they issued a second call with #WeWantOurselvesAlive. The Argentine collective also borrowed from Mexican feminists the phrase "If my life has no value, produce without me." The second call for a massive strike coincided with the inauguration of Mauricio Macri's neoliberal government, and the dramatic austerity cuts that it brought, particularly in the removal of subsidies for services such as electricity, water and gas. That is why in the second call for a mass mobilization in Argentina in June 2016 the slogan was "The government is responsible," politicizing the Not One Less demand. Once again, victimization was not an option.

The initial agenda of the mobilizations for bottom-up gender justice, called for a strike on October 2016 in alliance with fifty other organizations. Violence and economic rights were articulated by this broad coalition, which denounced the "democratically elected" government as responsible. The government is responsible, if my life has no value, produce without me. The call for that strike happened in an open assembly of the Confederation of Workers of the Popular Economy. Unions, collectives and political parties articulated the structural relationship between femicides and economic factors: 76 percent of unpaid domestic work is done by women; the tasks associated with the many forms of caretaking expose women to a more extreme form of labor precarity; in precarious jobs the gender pay gap between men and women is 40 percent; 20 per cent of women in employment are engaged in domestic work. This work is essential to the economy yet remains formally outside it. One of the speeches read during the march stated that femicide revealed "the most extreme expression of patriarchal logic, one that subjugates, objectifies and undervalues women across all spheres of life." Femicide brought them together, with a clear understanding that gender violence is a structural issue, determined largely by economic forces, as López remarks.

In the first pages of chapter 1, "Mourning: All Victims Count," López asserts:

> Not One Less is the outcry against a growing horror: it says that lives matter and that every body counts ... their stories should be recounted. Justice for these wasted lives is also narrative; it implies extracting them from the patriarchal discursive mechanisms that resound in the mass media and in courtrooms .... Faced with this reality, we have tried to ... use words as defense against violence; to commemorate the dead women in a kind of public act of mourning.
> ... The manifesto maintains that there is no substitution, no metaphorical representation where death is concerned, but that there must necessarily be a painstaking construction of common foundation, through acknowledgement of what has been lost.[10]

These reflections emerge from what has been the politics of mourning in the Not One Less movement from the very beginning. Woven into these words, López offers us a first-person chronicle of one of the first public vigils held by Not One less before the collective was fully formed, on 26 March 2015. Since then, López tells us, the movement has been working to transform grief into collective strength. In their narratives, their manifesto, their actions, the women have channeled public mourning into concrete demands. Claiming – or, indeed, performatively enacting – the right to grieve and be grieved, they reclaim the lives of those who were lost, fighting so that their names should not be further erased. Seen in this light, this haunting "ecology of death," to take Kashif Jerome Powell's powerful image, poses an ethical-political demand that has been taken up by Not One Less in a call that cannot be ignored. Not One Less transforms the work of mourning through collective affirmation of another possible life, a life where gender, poverty or marginalization would not entail fewer chances to live, and live well.[11]

Even though Not One Less is a response to the injury inflicted on bodies forced into universal categories created for the exercise of modern biopower and capitalism – gender, class and race – the mobilizations have always been in protest against the disappearance of particular bodies. Not One Less came together in

2015 and 2016 after the horrific murder of Chiara Paez and Lucía Pérez. In the collective's successive alliances with workers affected by massive layoffs, and with indigenous communities attacked because of their demands for land, they were again rallying for specific persons – the PepsiCo workers and Santiago Maldonado. All of the major mobilizations held by Not One Less have been organized around individuals.

This is also true of the Black Lives Matter movement, where the murder of particular black individuals at the hands of the police spurred the street protests that started in 2014, when the numbers and systematic racialized killings had reached a limit of unbearable proportions: Oscar Grant, Trayvon Martin, Michael Brown, Eric Garner, John Crawford, Tamir Rice, Walter Scott, Freddie Gray. Of the many points in common between Not One Less and Black Lives Matter, with the right to life at the center of both movements, is this galvanizing force of the singular name.

The singular name operates as the exact opposite of the individual subject who competes to be the most productive in the fast-paced pursuit of success imposed on us by our neoliberal times.

Perhaps echoing this ethical-political demand, Not One Less emerges as the name for the construction of a popular feminist social movement. In López's view, this is enacted partly through its capacity to establish alliances with other popular movements, "of finding truth in other struggles"[12] – hence not only its intersectional but also its transversal impulse. To talk about alliances here is essential to counter commonly held beliefs and presumptions about how struggles are to be played out. If a number of alliances have been possible, this is in large part because of the disobedient character of Not One Less, making its presence public, and in so doing disputing the public sphere as a space that emerges only in protest, contesting the conventional definition of strike or assembly.

Disobeying not only the patriarchal canon but also the normative definitions of gender that restrict the category "woman" to a dated binary logic, as well as hierarchical classifications that assign differential value to multiple "women" based on racial, cultural, national, class-laden, religious or moral factors, Not One Less calls, as López suggests, for new political subjectivities to emerge.

At the center of today's popular uprisings, straining against all forms of containment are bodies performing multiple, heterogeneous modes of agency, acting up, fighting back, demanding visibility, recognition, justice, self-identification, territory, infrastructure. In many of the most recent popular mobilizations these demands have a force that is both centrifugal and centripetal: the demand for the right to livable lives. These bodies claim an agency emboldened and strengthened through political and affective solidarity, never through victimization. These are bodies in resistance, bodies of resistance, pressing against the precarization of life in these neoliberal times. In their resistance they are not submissive: these are rebellious bodies that will not submit. They are expansive and they are incommensurable.

As Foucault and many others have argued, one of the crucial aspects of the political project of modernity can be summarized as the distinction between reason and unreason in order to delimit those who, as "fully moral agents," exercise reason in the institutional, limited, closed-off and constrained sphere of society and politics. This is the logic of biopower, biopolitics. As Mbembe has shown in his reading and discussion of Foucault in light of present-day global politics (and Palestine in particular), maximum destruction of persons and the creation of what he calls *death-worlds* are new and unique forms of social existence for vast subjected populations.[13] Speaking about the potency of Not One Less, the writer and activist Marta Dillon said: "We convert death into pure life, pure desire. "[14] Not One Less is a form of collective agency and collective subjectivity that resists the *raison d'état*, biopolitics and necropolitics, through the body. Not One Less mobilizes forms of life that proliferate, as Verónica Gago has argued, reorganizing the notions of freedom and obedience, projecting what she calls a "new rationality and collective affect."[15] To borrow Gago's term, Not One Less operates on the basis of a "persevering vitalism" that aims to safeguard the expansion of liberties, joy, pleasure and affects. Are there political forms that could keep up with these bodies?

It is precisely the life-force of these bodies that López conceives of as desire. This is a vitalist vision of desire that, according to López, allows us to see the ways in which Not One Less opposes a restricted understanding of politics. These bodies, these movements, and this plural writing, which includes López's voice, may well disrupt the way we understand the transnational women's revolt of recent years. While this is articulated from the Global South, these notions are not for that reason local. And neither is this book, which demands that we revisit what we think we already know about feminist embodiments and invites us to reimagine feminist potentialities in the midst of uncertainty.

Introduction: The Tide

Vision ceases to be solipsistic only up close, when the other turns back upon me the luminous rays in which I had caught him, renders precise that corporeal adhesion of which I had a presentiment in the agile movement of his eyes ...

> Maurice Merleau-Ponty, *The Visible and the Invisible*

... this encountered richness is infinite.

> Tununa Mercado

"Here, no one is dispensable," Nora Cortiñas said before hundreds of thousands of demonstrators on 8 March 2018. This sentence condenses a movement, a political commitment, an ethical proposal. The previous year we'd marveled at the massive march of women in protest of the conservative offensive led by Trump. The 8 March movements in fifty-five countries converged to become the first ever international women's strike. An army of women participated in the liberation of Raqqa, the capital of the Islamic State; and Brazil's female president was ousted by a coup. In Mexico, the Neo-Zapatista party launched a presidential campaign led by Marichuy, a traditional Nahuatl medicine woman. A large part of the huge country of Brazil was traversed by the Black Women's March. Marielle Franco, black councilwoman and favela activist, was assassinated in Rio de

Janeiro, becoming a symbol for these contemporary struggles. In Argentina a wave of massive, popular and intersectional feminism has repeatedly flooded the streets since 3 June 2015, when it marched under the slogan "Not one less." On 13 June 2018 hundreds of thousands of protesters, the majority young women, camped outside the National Congress in Buenos Aires to demand legalization of abortion. This surging tide is international and polyglot. It is capable of reinventing and transforming itself. Hydra of a thousand heads, a new political subject, a menacing force, an enigma to be solved, a challenge for our insomniac intellectuals and politicians.

Womanhood is not a biological trait but a site of political articulation: a name given to a multitude of existences that go beyond the traditional construction of the gender called woman to construct themselves as lesbians, *travestis*, transsexuals, transgender or more broadly trans*. "One is not born, but rather becomes, a woman," as Simone de Beauvoir wrote, although some feminists maintain gender essentialist strategies for establishing another order within the sensibilities historically attributed to feminine bodies. Essentialism does not serve as the basis for this book, nor does it match the experiences narrated herein. This practical and theoretical review affirms the historicity of "women" as a political subject and takes it as a category established by the social and discursive order. The political deconstruction of our bodies is at the same time a politics constructed from our bodies.

The subject of contemporary feminism is built on the recognition of gender and at the same time questions existing genders and its patterns of regulation of behavior. It overlaps with the materiality of trans feminism, which banishes any naturalizing meaning. Feminism today ranges from strategic essentialism to the surging demand for political recognition of socially available identities. Perhaps, like Marx's proletariat, feminism may be able to conceive of its own redemption only through a complete transformation of the social order.

There is not one feminism but a plurality of feminisms. Heterogeneous and conflicting. With distinct emphases and propositions. In modern-day Argentina, they converge in shared organizational goals. The writing of this book coincides with assemblies to organize the 8 March women's strike in Buenos Aires and as meetings held by the Not One Less collective draw over a thousand people every Friday. It is an unprecedented and powerful experience of organization across many sectors, with regulated speaking time and precise planning with a festive tone. It offers a break from everyday life, as the assemblies and meetings have an atmosphere of celebration, of change, feeling the women's strike like a tingling in our bodies. As I write, I hear the speakers, I see my colleagues, and we are dazzled by this coming together, from such diverse backgrounds, to create something new. What it will turn out to be we do not yet know.

Within the feminist revolution there are various rebellions. Breaking the glass ceiling and having our hands free for the battle of equals is not the only goal, nor do our dreams stop at merit without distinction of gender. Already underway are egalitarian and heterodox insurrections that see in feminism a contemporary means of communism – a communism that does not shy away from a radical rejection of patriarchal sexism – and these diverse ideas are woven into the design of a new fraternity, like a crowded tenement building, like the complex composition of existence. There are strains of feminism that draw on collective intelligence, understanding that the emancipation of women cannot be limited to the few, to the white or the rich. Adjectives swirl: intersectional feminism emphasizes the crisscrossed network of issues related to gender, race, class; popular feminism challenges the neoliberal translation of the movement.

This book is part of the tide. A fold. Conceived of and written in parallel to activism in the Not One Less collective and the experience of public mobilizations in the streets over recent years. It is part record and chronicle of events. But, fundamentally, it is an attempt to distill from these events some reflection that can be systematized and debated, opened up for discussion. Can a person write as an activist and as a theorist and critic at the same time? Is agitation so as to question people's wills and organize antagonistic to the analysis of obstacles and limits? It would be considered conflictive from the traditional conception of knowledge, where supposed objectivity overlooks the practical, historic and political conditions in which the very questions being studied here emerged. On the other hand, exposing these conditions, situating the questions to be answered among an archipelago of mobilizations and practical dilemmas, shows us that our words are always dependent on others' words, our bodies and existences entwined with those of others.

Far from having any illusions of full individual autonomy, my theories are in dialogue with the collective in which I have participated from 2015 up to the present. Rejecting the notion of the mind as separate from the body, conceptual and abstract, I write from sensory experience, from the memories of humiliations and harm, the euphoria of a massive gathering, the power of the occupation of a street, the challenge of conflicting organizational practices. My intention is not to project new images of comfortable plenitude but to contemplate the concepts and ideas that have been sparked by the mobilization of women in order to determine what they might tell us about our times, about neoliberalism and about power. To reflect on what we are doing, what is being achieved by this vast and heterogeneous movement, through its public demonstrations and its words.

The site of enunciation is complex. I write as a sociologist, essayist, novelist and activist who began to identify as a feminist on the streets only in 2015. I write also as a member of a feminist collective that shares a name with the greatest mobilization of women in the history of Argentina: Not One Less. The public demonstration is separate from the collective. We are no more heiresses and agents of that mobilization than any other activists. But we declare ourselves committed to its founding ideals. If the street is happily heterogeneous and multiple, if it unfolds diverse languages and tensions, so too the collective must avoid being univocal. Detailed herein is one singular intervention in a land of multiplicities, on a terrain of untested practice and disparate discussions.

The narration of this experience does not ignore the fact that in it the experiences of many forms of feminism in Argentina sediment: from the suffragist pioneers of the early twentieth century to the insurgent militants of the 1970s, from the organizers of the renters' strike to the women who took the factories in the chaotic Córdoba of 1969, the female writers who were brave enough to sign their texts and the tenacious activists who organized the national campaign for the right to abortion, from the journalists who created the first feminist publications to those who led the movements of the unemployed, from the *travestis* who demanded rights to the mothers of "the disappeared" who reinvented motherhood. All of these experiences in some way flow into the multifaceted experience of contemporary feminists in Argentina. They cannot be erased or made to disappear; they are woven into the massive public demonstrations we have witnessed in the streets over the past few years.

"Not one less" is a shared slogan that resonates with a wide range of women from different generations and social classes. The phrase expresses a common horizon that unites diverse groups; it is the name taken by the collective established to organize the first of the demonstrations and was instrumental in setting up the following ones. In 2016, during one of the many territorial disputes in Greater Buenos Aires, existing occupants disputed with a new group who employed violent practices. The local government didn't want to get involved. In a meeting, an activist from the Greater Buenos Aires collective told the local Secretary of Security that they were part of Not One Less, which had already organized two strikes. The tone quickly changed. Behind the small group was a national and international force, implicit but well known. Days later, a meeting was held among feminist groups in the area to discuss the conflict. In the round of introductions, each woman declared her dual membership: to a specific collective and to Not One Less. The phrase is at once essential to our times and a point of unity for Argentine feminisms.

Contemporary neoliberal governance appeals to emotion; it places individual experience at its center and constructs its dominion on the basis of agitated feelings. In contrast to modern modes of government, aimed at a supposedly contemplative public, the new right wing distances itself from political rationality. The old illusion of ideas without a body, of spiritual life prevailing over the corporal, is reversed by the notion of a body without ideas, of pure sensitivity, bare life, an existence without qualities. But this emotional life held up as the opposite of rationality is a damaged life, stripped bare, turned into a marketing device. They invoke the joy of living – wrote Adorno[1] – as the antechamber to the slaughterhouse.

Certain strands of feminism could be written off as "purple marketing" or as part of the model that appeals to the emotional, but at the same time they have the power to subvert the established order. They are able to do so because they are wise to these emotional appeals and understand both abstract words and pure rationality as inventions that legitimize an unequal order. The contrast of private–public, body–reason, reproduction–production, feeling–ideas, as they are articulated in modernity, condemns women to subordination and the systematic exploitation of their strengths upon tasking them with the socially necessary but habitually unpaid domestic work of reproduction and carework. Discussion on sexist exploitation aims at overturning these underlying axioms. That the new right wing appeals to the primacy of emotion should not erase this critical genealogy.

Writing this book has a political objective: to further understand the actions and achievements of contemporary feminism; to impede the conservative appropriation and stop the work being done from devolving into something purely ornamental; to describe the powerful process of constructing a feminist political subject. We are witnessing the dawn of feminism in real time, hearing the questions it poses and seeing the disobedience it incites. Bearing witness to the dawning of this movement turns the story we write into a story about ourselves. A girl cries inconsolably at school. She is referred to a social worker. The girl is too upset to speak, until finally she says: Not One Less happened to me. The phrase provides a starting point for reporting sexual abuse in the home. Another girl speaks with her grandmother. She is eight years old and asks about a lesbian couple. She is surprised to learn that this kind of relationship could only recently be expressed publicly. She ventures an interpretation: now they can show it because Not One Less is here to defend all the rights of women.

What is this phenomenon, encapsulated in a single phrase, which has become password and symbol, common code, filled with multiple meanings, tool employed by diverse political constructions, contested territory? A movement is occurring which, as we say in the assemblies, has no boss, no leader, no owner. Nor does it have one singular or legitimate interpretation. The pages that follow are an attempt to contribute to the discussion on how to conceptualize this movement and also an attempt to gather some "strands of thread" with which to weave our political imagination.

1

Mourning: All Victims Count

I'm not the woman in the bag. That's why I'm here, standing before you, reading this text and breathing in all our pain, our struggle and our hope.

Marta Dillon and Virginia Cano

I don't want to leave her alone. I want my book to be phosphorescence, the trail of sequins and laughter she left in the air one summer afternoon, a wake of words that express her grace and her elegance, as well as her spelling mistakes, her defenselessness and her tragedy, as well as her Facebook selfies and her karaoke nights at Le Girafon.

Iván Jablonka

The body as rubbish

On 25 August 2014, Melina Romero was found in a rubbish bag, murdered. The country's largest newspaper called her "a party girl who dropped out of high school." A year earlier, on 10 June 2013, the body of Ángeles Rawson was discovered in a black bag. On 28 December 2014 Lola Chomnalez was murdered in Valizas, where she'd gone on holiday. Daiana García was nineteen and was forcibly disappeared on her way to a job interview. Her half-naked body was found in a rubbish bag on 16 March 2015. A group of activists carried out a street performance to raise awareness of the string of murders. Some writers and journalists held a reading marathon in the Argentine National Library's Museum of the Book and Language.

The feminist writer María Moreno wrote a kind of manifesto, which said:

> we are all the woman in the bag, and we are coming out of it so that there will be not one less. ... And the rubbish? Taking it out implies banishing from the home the leftovers of productive life. When rubbish bags first appeared, the object shifted from the space that feminism called invisible work to part of the building supervisor's work equipment; the murderer's toolkit today includes the rubbish bag and the dumpster, the sewer and the manhole, where practicality reveals a semiotic horror: women are rubbish.[1]

The reaping has not stopped: the lives of young women are repeatedly harvested, from diverse social classes, and converted into sacrificial victims. The hands of the murderers say that the bodies of women and *travestis* are rubbish, waste, leftovers. I've named just a few women, but we must remember that the statistics compiled by several social organizations, at the start of 2015, estimated one femicide every thirty hours.[2]

Not One Less is the outcry against a growing horror: it says that lives matter and that every body counts, should be valued, counted – one of the movement's initial demands was the creation of a public register of femicide – but also that their stories should be recounted. Justice for these wasted lives is also narrative; it implies extracting them from the patriarchal discursive mechanisms that resound in the mass media and in courtrooms, dissecting the victims and not the system or the criminal logic. Faced with this reality, we have tried to produce a narrative and create meaning; to use words as defense against violence; to commemorate the dead women in a kind of public act of mourning.

The speech was controversial; it sparked interpretative disputes. Marta Dillon and Virginia Cano shouted, during a protest that lasted all night, "I'm not the woman in the bag. That's why I'm here, before you. That's why I'm here, standing before you, reading this text and breathing in all our pain, our struggle, and our hope." This shift challenges various means of representing the murdered women, even the drawing of portraits. The manifesto maintains that there is no substitution, no metaphorical representation where death is concerned, but that there must necessarily be a painstaking construction of common foundation, through acknowledgment of what has been lost. Every body counts because it is irreplaceable and death is irreversible. Those of us who are still living may mourn, but we cannot put ourselves in the wretched place of the murdered women. We may identify commonalities in our mutual vulnerability, in the fragility that puts us at risk, and in our empathy for the victims. And upon doing so we inscribe that act in a singular historicity.

The reading marathon took speech as the generator of a collective narrative – the retelling around the bonfire, words circulated and absorbed, creating feelings of recognition or sparking dissent – debating the association between body and rubbish. A group of people decided to take a literal interpretation of the murderers' equipment to declare that we are not disposable. If the murderer uses signs that must be interpreted (as maintained by Rita Segato: femicide violence is expressive),[3] the response is the resistant circulation of other signs and the controversy, among the activists themselves, over the meanings at play.

The second demonstration was extraordinarily massive. On 3 June 2015 hundreds of thousands of people mobilized in the plazas outside of Argentina's Congress and in over thirty cities across Argentina, united by the message "Not one less." The first speech declared femicide to be a "political category, a word that denounces the mode in which society naturalizes something unnatural: sexist violence. And sexist violence is a Human Rights issue."

The polemical nature of this statement should not be overlooked: femicide is not merely a public safety issue to be dealt with using the logic of punishment and prison sentences. It is the bloodiest expression of patriarchal control, which assigns each person a position and a normative definition and kills those who do not comply. Upon stating that this is a human rights issue, the movement establishes a genealogy in which the Mothers and Grandmothers of Plaza de Mayo figure as the central node. Both movements draw nourishment from the practice of public mourning.

Between human rights and public safety: the social archive

The present is always jumbled: it implies distinct temporalities; it inherits multiple strands. The circumstances in which Not One Less emerged have a diverse historicity, with legacies from the women's movement and the activists for sexual diversity, certainly. But I will first address not that legacy but another that may seem further removed and yet is essential to thinking on how the movement arose and what it rails against, linking various issues on an unprecedented scale. It creates meaning in dialogue with other movements and with pre-existing struggles. To understand it requires delimiting this zone of emergence, since its character is relational and its meaning is constructed through affinity and antagonism with other movements.

In 1983, democracy was re-established in Argentina after years of state-sponsored terrorism that, starting in 1976, murdered tens of thousands of persons in concentration camps after submitting them to torture and brutality. The corpses were hidden, producing the specter of the detained-disappeared. The search for a forcibly disappeared person began as soon as they were kidnapped. The families and friends made the rounds of police stations, courts, churches, barracks, in search of information. The mothers of the forcibly disappeared began to organize one year after the military coup, demanding the return of their missing daughters and sons. They invented powerful and foundational protest methods. They met one day of every week – and still meet every Thursday – to protest together. When a "circulation ordinance" was passed in an attempt to disperse them, they began to walk in circles as they protested. To identify themselves, they wore on their heads white scarves that alluded to the diapers in which they'd dressed their lost children as babies. These women stood up to a terrifying dictatorship. Some of the mothers were themselves kidnapped and murdered, as their daughters and sons had been before them. Many were housewives, some were professionals or professors, but only a handful had prior experience in political activism. They were born as activists in the search for their children. Shortly after the mothers organized, they were joined by other women with missing granddaughters and grandsons whom they knew had been born in prison or who were also missing. The Mothers and Grandmothers led this desperate and sleepless struggle, breaking the pact of silence that society had made with the military dictatorship.

Like Antigone, they couldn't let their dead go unburied. They went even further: in the face of the unknown status of their detained-disappeared loved ones, they demanded that they be returned alive. The most emblematic general of the genocide said in 1979: "It's a mystery, it's a disappearance, there is no entity ... dead or alive, they have disappeared." The Mothers responded with their turns around Buenos Aires's main square, the political heart of the country. They were firm in their demand – "They were taken alive, we want them back alive" – even though the magnitude of the massacre and the scant number of survivors was common knowledge. Their message underscored the incommensurability of their loss. No identification of bodies, no compensation, no trial, no punishment would be enough, even if all that were possible.

These movements led by women were based on the notion that only in keeping the memory of past criminal injustice alive could we face the injustices of the present. They never stopped translating and updating their struggles to each new present, always sympathetic to new forms of suffering. In the absence of a body to mourn in private, they made their mourning public. Every Thursday of every week of every month of every year. More than four decades. This mourning included all mothers (and they mourned not only their own children), socializing maternity, demanding justice, not vengeance. They never asked for the murderers to suffer as the victims had suffered and they upheld an ethical standard that made it possible to establish the new Argentine democracy that defended the principles of human rights. In 1983, the majority of the population and political representatives supported democracy over the military dictatorship. The Never Again movement, decrying government terrorism, was key to the restitution of legitimate power. *Never Again*[4] was the title of a compilation of reports from survivors of the clandestine detention centers and relatives of the forcibly disappeared. It was an attempt to reconstruct what had happened and produce an understanding of events. It stirred controversy through seeming to configure resistant violence as equal to government terrorism; but, even with the publication's limits and controversies, it sparked a movement that, in a kind of implicit pact, emerged during the trials of the military leaders. In the 1990s the trials were suspended and the military leaders pardoned.

In 2003, after a devastating social crisis that left political institutions destroyed, Néstor Kirchner assumed the presidency. He met with the Mothers and Grandmothers of Plaza de Mayo and made many commitments. He ordered the portraits of the condemned military leaders removed from the presidential gallery and offered an apology on behalf of the government for the crimes committed in the concentration camps. He decreed that social protest could not be criminalized. The "human rights" movement played a dual role: demanding justice for past crimes and upholding the memory of what should never again occur. Meanwhile, society was being shaken by new violence, surging from economic exclusion, social inequality, the widening of zones of exclusion, and illegal economies that often included corrupt police and hopeless youth. The deindustrialization and emptying out of public institutions in the preceding decade had created a pressure cooker. A year after Kirchner took office, a young man named Axel Blumberg was kidnapped and murdered. More than 150,000 people mobilized, answering his father's call to demand harsher sentences and stricter security measures. In response to this kidnapping and murder, a new movement emerged, opposed to the focus on human rights. The movement for public safety tried to discredit human rights activists, accusing them of only defending the human rights of criminals.

The Mothers and Grandmothers, when they talked about human rights, didn't discriminate between valuable lives and disposable ones. The mobilizations demanding tighter security stemmed from a distinction between lives with merit (with the right to live and be protected) and lives that could be disposed of. This anticipated a more general transformation whose political consequences can be vividly seen in Latin America today: life is not a right and does not bring with it rights; one must first be worthy of them. The lives of young people in poor neighborhoods, *travestis*, transgender persons, working-class women, migrants, criminals, are lives that are not deemed deserving of protection. The line that divides lives based on merit and does not unite them based on law, writes Alain Badiou,[5] leads to demands for the state to guarantee the safety of valuable lives against the threat of others.

Femicide could be interpreted from either of these stances; its translation is still contested territory. The conservative powers try to translate it in terms of public safety and respond to its increase with harsher sentences, with punitive demagoguery centered around prison less as a means of resocialization – with all the surrounding debates as to whether that is even possible – and more as a means of punishment and torture. In 2016 Micaela García was murdered. Her murderer was on parole from the prison where he'd been incarcerated for a previous rape. Parliament modified the Law of Execution of Sentences to prohibit parole and reduction of prison time for certain crimes, such as gender violence and drug trafficking. The majority of imprisoned women are "mules": caught smuggling drugs hidden inside their bodies. The lowest and poorest rung of the illegal economy. Many are migrants and have no papers or family network. They are left abandoned in prison. The Not One Less collective, activists who carry out projects with female prisoners (such as "Yo no fui" [It wasn't me]) as well as human rights organizations, declared their opposition to this reform measure that would deepen the division between bodies of value and disposable lives.[6] They said: "Not in our name." The parents of Micaela, whose murder sparked the reform, did not support the measure, insisting that respect for the memory of their activist daughter required them to conceive of justice in other terms. The dissidents were ignored.

From the first massive mobilization, in June of 2015, the movement has maintained that femicide is a human rights issue, not a public safety issue.[7] The fear of street crime locks people behind the bars of their homes and alarm systems. Femicide occurs, oftentimes, within the home. Murder comes at the end of a spiral of violence that the woman is not able to stop and which there are no effective public policies to combat. The logic of punishment is perpetuated, pushing aside strategic programs that would decrease patriarchal violence.

Harsher sentences increase the production of disposable lives: certain bodies are marked as disposable under the pretense of saving the lives of women or compensating for damage incurred. Thinking of femicide as a human rights issue implies demanding rights and liberties for everyone through the strengthening of community ties. Only by understanding the meaning of the rubbish bag, translating what the murderer is stating – unknowingly, Marx would say – as they toss the body in the dumpster, will we be able to state that no body is disposable. Only from a gendered perspective – we are sentenced to death because of our sexual and gender identity – is it possible to understand the drama playing out in the production of lives destined for sacrifice.

Reactionary sectors condemn gender violence in order to legitimize institutional violence against vulnerable groups. We are witnessing social and economic violence that produces a mass of disposable bodies (poor youth, migrants, indigenous peoples, black populations, transgender people, women). This violence is not directed toward all bodies with the same intensity, and in the relationship between genders those vulnerable in one dimension (class or ethnicity) could be the aggressors. The experience of a young woman in a poor neighborhood is not the same as a young man's, because social and institutional violence is compounded by sexist possessiveness; the framework of power is inscribed onto a woman's body; the logic that confines women and configures them as property sometimes leads to death. These boys – just like men in more privileged positions – are invested with gender mandates that may even require them to play the part of *machos* to such an extent that it can lead to their own or another's death. In the relationship between genders, the social configuration of masculinity implies the potential and transversal position of aggressor.

The public demonstrations carried out with the message "Not one less" sparked debate over the violence that produces bodies as rubbish (whatever bodies they may be) and that creates zones of exclusion in which no legal protection exists, while simultaneously emphasizing violence against women, trans people and *travestis*. If the first aspect were not present, feminist demands could be used to support the contemporary neoliberal separation between lives that have merit and should be protected and lives that should be disregarded: save our lives, it doesn't matter how, even if you have to use prisons that are torture centers and police officers who shoot with a terrifying ease. But if the attention is not placed on the specificity of sexist violence, gender inequality could be taken as a secondary concern, less relevant than the violence created by classist society. Violence against women and feminized bodies is a disciplinary tactic employed by men from varied social extractions, themselves products of the same social violence. While forgetting this systemic violence is typical of liberal feminisms, overlooking its gendered character dilutes the criticism of the patriarchy in the discussion on neoliberal violence.

Public mourning, private melancholy

On 3 June 2015, the street was crowded with handmade signs. One of them read: "Pardon the inconvenience, we're being murdered." The sentence underscored a threat felt by an entire population. The signs echoed what the bodies said with their very public appearance: that these crimes could not be classified as personal or individual tragedies (up to that point the media classified femicides as crimes of passion perpetrated by persons who had romantic links to the victims); that a person's gender can make them vulnerable and place them at risk; that our lives are not disposable.

The mobilizations implied a kind of collective mourning for the deaths. It was acknowledgment – as Judith Butler[8] theorizes – of the human interdependence that is at the very origin of life and remains like an unconscious trace, veiled behind the notion of individual autonomy. Mourning recovers a shared corporal condition: vulnerability. This mourning is not melancholia if, as Elias Canetti writes, "a person in a state of melancholia feels that pursuit is over and he has already been captured. He cannot escape; he cannot find fresh metamorphoses. Everything he attempted has been in vain; he is resigned to his fate and sees himself as prey."[9] For Freud, in his famous 1914 article, mourning and melancholia imply the same state of depression and the focusing of all one's energies on a single point. But mourning is a short phase, ended by griever's detachment from the lost object. Melancholia implies reversion to the subject: "The distinguishing mental features of melancholia are a profoundly painful dejection, cessation of interest in the outside world, loss of capacity to love, inhibition of all activity, and the lowering of the self-regarding feelings to a degree that finds utterance in self-reproaches."[10]

Public and collective mourning does not compare to the mourning of the individual who has lost someone and must reconstruct their splintered self, subtracting what remained of the connection that was ended by death or separation. Collective mourning for victims of femicide is a ceremony, a sharing in the pain over the loss of a person we did not know,[11] for someone who was not part of our lives until the moment they were reported missing, kidnapped or dead. Nevertheless, this mourning is real and is made stronger as it establishes a shared belonging. The Freudian notion of melancholia – the disappearance of the feeling of self – or the Spinozian sense of melancholia as feeling of powerlessness,[12] which hinders active life, or Canetti's notion of melancholia as a fixation, allow us to pose the question of its political effects. Because this sequence, which goes from inhibition to powerlessness and repetitive fixation, would end in the construction of the victim as inextricably victimized, as an unavoidable condition. Feminist strategies imply avoiding the crystallization of that position. Virgine Despentes, in *King Kong Theory*,[13] tells how she hid the fact she was raped while hitchhiking because she didn't want to be trapped in the role of victim and see her travels, outings and adventures limited. The options are clear: silence or restriction. Public mourning allows victims of gender violence to declare themselves active, powerful women, to expand their freedoms and not their limitations. The expression "Sister, I believe you," uttered at mobilizations and by feminist networks, separates denouncement and victimization, constructs a "we" that is supportive and welcoming, a political community.

Diego Tatián, reading Spinoza, writes: "If melancholia is absolutely bad – it's not possible to imagine a melancholia that is not excessive – in that it totally blocks active life, it is also a solitary passion par excellence: it implies an elegy to 'uncultured agrestic life,' a 'disdain for man' and an 'admiration for beasts.'"[14] It is the rejection of the social ties that dispossess us, that link our bodies with others. Melancholia and narcissism are forms of crazed individualization. Mourning is an acknowledgment of commonality, but it is not a pre-existing commonality; it is, rather, one that is forged through mourning, through the power to find ourselves in others, with others, to sympathize even with people we don't know. The shared is established through political experiences and public actions.

Mourning and melancholia form the basis of different strategies. Mourning allows freedom from the category of victim and, at the same time, detachment from the unambiguous association between reparation and punishment, opening the way for other reparatory modalities and other images of justice. Melancholia confines us to the position constructed by the disciplining power and criminal action: the position of victimhood.

Mourning and desire

Mourning implies crying together over the deaths, sharing in the pain, the fury and the decision not to be victims. In Uruguay, Feminist Alerts are sent out. A network of activists is called to march whenever a femicide has occurred. In countries such as Argentina, where the rate of femicide is much higher, we are not able to respond with mobilizations for every case (the body count has risen to one per day), but several marches were carried out in response to crimes that caused public outcry. On 3 June 2015 a march was called when Chiara Páez was murdered. She was fourteen years old and her body was buried in the backyard of her boyfriend's house in Rufino, in the province of Santa Fe. In 2017, the murderer was sentenced to twenty-one years in prison. The National Women's Strike on 19 October 2016 was incited by the horror of the crime against Lucía Pérez, sixteen years old, raped and murdered by several men in the city of Mar del Plata. In some cities, marches were held when the body of Micaela García was found (twenty-one years old, social activist and feminist) and her funeral became a public event. The murderer was sentenced to life imprisonment. On 5 August 2017, after Anahí Benitez, sixteen years old, was raped and murdered, her body found after a six-day search, her classmates called for a protest outside Congress. During the demonstration, the students denounced the justice system, the security forces and the media. Anahí's classmates participated in the assemblies to organize the international women's strike on 8 March 2018.

Not One Less puts words and images to the murders, draws connections between them. Where others classify the crimes as unacceptable violations of norms without debating the norms themselves – ratifying the social patterns that regulate behavior and bodies – Not One Less says that we must break the cycle of crime. Several of the murdered girls – Micaela, Anahí – had been photographed wearing shirts that read "Not one less." They identified as part of a very broad movement that included those who later mobilized for them. A shared learning experience and multiple lines of activism are present in contemporary strains of feminism.

The logic of punishment and safety treat vulnerability in a reactive way. They give in to a desire for vengeance or the notion of individual compensation: that a person must pay for what they did. Making mourning a public event, sharing this fragility and exposing it, questioning who we are in the wake of each death, establishes a new notion of political community, sustained by the recognition of what we have in common and not by the illusion of individual competition and solipsistic autonomy. Capitalist subjectivity puts forth a separate and autonomous individual. Any feeling of fragility is treated through protective technologies – medicine, security – or is remedied with vengeance and punishment: "He should pay for what he's done." The feminist movement tries to connect what is unique about each life – our personal lives – and desire as the foundation for shared political experience. It affirms that, when one woman is killed, all women are affected, that our sense of community is jeopardized, that acknowledgment of shared vulnerability confirms the unprecedented power of joining together. Desire is a problematic word, its meaning slippery, a name for what is lacking, sometimes limited to the exposition of subjectivity. In political terms, it is the exposure of what we are in and with others: our truth emerges through connections. It is a desire to share. Desire, then, not as neoliberal impetus or affirmation of a solitary decision.

Mourning and desire are experiences of dispossession, exposing to what point our relationships constitute who we are and to what extent – Butler writes – we are "disposed by them." Collective mourning takes pain as a public issue and connects it to the question of what the community we desire looks like. Feminist mobilizations create a kind of ecstasy, a leaving of the self, a break from private individuality. Not One Less produces politics from the corporal experience, from fragility, and from the unconsciousness of desire. The experience on the street encompasses both fragility and strength. During 2016, the Not One Less collective incorporated a phrase taken from the Mexican feminist mobilizations: "We want ourselves alive." In reference to the 8 March international women's strike, the group specified: We are moved by desire. The mobilizations include mourning, empowerment, transforming defense of life in the biological sense to the affirmation that living implies freedom, autonomy and desire.

The international Women in Black movement incorporates elements of mourning rituals. Women dress in black and march in silence. Mourning is the equalizer, and no chants emerge from the resolute crowd. Not One Less called for women to march – during the first National Women's Strike – in black or to dress in black if they were unable to strike or march. Everyday life was disrupted by the appearance of black clothes in all public spaces: offices, public transport, businesses, schools, television screens, the streets. It was pouring rain that afternoon, but a crowd of furious women dressed in black marched anyway. Some women of African ancestry objected to the use of the color black as a symbol of tragedy, although, for the organizers, the most powerful resignification was the color black as emblematic of battle and recovery of the Black Power movement. In Brazil, after the murder of Marielle Franco,[15] a new chant spread: "luto es luta" – mourning is fighting.

The right to mourn and the speech of the bodies

In *Notes Toward a Performative Theory of Assembly*, Judith Butler analyzes the meaning of the contemporary gathering of bodies in the street: "What does it mean to act together when the conditions for acting together are devastated or falling away?"[16] Even in the current neoliberal climate, mobilization is not, in itself, a radical expression of democracy – the right wing sings its own collective chants. Mobilizing may be radical when it fights precariousness and unequal structures (racism, misogyny, classism). Bodies gather in the public space, exposing the interdependence denied by individualist apologists, more emphatic as life for the majority grows more precarious.

Just as femicide is the cruelest level of machismo, the blaming of victims is the culmination of the false attribution of responsibility to those who suffer misfortune. The illusion of individuality legitimizes inequality. It hides the fact that we do not all suffer vulnerability in the same way: in a racist society a person of color or of indigenous origin has much greater chances of being unemployed, homeless or imprisoned; in a male chauvinistic

society a woman, *travesti* or trans person has much greater
chances of being murdered. We live in interdependence and we
need things from each other. This is ignored in the neoliberal
dictate that marks persons as either lost or salvageable. The
lost, bodies without merit, disposable lives, are not worthy
of mourning. When these bodies gather – writes Butler – they
demand their right to have rights.

The bodies *say* that they are not dispensable. And that we
all count. Bodies gather on the street to declare that their lives
deserve to be lived, that they are worthy of living and of being
mourned if they die. Migrants mobilize to declare that the bodies
drowned in the Mediterranean also have value. When the funeral
for a boy shot by the police becomes a large mobilization, it
proves that his life was not disposable. Not One Less emerged
to say that the girls found murdered and discarded in black bags
are not rubbish or waste. That their lives should count and be
counted. Each time a woman disappears, and the media, the
judicial apparatus and the security forces look the other way
because she is poor or she uses drugs or she is not a good victim,
women's organizations will be there to search for her.

Gisela Catanzaro states that "We must persist in the difference
between our vulnerable nature as individuals and the precarization socially imposed on us that exploits our dependence."[17]
We will always be interdependent, fragile, and we will always
need others; but not all historical moments and regimes of
accumulation deepen this precariousness. It is a symptom of
the present climate. Feminism becomes more powerful when it
understands vulnerability as openness, dispossession, willingness
to be affected by others, exposed to history and passion,
spontaneous happiness and sudden loss. It is political agency
and shared potential for construction, a break with the sensory
regulation demanded by individualism. Starting from a place of
vulnerability is not to appeal only to a protective legislation or
a judicial strategy; it also implies building support networks,
modes of organization, popular and illegal resistance.

I've often felt that the gatherings in the street created spaces
in which the pain of each one of us – our wounds, our humiliations – was made bearable, similar to the way we may produce
a protected space in our own body where pain, love and desire
can coexist. Non-domesticated interiors, shared in public and
produced through the gathering. Understanding what we are

experiencing demands consideration of our constitutive dispossession. The Not One Less movement established the political realization of that experience. I read, alongside these writings, the extraordinary book by Iván Jablonka, *Laëtitia, ou, La fin des hommes* (Läetitia, or the end of men).[18] After the murder of a young woman, the historian tries to understand and narrate her story, the violence she endured, the brilliance of her desires. He ponders the law and its limits, the state and its processes, public opinion, the media, the criminal justice system and political power. He thinks, even, about the murderer, trying to understand him, and, especially, lovingly, about Läetitia and her sister Jessica. I read and I think about how our steps on the street express a similar attempt to contemplate, narrate and achieve justice.

2
Violence: The Role of Crime

It would've been nice if murder hadn't been the catalyst for Latin American feminism, ever more porous to political narratives, to heterogeneous but always anti-capitalist alliances, unctuous, libidinous. In the organization, violence is de-privatized and called out so that it might be undone. If violence is expressive, Not One Less is a teacher.

María Moreno

We discovered, as other feminists had before us, that the kitchen is our slave ship, our plantation.

Silvia Federici

More freedom and more punishment

In 2012 the term "femicide" was incorporated into the Argentine penal code, defined as a murder perpetuated by a man as a form of gender violence. The creation of this new category of crime was contemporary to its specific acknowledgment in the language. In the first Not One Less summons it was spelled out: death for the mere fact of being a woman or *travesti*. The call also demanded official public records be kept. The only statistics that existed had been gathered by social organizations, such as Casa del Encuentro. The problem is quantifiable and interpretable:

the statistics show sequences, patterns, regularities, continuity and change.

Between 1 January and 31 December 2017, according to the investigation carried out by the Supreme Court of the Nation of Argentina, there were 251 cases of femicide. Feminist organizations, such as Mumala or Casa del Encuentro, cite a higher number, but I use the official data, which indicates that 93 percent of the accused murderers, in cases across the entire country, were men with whom the victims had a previous connection. In 60 percent of the cases, the murderer was a partner or former partner. In 71 percent of the cases the crimes were committed inside the victim's home. In February of 2018, the Gender Violence Unit, a branch of the Public Prosecution Office, carried out an analysis of the first fifty sentences for femicide in Argentina. They indicated that, "in 85 percent of the sentences, the author of the crime was a partner, an ex-partner, or had some romantic relationship with the victim. In 55 percent of the femicides, the crime occurred within the victim's residence or a residence that was shared with the victim."[1] These data speak of the predominance of traditional gender violence, where the crime occurs as the culmination of a pattern of violence and abuse that employs the logic of patriarchal possession, converting the woman into an object.

The growth of femicide coincides with the transformation of normative models. Changes in practices and increasingly visible sexual diversity activism were accompanied by the legal recognition of self-perceived gender identity and the broadening of the institution of marriage to include same-sex partners. The inclusion of integral sexual education (education with a gender perspective) across the entire scholastic curriculum went hand in hand with a deep cultural shift. This expansion of rights which fissures the heteronormative model concurs with the criminal reinforcement of heteronormativity. Concurrence is an ambiguous term. It can indicate causality or mere chance, overlooking other elements that could explain it (such as economic factors or political and social conflicts). The rise in femicide cruelty seems to be an objective response to the weakening of the patriarchal model, to the shift in customs, to non-submission. A response to experimentation and social transformation: the growing power of saying no and the proven distance between biology and gender. Submission to norms in the

name of biology and the acceptance of biology as destiny have
been challenged.

Luciana Peker refers to the shifts in everyday life and
sexuality over the past decades in Argentina as *The Women's
Revolution*.[2] This revolution does not have explicit program-
matic or ideological precepts (like the revolutions we remember
with dates and names, the French, Soviet and Cuban revolutions, which shaped the world's political imagination): this is a
disruption that implicates technology, medical laboratories and
collective creations, as it forges its own stories and symbols.
It emerges from the debates over access to birth control for
women of all social classes, the right to public exhibition of
non-heteronormative lives, the incorporation of women into
the labor market, from the economic crisis of the 1990s that
left everyone outside that labor market as it produced a kind of
militant feminine subjectivity, with new kinds of leaders. If we
are contemporaries of the rebellion against traditional gender
divisions and prescribed hierarchies between them, we are also
contemporaries of a cruel backlash, of a disciplinary sanctioning
inscribed on the bodies of victims and disseminated as a way to
educate all women.

Rita Segato coined the powerful term "pedagogy of cruelty"[3]
to refer to this violence, which is not individualized, although
femicide is committed by individuals. Perhaps no pedagogy is
individual. Even Rousseau's *Emile, or On Education*, seemingly
directed to one person and incarnated by a teacher, has a social
function: it aspires to become a methodology. The pedagogy
of cruelty is a system. It intersects with other modes of speech,
with symbolic and material degradation, with privation and
dispossession, with exclusion and domination. It influences and
entwines with individual actions. It speaks not only to the victim
but to the collective group of which she forms part, as well as
to the brotherhood of men from which it seeks recognition.
For this reason, part of the feminist struggle against violence
implies a persistent cutting of ties: removal of acts from the
sphere of social acceptance, of jokes that make sexism funny,
of the knowing wink, of covering up or tolerating abuse, of
distrusting the victim's word. With this shift, the derogatory term
"feminazi" is thrown around (describing an intransigent feminist
who roots out misogyny in every inch of everyday life) in an
attempt to separate murderous violence from the narrative of

social misogyny, which is discriminatory and denigrating. These murderers, rapists and abusers are not isolated cases of mental illness, expressions of a pathology that could be cured through psychiatry or punishment: their actions are understandable as part of a social narrative that supports them and justifies them through modes of speech, action and thought.

Sedimentations

What punishment does a murderer inscribe on the body of the victim? In what historicity is it forged? Can we think of gender violence in Ciudad Juárez as the same as in the city of Buenos Aires? Ciudad Juárez, border town, sweat shop, migrant girls in the factories and their bones in the desert (as Sergio González Rodríguez wrote),[4] drug cartels and the dream of crossing to the United States. There are many hypotheses about the murders, which, beyond singular acts, insinuate a shared logic.

Rita Segato believes it should be considered a femigenocide, because the violence is directed toward the entire gender group, not implying a personal relationship:

> What is a femicide, then, in the sense that Ciudad Juárez has given the term? It is the murder of a generic woman, a type of woman, merely for being a woman and for belonging to that type, in the same way that genocide is a generalized and lethal aggression to all those who belong to the same ethnic, racial, linguistic, religious or ideological group. Both crimes are directed toward the category, not the individual subject.[5]

The murder does not target an individual, it targets a social group. It is, from the outset, serial. Segato makes a comparison: "If in genocide the rhetorical construction of hatred of the other drives the action of their elimination, in femicide the misogyny behind the act is a feeling more akin to that of a hunter toward his trophy: it is a disregard for the victim's life or the conviction that the only value her life has lies in its willingness to be appropriated."[6] Segato proposes creating a penal category that would allow the cases to be heard in international courts.

The Jewish genocide perpetuated by Nazism implied the creation of the linguistic and ideological conditions that made it possible.[7] The colonial genocide was furthered by the distinction between humans and non-humans. Ethnic difference becomes an argument to legitimize extermination. In the sixteenth century, Bartolomé de Las Casas and Juan Ginés de Sepúlveda struck up a controversy over the treatment of indigenous populations. Las Casas called for curbing of exploitation in order to avoid extermination. The case he made was that the native people had souls – something that Sepúlveda denied. They debated the line that defined which lives were human through the racialization of bodies.[8] The same occurred in the justification of the slave trade.[9]

The discursive legitimization of criminal violence functions very differently with femicide. It is not constructed around the notion that the entirety of women and feminized bodies or dissidents should be exterminated. The crimes are treated as insanity or abnormality, even though they imply a certain degree of complicity and tolerance. The social narrative utilizes modes of language and social practices, in which objectification and appropriation come in many shades: the pink of romantic love, the red of jealousy, the grey of maniacal control. The patriarchal logic that ranks practices and statements by degree of offensiveness makes the crime possible but at the same time does not specifically justify it. The patriarchy is fully capable of creating inequality between genders without a massive wave of murders. This web of arguments has had moments in which it functioned as the hegemonic and undisputed logic of interpretation and regulation of behavior, making murderous violence less common. Now, as inequality and oppression are disputed because the patriarchy has ceased to be seen as a self-evident phenomenon, the crime rate grows.

The most powerful attempt to unravel this phenomenon is the one undertaken by Segato[10] as she analyzes violence in its expressive form (producing signs, directed at others, to a brotherhood by whom the murderer wants to be acknowledged) and abuse and rape as crimes of power: the body as a territory to be conquered, colonial booty, hunter's trophy. More debatable is the use of the expression "war on women" to denote the construction of feminized bodies as sacrificial victims, in which "a pact of complicity is sealed in power and its exhibitionist judgment is made a spectacle."[11] The notion of war permeates contemporary political strategies – for example, "the war on drugs" or "the war on terrorism." Far from the Clausewitzian confrontation of combatants, of dueling nations, the new wars emerge through the government's targeting of diffuse threats, which include economic and social practices, collective narratives. The translation to battle terms implies governmental strategies of extensive and multiple interventions aimed at diverse populations.[12] The notion of the "war on women" implies an inverse movement. It supposes a dispersed group lumped together by those in power (governmental or Mafioso) as the target of the attack, and the aggressive faction does not follow any plan or common strategy. The notion of war buries the inscription of violence in a narrative that produces regulated bodies such as women and at the same time places them at risk. It is a productive chain that becomes increasingly violent as it breaks down, but whose logic is widespread, perpetuated by men, transformed into machos by the very sexual and gender norms that are being splintered, against women, constructed as such by the same molds and abused for being women or for embodying dissidence.

Women held captive

Between 1996 and 2000 in Peru, the National Program of Reproductive Health and Family Planning (PNSRPF for its initials in Spanish) was implemented under the rule of President Alberto Fujimori. It was adorned with rhetoric taken from feminism: it would allow rural women to escape their destiny as incessant reproductive machines. The actual implementation was the opposite of any construction of female autonomy. More than 300,000 Quechua-speaking women were sterilized by force or through deceit or deficient information. Alejandra Ballón carried out an extraordinary investigation on the forced sterilization, in which she warns of the articulation between repressive political power, ideological Malthusianism and authoritarian practices by medical corporations.[13] And, to a lesser degree, she highlights the initial enthusiasm and lack of sufficient scrutiny on the part of some branches of feminism beguiled by the government's "attractive populist feminism" – as Jelke Boesten describes it.[14] The bodies of these women were mutilated through an intervention to which they did not consent. They were not informed in their own language;

no post-op care was offered. Doctors and politicians acted as if these bodies were the booty of a conquest which they still recognized themselves as heirs to and perpetuators of. Racism, classism and misogyny played out, dramatically, in the guise of progressive programs.

Under Fujimori's plan, native women are taken as "uteruses subject to control": bodies to which medical intervention could be applied with or without their consent. A well-worn notion and persistent practice was put into play so that a campaign of this type could be supported or tolerated. Latin American societies are products of the colonial past. The nations that emerged from the battles for independence have been unable to break fully the class-based logic of colony or slavery, which became the principal organizer of hierarchies and inequalities. Women's bodies are woven into the bloody tapestry of this history. Among the Latin American origin stories is the tale of Malinche, a native woman, able to speak several languages, given as a gift to Hernán Cortés. This conquest trophy, gift to the conqueror, becomes key to colonial expansion, because she is able to decode the native world for those who had come to destroy it. At the same time, she is the raped, submissive woman, forced to participate in the logic of exchange between masculine communities. Mestizo symbol and persistent emblem of submission that plans treachery through translation. But who did she betray – the community that gave her away like an object, who disposed of her like merchandise, who handed her over like a slave?[15]

The history of Argentina is, in part, a war of borders: the struggle against the colonial empire – the Spanish metropolis – to become a new state and wars with the indigenous, to convert them into subjects of the new state or annihilate them. Indigenous women are captured, destined for a life of domestic servitude or the rural whorehouse. Despite the effective transaction of indigenous bodies, in the Argentine imaginary they are not an erotic object; there is no mythology of voraciousness surrounding their sexuality. Just the opposite: the native woman would seem to be something flattened out, emptied of its becoming nature, set aside in favor of the white woman who is captured and forced to submit.

The white captive, stolen in a raid and taken back to the indigenous village, populates folk tales and fables. The story of Lucía

Miranda, told in a 1612 manuscript by Ruy Díaz de Guzmán, captured by an enamored native man who attacks only to take the girl, is as powerful as the story of Malintzin, who was given away by her people. During the nineteenth century this tale functioned as an ideological statement and a pictorial and poetic image.[16] On both sides of the border, the feminine body circulated, like stolen livestock, a kind of movable boundary. This historic violence is recycled today in the enslavement of women, human trafficking, the stealing and sequestering of girls destined for sex work.

The captive woman is a national emblem (the scarred body of the white country) which served as legitimization for the indigenous extermination campaigns. The way they treated the snow-white and fragile feminine body was evidence, for their opponents, of an inhuman savageness that made any peace treaty or negotiation unthinkable. In the name of the victims, they canceled all possibility of coexisting with the native populations. This same operation is, in a certain sense, repeated in the denouncement of femicide violence.

Micaela García, a twenty-year-old university student and political activist, was murdered in 2017. She was missing for several days, and, in the search for her, news outlets and social media were plastered with images of a pretty, responsible young woman. Her body was found and it was quickly discovered that her murderer had been previously convicted of rape and was back on the street after receiving a reduced sentence. The public outcry was aimed at the system that had created another victim. The contrast between the valuable life of this victim and the disposable life of her murderer was overwhelmingly clear. Prison, useless as a means of reform or re-education, exists as a place to confine bodies deemed dangerous. Micaela and the victims of femicide are used, like the captive women of old, to legitimize a process of social exclusion. She was construed as a good victim, different from other murdered young women who used drugs, or lived in a criminal environment, or were "party girls." The "innocent" victim is the only body worthy of being mourned. The feminist movement struggles, through a forest of meanings, to establish the notion that there is no line separating bodies of value and disposable bodies, that this difference established by neoliberal cruelty is unacceptable to popular feminism.

Terror and normalization

Between 1976 and 1983 the threat of forced disappearance gave
absolute control to the torturers in power. Inside the concentration
camps, the perpetrators of genocide declared themselves masters
of life and death. The majority of people who passed through
the camps were murdered. The few survivors gave testimony
to the endless stream of cold-blooded tortures, the efforts to
strip the prisoners of any will to live, the sexual violence and
specific brutality directed toward rebellious female bodies. In *Ese
infierno* (That hell), five women who survived imprisonment in
the ESMA torture center told of the pressure from their torturers
to prove they were in the process of recovery. Their life seemed
to depend on it, but the arbitrariness with which death was doled
out makes their survival nonetheless almost unfathomable. The
proof of their transition from the combatant mind-set to a more
traditional mode of femininity was seen in their use of jewelry,
perfume, feminine clothes, makeup. They were imprisoned,
shackled; they'd been savagely tortured; they lived among other
kidnapped people, in inhuman cells. But their captors brought
them dresses and toiletries:

> ELISA: "It was the same as the French perfume the marines brought
> for the female prisoners to wear."
> MUNÚ: "What?"
> ELISA: "I remember, in the Hood torture center, the smell of rats and
> the scent of French perfume."
> ADRIANA: "They wanted to see proof of our femininity."
> ELISA: "Shackled, darling! In chains but wearing French perfume!"
> MIRIAM: "They wanted us to show them ..."
> ELISA: "... that we wanted to be very feminine women!"[17]

Interpreting the guards' wishes allowed these women to
employ careful tactics. Lila Pastoriza, another ESMA detainee,
remembers: "One day I recognized el Tigre's footsteps and I
pulled out a piece of lipstick that I'd gotten back from my purse.
El Tigre looked in and I saw that he had a kind of satisfied
smile."[18]

   In a context in which life or death was at stake, in which people
were subjected to the cruelest exercise of power, conforming to
the prescribed gender mold was still expected: modes of dressing,

movement, presenting one's self. Trans women often emphasize feminine attributes and in doing so break with moral norms: presenting themselves as women, appealing to the traits socially attributed to feminine sensuality, defying biology's initial classification of their bodies. The importance placed on femininity inside the concentration camps was an attempt to cure the women's militant deviancy. Pilar Calveiro, social scientist and survivor of the Argentine dictatorship, reconstructs the torturers' mentality toward the female militants: "The women flaunted their enormous sexual freedom; they were bad housewives, bad mothers, bad wives and *cruel* women."[19] Punishment was applied to these dissident subjectivities. Their activism undermined sexual and gender norms and put family hierarchy in jeopardy. This was one of the reasons they were condemned to death or to the brutal corrective pedagogy that combined the cattle prod and French perfume.

Recognition of the sexual violence carried out inside the concentration camps was late in coming. Judges turned deaf ears, sentences classified rape as merely another form of torture, literature portrayed women prisoners as traitors, as if inside the camps anyone was free to decide.[20] There is no possibility of consent inside a concentration camp: when a woman says no it means no – Miriam Lewin recalls[21] – and when a woman says yes inside a concentration camp it also means no.

The violence inside the concentration camps inscribed the patriarchy's punishment onto the bodies of the women rebels. It punished disobedience, political rebellion, insurgent desire, deviation from traditional roles and abandonment of family as "the basic unit of society." Later interpretations of events, while acknowledging the women's political commitment, failed to recognize the subversive effects they had on the familial structure. The hearing of the testimonies on misogynist violence within the process of genocide emerged only with the social recognition of femicide. Ripping away the existing veil of sexist power allows us to see what was hiding beneath. The safe space for expression of pain created by bodies gathered in the streets assures that these testimonies will not be soliloquies. To the contrary, the critical efforts of survivors and activists to break the silence of the past allows us to hear better the victims of today.[22]

How much persists of the decision between lethal cruelty and a gift that reinforces traditional feminine traits in modern-day gender violence? How much of that cycle can be seen in the gesture of the violent husband who beats his wife and then gives her flowers, with the same message: behave? Can that lineage be traced or does the extremeness of the violence produced in the concentration camps have no heritage? While not diminishing this singular cruelty, we must recognize that the current treatment of women's bodies connects to a history that precedes the concentration camps where it showed its cruelest expression. Corrective violence confines bodies and desires to the Procrustean bed that is the gender mold, doled out by the hand of the torturer and articulated in the political and ideological motives of the counterinsurgency as well.

On 8 February 2018, the feminist activist Marta Dillon testified in court on the forced disappearance of her mother, Marta Taboada, in 1976. The Not One Less collective accompanied her to emphasize the connection between the two forms of violence:

> We refer to misogynist violence in all its forms, including the specific cruelty toward women that was applied to the bodies of our political mothers, the female activists of the 1970s, during Argentina's years of state-sponsored terrorism. Their rebellions aimed at undermining the traditional family as authoritarian nucleus and the state-sponsored terrorism violently systematized patriarchal control over the bodies of the detained-disappeared women. This message is inscribed on all our bodies and resurges as a collective fury and demand for justice.[23]

The aim of state-sponsored terrorism was to keep society on its traditional track. It continued the policies of previous military coups, repressing, almost indiscriminately, political activism, countercultural activism, public eroticism, and academic and scientific research.[24] It made violent attempts to impede any change in customs, except those introduced by technology or the market. It defended so-called Western and Christian civilization. Segato affirms that "it is possible that the dictatorships ended once they had finished laying the groundwork for new forms of terror. No longer state-sponsored terrorism, but in the form of entertainment that desensitizes existence to outside suffering, an existence without empathy, without compassion, achieved through the encapsulated pleasure of the consumer."[25] In this sense, new forms of violence would be part of the same process of discipline and of production of an isolated and selfish individuation, hemmed in by fear and for which equality is less a material experience than a moral premise.[26]

Analba Brazão, in *Violência contra as mulheres*, suggests that the institutional coup against Brazilian president Dilma Rousseff, disguised as a response to corruption in the management of public assets, was in fact a neoconservative attempt at deep transformation of the social order, ratifying the "enslaver culture that, confronted with the possibility of loss of privilege, pushed the class struggle to the forefront, revealed in the intensification of racist, misogynist and conservative ideas."[27] The rulers who emerged after the coup undertook a series of measures that aimed to empty the government of egalitarian policies. It attempted to modify the Maria da Penha law, for prevention and eradication of gender violence in Brazil, in order to confer more power upon the police and the penal system. The women's movement opposed this change, in order to "guarantee the rights of women without violating the rights of the accused or convicted."[28]

The current climate in Brazil exposes the knots and tangles of traditional logic (slave heritage, misogyny, the persistence of colonial hierarchy) and anti-egalitarian principles (racism, misogyny, classism) and calls for tighter security as an answer to feminist demands. In response to the intensification of violence against feminized bodies, the social elite, in defense of an order that exerts systematic violence on subalterns, takes public outcry as an opportunity to strengthen their means of control.[29]

Economic violence

Silvia Federici narrates the origins of capitalism through the articulation of various processes: "the expropriation of European workers from their means of subsistence, and the enslavement of Native Americans and Africans"[30] (analyzed by Marx in *Capital*); "the transformation of the body into a work machine, and the subjugation of women to the reproduction of the work-force" and an *"accumulation of differences and divisions within the working class*, whereby hierarchies built upon gender, as well as 'race' and age, became constitutive of class rule and the formation of the modern proletariat."[31] The production of the free worker is woven into a tapestry of egregious exploitations, which include – when the perspective becomes global – slavery and servitude, and where the home is revealed as the factory's necessary counterpart. Production of bodies subjugated to salaried work, slavish exploitation, or domestic reproduction implied contingent and confluent processes.

The witch hunt was the strategy for expropriation and privation of knowledge held by women, persecution of their community agency, a wedge in the heart of the lower classes: the creation of a hierarchical structure that allowed for the plunder of all workers. The bonfires cleared the fields so that a new regime of accumulation could once again flourish. Patriarchal violence was directed toward women and against the communitarian narrative. Women would be condemned to domestic work, excluded from access to money and made invisible as workers: "it was in the torture chambers and on the stakes on which the witches perished that the bourgeois ideals of womanhood and domesticity were forged."[32] This dispossession is reproduced each time those ideals are affirmed to condemn women to unpaid and invisible domestic work.

León Rozitchner, in *La cosa y la cruz*,[33] states that material and emotional dispossession was fundamental to establishing the logic of the market across all of social life. This expropriation occurs also on the symbolic plane, with the primacy of a religion that denies the maternal body (that is to say, the material reproduction of the species and the nurturing that allows for persistence of life) to substitute it with the law of the father, abstract symbol of control of nature and the body. The central myth of Christianity includes the story of the mother who gives birth to a son destined for sacrifice, torture and death. A virgin mother, not marred by desire or pleasure. All materiality dissolves in the face of religion and its general equivalent. In his later texts,[34] Rozitchner emphasizes the link between the material and the maternal, anchoring there the possibility for an anticapitalist worldview. The condemnation of being "queen of the home" correlates with the dematerialization of existence, which diminishes and hides the fundamental work of reproduction of life. We must add another dimension: violence exerted on the body as a productive force, to produce goods and offspring in slave-holding societies,[35] and with mediations in capitalist societies. Weavers, textile workers, were emblematic figures of early exploitation. The women who made lace went blind to produce the most beautiful fabrics, tailors suffered consumption from being always shut inside and died at twenty years old, the working women were hired in England for half the salary of the men.[36] Graciela Rodríguez states that the great waves of accumulation implied the massive entry of women into the workforce, the feminization of factories and wage depreciation. The last wave was birthed in the sweat shop by millions of young women denied workers' rights and granted meagre wages.

Federici discusses the limitations of the typical definition of gender violence as something that happens in a domestic environment, because "it has ignored the violence inherent in the process of capitalist accumulation, the violence of famines, wars and counterinsurgency programs that, through the '80s and '90s, have cleared the way to economic globalization."[37] This limited definition of gender violence converts feminism into an ally of the new international economic order and keeps us from addressing the complexity of the violence and its points of convergence. What does Ciudad Juárez tell us about the relationship between exploited bodies and sacrificed bodies? Or about the link between illegal economies, neoliberal accumulation, new manufacturing methods and violence against women?

In some Latin American countries, at the start of the twenty-first century, government policies attempted to erase the division between bodies with merit and disposable lives. The implementation of reparatory and redistributive policies had direct consequences on the lessening of poverty and the inclusion of new sectors in the internal market. Economies grew, sparking heated discussions on the coexistence of these elements with extractive and neo-developmental logic that had produced new modes of exploitation.[38] In Argentina and Brazil these policies were terminated as new governments took over, established on the direct link between political power and economic powers. The fact that under Mauricio Macri's rule government ministries were populated by businessmen and CEOs is not anecdotal but serves as proof that the logic of the market can be translated to government and used to define policies based on strict criteria of profit and loss. Social security and labor reform, the lifting of controls on financial capital, the systematic taking on of debt, austerity policies that imply cancellation of social programs and the reduction of public employment, greatly impact the life of citizens. The increased presence of police and military forces in poorer neighborhoods shows the government's extreme shift toward repressive policies.

Political activists, young people from poor backgrounds, women and feminized bodies are victims of ever worsening violence. These are not necessarily oppositional identities but often overlap, as an activist may see repression exacerbated by her condition as a woman.[39] We must consider the complexity of the contemporary production of violence, taking into account the patriarchal relationship with racism and classism, to denounce popular machismo while also defending men against institutional violence. But we must keep in mind that there is a specific violence, incarnated as appropriation and denial of autonomy, directed toward the female body as something to be possessed or destroyed, a territory to be colonized.[40] Men may be tortured and murdered, but the torture (even rape) and the crime are exercised on a male body taken as an adversary or a defeated enemy, as a subject who was recognized as such before being racialized or feminized. In violence against women the prevailing notion seems to be that of impeding something perceived as an object from becoming an autonomous subject.

Popular feminists walk the line between achieving their agenda and keeping it from being used as an argument to legitimize new exclusions and privations. In this context, the Not One Less collective affirms that feminism should be intersectional, capable of sharing common objectives with all other popular movements and causes, of finding truth in other struggles against hierarchies and established classes. It aims to be a feminism of unprecedented alliances, not a liberal varnish applied to white power.

Forms of violence

What if, instead of finding a rationale to explain away violence, we were to focus on the broad range of violent situations and contemplate the various forms of violence at play in femicide? An issue of interpretations and political strategies. Naming is a political act. It characterizes, situates, describes, chronicles, intervenes. To think, as Jacques Derrida says, is to name.

One type of recurrent violence occurs within romantic relationships. It ranges from abuse, to control, to death. It is expressed in "things got out of hand," meaning the hand became a fist. In this cycle of violence, beatings are followed by gifts, apologies and promises; then the cycle starts anew. Many women sustain these relationships, in part influenced by the idea of passionate love, which implies jealousy and possession. It is a common theme of our collective imaginary made explicit in literature, television shows, songs, plays: "He hits you because he loves you," or "He does it because he cares about me." The woman is, at the same time, subject and object. A subject who is limited, conditioned, controlled, required to submit and at the same time to love. In many Latin American countries abortion is illegal,[41] and in this government regulation the same restriction of autonomy is at play.[42] A woman does not have total legal authority over her body. She is subject to outside law. Femicide creates a murderous act of that affirmation. If she doesn't submit to the norm, she doesn't deserve to live. "I killed her because she was mine": that possession is singular, individual, invested with objectifying desire.

The mobilizations of women in Argentina correlate with a notable increase in reports of domestic abuse. Calls to government violence hotlines have increased, as have the number of women seeking support from social organizations and networks.[43] Yet femicide has not ceased, and an explanation emerged from conservative branches: the mobilizations create more violence, and they don't give people any tools to protect themselves. At the root of this argument is the idea of accepting habitual violence in order to remain alive, that it is preferable to strike a deal with the domestic murderer. This interpretation belies the fact that the circle of violence often ends in murder, whether or not a police report is filed. A woman who puts up with abuse, in many cases less out of conviction than of an absence of concrete conditions to extract herself from the abusive situation (economic resources, a different place to live),[44] may still be beaten to death.

Some time ago, after a lecture I gave on sexism, language and violence, a woman in her mid-thirties approached me. She showed me a photo of the first women's march, and she said "Not One Less saved my life." The mobilization on 3 June 2015 gave her the courage to leave the man who beat her. She had been in that relationship for fifteen years. He wouldn't grant her a divorce. He stalked her and attacked her on the street. She filed charges. There was a trial and he was imprisoned after an attack that left her seriously injured. On 19 October 2016, the day of the first national women's strike, the woman attended a demonstration for the first time in her life. The gathering of bodies in the public sphere creates a welcoming space and at the same time constitutes a site of conversation and discovery for those who hadn't dared to speak up until they recognized themselves in the shared fragility and pain.

Being hospitable means creating a space in which the power of speech, a victim's word, is believed and recognized as valid. When does a person decide to speak up about the violence they've suffered in the past or that they are still suffering? When social conditions are hospitable. In this sense, the massive mobilization of women is the echo chamber for the individual voice.[45] Decontextualized facts say little. I reference them only to indicate the increase in reports of abuse, which suggests a shift: it is possible to speak of what happens behind closed doors, of what is inflicted on children or was suffered in our already distant childhoods. In a meeting to organize the 8 March women's strike, young people testified to abuse they suffered in childhood. They shouted that they did not want pity, merely to be recognized as political subjects.

Beyond domestic abuse are other common forms of violence. The Equipo Latinoamericano de Justicia y Género (Latin American Council for Gender Justice) reports that 56 percent of young women murdered between the ages of twelve and twenty-one years old did not know their killers.[46] Agustina Paz Frontera and Romina Zanellato use this fact to show that the home is not always the most dangerous place once data on age and class are factored in. Girls "are exposed to a chain of violence that is established on a communitarian continuum and in a misogynist pact." The lives of adolescent women from poorer sectors of society are lived in the streets, in the clubs and at house parties, and the girls are taken as "community property by the young men of the neighborhood."[47]

These crimes are not directed at one specific person and driven by desire or passion; instead they take the woman as a mere object – a hunting trophy. If domestic forms of violence are based in colonial logic – which includes the right to sovereignty over other persons – the youth culture in poorer neighborhoods views girls as goods: they circulate, can be taken, used, disposed of. Neoliberalism produces disposable lives; the murderer inscribes this maxim onto the body of his victim. Sometimes, he does so using knowledge gained in prison, involving torture or suicidal intentions. The act seals two fates: the victim's and the victimizer's. The statistics scream out: in 2016, 1,917 cases of femicide were registered across seventeen Latin American countries.[48]

Precarious lives

Girls from poor neighborhoods disappear and are sometimes rescued from whorehouses or human trafficking networks. Other times, their families and friends search for them in vain. In Bajo Flores, a poor neighborhood of Buenos Aires, the Network of Teachers, Families and Organizations was created to help find girls when they disappear, as well as to gather first-hand information to aid the search for them. The young women are considered not as helpless victims but as individuals looking to extract themselves from oppressive lives, often falling into much more dangerous circumstances. Young women or girls who want to flee from domestic entrapment, from being required to care for siblings or forbidden from going out in their family's attempt to shield them from the violence outside, run away with a man, often older, the connection often made through social media, who prostitutes them. Silvia Herrera says that "the girls function as objects of consumption in this area because in Bajo the drug trafficking network is very prominent; there are places where only a few families may enter, governed by codes we don't understand. In the 1-11-14 slum it is common knowledge that, on a weekly basis, boys are killed and girls are pulled into a circuit where they are consumed."[49]

Violence builds up, and what looks like a plan to escape family entrapment and punishing poverty leads the women into new forms of submission. Thousands of young girls in poor neighborhoods live precarious lives and are considered either an object for consumption or rubbish to be disposed of. Government institutions do little to counter this selection process. To the contrary, the placement of recovered girls in shelters often only increases their vulnerability.

In the early twentieth century, Argentina was the destination for waves of migrants. European women, deceived through promise of marriage, or in some cases actual marriage, were taken to a country that received them as sex slaves. The largest of these networks, known as Zwi Migdal, brought young women from Eastern Europe, leaving them stranded in an unknown land that spoke an unknown language. White slavery: women fleeing poverty, beguiled by the romantic promise of a bright future, discover their true destiny once they arrive. The prostitution ring functioned until 1930, when one woman's testimony pushed the authorities to investigate.[50] These networks of human trafficking have always been accompanied by a range of conditions, from romantic exploitation of economic necessity to recruitment by a man who exploits his partner as a prostitute. From a large impersonal kidnapping scheme to submission in the context of romantic connection.

The violence to which kidnapped or recruited women are subjected in poor neighborhoods also spans a range of situations. Ileana Arduino maintains that, whether the young woman ran away or was co-opted through deceit, it is necessary to emphasize the situation of "physical, emotional and sexual enslavement that is produced in these circumstances even if they are not always preceded by a situation of deceit or sequestration, or exploitation in terms of the traditional configuration of the crime of human trafficking."[51] Many forms of violence intersect on these marginalized bodies, revealing the fundamental nature of the function of violence in contemporary society. Violence not only molds sexuality and gender, domesticating women, producing housewives and mothers; it also draws a line that divides valuable lives and disposable lives. If all women, for the mere fact of being women, are vulnerable to violence, we are not all equally vulnerable.

In recent decades, the moral force of sexual and gender regulation has weakened. For a woman of my mother's generation, virginity was a merit and monogamy was destiny. To the extent that the horizon of freedoms has now broadened, there should be no need to fear that a report of harassment will feed a puritan vision of sexuality. The pushback to the Me Too campaign, led by a group of famous French women, points out the risks of coercive regulation of behavior in the name of feminism, a denouncement used as a battering ram to impose order, particularly within institutions and working environments. These French women condemn what they call the excesses of a movement they see as being punitive and at the same time victimizing women, ignoring the multiple modes and situations in which a woman can say no and also ignoring the link between eroticism and certain modes of sexual objectification. The debate highlights the more complex points of the current situation. A rebellion has occurred against accepted behavioral norms and sexist practices. This poses many risks, but these risks are recognized by feminist activists themselves in the debate over punitivism and victimization. Far from proposing a puritanism empty of all eroticism, it seeks a reconstruction of the limits of the erotic, increased connection, and the breakdown of sexual and gender impositions.

To deny the fact that only a certain sector of women actually have the authority to speak out against practices that have been normalized, to say no and remain respected, is to ignore the question of power entirely. Who has the power to say no? Who is not in the position to do so? When can acceptance of certain situations of subordination and exploitation be seen as part of the subaltern's tactics to improve their living conditions? Does a university professor have the same autonomy as a girl from the slums, exhausted by forced domestic work and poverty? As regulatory morals and the crisis of gender construction fall away, freedoms flourish, but they also reaffirm the brutal logic of dispossession of bodies. If the witches were the sacrificial bodies of the first process of accumulation, girls and *travestis* transformed into discarded flesh are the most extreme victims of neoliberal accumulation; their bodies pile up beyond the zone of rights as their lives are made more precarious. The breakdown of empathy for these murdered young women – produced in the notion that "they must have done something to deserve it," the questioning of their conduct, the mention of their involvement in drugs and prostitution – is the foundation upon which tolerance toward all violence inflicted on their bodies is established.

3

Strike: The End of the End of History

"Finally one can breathe. There is a strike ..."
                    Simone Weil, *La condition ouvrière*

International feminism

Flora Tristán was persecuted until her ex-husband attempted to murder her. Her children were taken away. Conservative judges accused her of dissolving the home and refused to hear her complaints. A bullet remained lodged near her heart; the doctors recommended she try to lead a quiet life but she ignored their advice. Her ability to understand the pain of others did not radiate from the bullet that sought to kill her but came from her own urge for freedom. She contemplated the intersection of injustice, economic exploitation and the crushing weight of the patriarchy. And she knew that beneath all other forms of oppression is that of gender. Every woman, rich or poor, is regarded by her husband as his property, like a piece of furniture that must serve only for his use, a baby-making machine.[1] She defends Robert Owen but also Mary Wollstonecraft, astute writer on the rights of women.[2] She thinks of them as precursors to another category of words, more powerful or more irate, individual or collective. Emancipation is still underway and the last word on it has not yet been said.

Tristán herself is considered a precursor. Every break in language, in knowledge and in politics, Borges believed, reinterprets what has come before and invents its antecedents. Flora was read (or under-read) from Marx's great intervention, in particular through the link between what she proposed in *The Workers' Union* in 1843, tinged with philanthropy and reforms, and his *Communist Manifesto* in 1848[3] – two proposals for constructing an international association of workers. Lorenz von Stein states that the awareness that the working class is an entirety is manifested in her with more force than in the other reformers.[4] Tristán's book opens with two epigraphs: one affirms that everything of value is created by the worker and the other indicates that union creates strength.

Flora had the idea of unionization and decided to print a pamphlet to spread the notion. She couldn't find a publisher so she started a subscription campaign to finance it. Then she began to travel from town to town – an itinerant red prophet. Her writing may not have the force of Marx's *Manifesto* but it is not merely a precursor. It's a specific dissidence which was pushed aside.

Tristán's call is directed to men and women, male and female workers. She makes the distinction, avoiding the French universal masculine. She proposes the construction of a universal union of male and female workers. In chapter 3 of *The Workers' Union* she explains why women are the true pariahs, the uncounted in any organization, un-nominated in all politics. Tristán summarizes millennia of arguments that emphasize feminine inferiority, from Aristotle to Buddhism, numerous Christian quotations and scientific affirmations. The chain of citations cannot be chains on our lives. She ponders: what would happen if we recounted all the literary insults about the proletariat? Wasn't it said that they couldn't govern themselves or have rights? But 1789 came, and, through the revolution, the group gained knowledge of themselves and recognition as citizens. Women still need their (own) revolution.

The writer explores the bleakness of an everyday life made bitter by female servitude. Women suffer as their anguished masters drown their unhappiness in alcohol. She contrasts the home full of arguments and abuse with a life shared by equals. And she specifies: "I demand rights for women because I am convinced that all the ills of the world come from this forgetfulness and scorn that until now have been inflicted on the natural and imprescriptible rights of the female."[5] This text disappears after publication of *The Communist Manifesto*, five years later. It's unfair to view Tristán as a romantic dreamer of unionization, a philanthropic precursor to others considered to have more critical weight and political commitment. To do so would be to ignore her radical affirmation that the brick and mortar of inequality between the genders is what upholds the social order.

Today the specter of feminism haunts the world. Many activists, dreamers, imagine the creation of a Feminist International. Carrying the torch lit by Flora is no longer a solitary act but a network woven from joint actions, personal encounters and online contacts. The time has come to replace what was forgotten by the great majority of the left wing when *The Communist Manifesto* erased from the scene *The Workers' Union* and its call to male and female workers was set aside in favor of an appeal to the proletariat of the world. The female proletariat was doubly neglected: by Marxism, which thought only of the masculine, and by feminism, which overlooked the working class.

8 March

The international day of the female worker is commemorated on 8 March. The date was set in 1910 by the International Socialist Congress, gathered in Copenhagen, and the following year mobilizations were held to demand rights for female workers and all women's right to vote. A week later more than 140 female workers, mostly migrants, died in a factory fire in the United States. In 1917, Russian women declared a strike against the war. The date was 23 February according to the Julian calendar used in Russia and 8 March on the Gregorian calendar. Four days later the tsar abdicated and the new government extended the right to vote to women. In the 1970s the United Nations made the date official. In Argentina, the day was formerly an occasion for gifts – insistent flowers and chocolates – and a day for feminist mobilizations. On 8 March 1984, the first women's day after the end of the military dictatorship, a multi-sectorial women's group called for a demonstration outside Congress. One activist, María Julia Oddone, carried a sign that read "No to motherhood, yes to pleasure." It sparked a huge controversy within the group itself.[6] In the years that followed, the 8 March commemoration was attended primarily by activists.

The call for an international women's strike on 8 March 2017 brought new life to the date. In Argentina, the first national women's strike was organized after a horrendous crime. A young woman had been raped and murdered in October of 2016. This occurred days before the annual National Women's Conference was held, drawing in over 60,000 furious women. A group of organizations and activists, gathered together, decided to strike on 19 October. The meetings and interactions brought a key notion to the forefront: gender violence correlates with social and economic inequality; the strike is a means of sparking debate over these connections.

Can a women's movement call for a strike? The union organizations objected to a supposed lack of legitimacy to invoke a measure specific to the world of labor. Without a union to call for the strike, there is no protection for the strikers and employers can sanction them for abandonment of their positions. The women's movement provided a repertoire of actions which were considered forms of striking: assemblies in workplaces and neighborhoods, displays of solidarity through the wearing of black clothes (which allowed many women who went to work to do so while still observing the strike: television hosts, shop assistants, who worked wearing black or with a black ribbon on their uniform). Women took to the streets as well. In the city of Buenos Aires, an incessant freezing rain fell over the massive march. The movement's narrative draws powerful nourishment from these images.

The resignification of 8 March as a day of strike produced international articulations and a national structure that emerged from networks across cities. A group of Polish activists promoted the PIM (Paro Internacional de Mujeres [International Women's Strike]) network to help organize actions for the day. In Argentina, the huge turnout was credited to the Not One Less collective, active in several cities, and to alliances forged throughout Latin America. In the city of Córdoba, an Inter-Syndicate Women's Panel joined activists from more than twenty different union organizations.[7] Agreements were signed across rifts that union leaders could never have otherwise dreamed of bridging were it not for this cross-section of feminists and their commitment to forging alliances. Female union workers participated in assemblies that included social movements, political parties, feminist collectives, and cultural and artistic activist groups. At the same time, they began to form alliances, not devoid of all conflict, but which were sealed in joint actions such as press conferences and organizational meetings. The debate over the right to call a strike allowed for collective reflection on the definition of work, expanded beyond paid labor to include the reproductive duties and tasks carried out in the informal economy.

Work

A union may declare its right to strike in a sector of the formal economy, a declaration that carries with it labor rights and union representation. Across Latin America, the number of workers in the informal economy equals the formalized labor force.[8] In Argentina, organizational processes surround the so-called popular economy, a name used to avoid the value judgment implicit in the distinction between formal–informal and to include the popular entrepreneur, emerging from co-ops or micro-enterprise. Verónica Gago, in *Neoliberalism from Below*, analyzes proletariat microeconomics, in order to understand that

> All the vitality involved in the creation of a space of popular commerce and consumption, with its tactics and hierarchies, transactions and appropriations, comes undone if there are only victims (of neoliberalism, of unemployment, of mafias, etc.). This does not deny the violence of social relationships nor romanticize their transactions, but neither does it unilateralize them.[9]

Part of the female workforce participates in this type of economy – through domestic service, non-formalized textile production, the popular markets, recycling – jobs which do not always imply wages.[10]

Traditional syndicates represent only a part of the labor force and one sector of workers. Some seek to build representations that are able to breach that barrier. There are many modes of work and the working subject is multicolored. In the groups assembled before 8 March, the definition of work was debated.

Does it include the popular entrepreneur? Does the woman who sells food she cooks in her home count? And sex workers? And homemakers? And unemployed women or those active in social organizations? The debates were conceptual and political. The prevailing notion was to broaden the concept of work, recognizing that it is multiple (that there is not one single paid and formal mode, with union representation) and that it is carried out in diverse ways that require distinct modes of contemplating exploitation and resistance.

On the one hand, post-Ford societies are characterized by jeopardizing the regime of paid, localized and stable work. What emerge are flexible economies, which subject workers to uncertainty. Richard Sennett proposed the notion of corrosion of character as a way to think about the subjective effects of precarization.[11] In globalized enclaves of the economy, an elite and well-paid workforce in the world of services cohabits with the harshly exploited labor force in manufacturing territories. These contrasting forms of economy often coincide within one organization, with profitability built precisely on this division between executive elites and exploited masses in other regions. In many cases, the childcare and domestic reproduction services for these more comfortable nuclei belong to the informal economy. The women's strike, with its inclusivity, incorporates in the same process migrants who work in childcare and bank employees who are eligible for social security, paid vacations and bonuses. Unions have a role to play; they can form defensive and conflictive alliances, but their voice is not loud enough to make the complexity of this social narrative heard.

On the other hand, feminist activists and theorists have established a non-salaried concept of work in order to acknowledge the reproductive and social effort that is necessary for a productive society.[12] The socially necessary sex–gender division of labor left a substantial part of these tasks in feminine hands. These are jobs that do not imply monetary compensation (except in cases where they were delegated to other women, outside the network of family and friends) but do imply a double workday for women. Questions arose in the assemblies to prepare for 8 March: Can a person go on strike from childcare? When we strike, are we just unloading onto other women the chore of that never-ending effort? The discussions that took shape, the path that led the collective to strike, are as fundamental as the strike itself because

they served as a debate on work, its modalities, its gender differ-
entiations, the paid and the unpaid, time, and the right to free
time. Neoliberalism, ignoring any distinction between work and
free time, converts all time into opportunity for market valorization, makes evident the production of value that was already
present in the regulation of women's work.

For feminism, the notion of work goes beyond the presence
of wages to the experience of the unpaid but socially necessary
work of reproduction. This unpaid job disguised behind love for
family is central to the accumulation of wealth. In Argentina,
and according to official data, the average time women devote to
unpaid domestic tasks is 6.4 hours a day.[13] This fact, added to the
high percentage of women who make up the labor force in the
informal or popular economy,[14] demands a notion of work that can
accommodate this broader definition. A notion of work capable
of encompassing diverse situations, the dispossession implying
the precarization of lives and the specific violence that entails.
A century after the Russian women's strike, the term "female
workers" names a radically diverse subject, inscribed across very
different contexts and national belongings and migratory destina-
tions, languages, cultures, religions. It is a subject whom no single
union or political party may ever fully represent.

The map of union leadership in Argentina is masculine. The
highest positions in the unions are occupied by men. Women
hold, in the best cases, the position of gender secretary or head of
cultural activities.[15] After 8 March 2017, several unions created
branches for gender as part of their response to the women's
strike. The impact has yet to modify the leadership profile, but
discussions within unions are underway and building steam.

Immeasurable

The film *The Intense Now* (2017), directed by Joao Moreira
Salles, recovers footage from the archive of the French May
events. Among the fragments selected is the return to work of
employees at the Wonder factory after three weeks on strike.
One girl cries and protests: the factory is a cruel place to which
she does not want to return. Two union delegates try to convince
her that the 10 percent wage increase is a victory. She insists: this
is not what we went on strike for.

Union strikes usually aim for specific, quantifiable results – a certain percentage of wage increase, a list of working conditions, curbing firings, exemption from certain fees. There is calculation and measurement. It is won or lost. And it is directed at an employer, private or public. In contrast, the international women's strike pushes for something immeasurable. Although it proposes an agenda of concessions, it goes beyond any possibility of measurement. Its immeasurable nature emerges from the strike as a collective experience, a privileged moment in which political subjectivity is forged. The women's strike is immeasurable because the notion of work that it acknowledges and aims to interrupt is not unidimensional. It does not accept the reduction of work to its paid incarnation but encompasses all productive labor, creative force, molding of material, weaving of community ties.

"We are all workers" was the slogan of the 2018 strike: whether at the machines in the factory or sewing at home, in a neighborhood organization or in the family kitchen, in the classroom or behind the wheel of a truck, caring for other people or writing about them. To strike is a diverse, multiple interruption. Its modes are as diverse as the female workers. The key notion of socialist struggles, "equal pay for equal work," is insufficient. Beyond equivalence, we must demand the recognition of all productive and reproductive work.

Toward whom is a strike of this nature directed and whom does it challenge? It shakes the very foundation of the social order: it confronts the notion of domesticity and the gender norms that condemn women to domestic chores and submission, to badly paid work in exchange for the freedom afforded by wages. It denounces the invisible ceilings in professional careers and at the same time proposes a notion of equality that will make these very hierarchies quiver. It is directed at all employers with an agenda of labor concessions, and it is directed at a government that criminalizes protest. The same strike affects marriage, politics, family, the sphere of work, art, science. Unlike individual strikes for specific sectors or spheres of life, this strike is disobedience, interruption and desire for foundation.

The women's strike reveals that the accumulation of wealth is not only an appropriation of what is produced in the spheres of paid labor; it also hoards surpluses created through community knowledge and the work of domestic reproduction.

Acknowledging all these varieties of work reveals that the collective production of wealth has been privatized, leaving its very creators with little or nothing. The strike is a collective political action because it makes evident this social articulation. It targets all appropriation of creative force and the misogynist hoarding that permits men to make use of free time thanks to their partner's domestic efforts. It is directed at the businessman who gets rich thanks to the meagre wages paid to his employees, at the political leaders who shine by obscuring the activism of women, at the governmental translation of feminist demands that uses them as campaign publicity or justification of reforms that reduce rights.[16]

How can a nurse in a neo-natal unit strike? She and her co-workers can decide to treat patients dressed in purple uniforms to represent the women's struggle. And how can a person strike in a soup kitchen in a poor neighborhood? Women resolve the issue at a meeting: we will hand out raw foods, we won't add on more work. These are two very different creative solutions to the challenges of striking. Female subway workers wore a sash that read "I strike." Male university employees hung a sign that said "They strike, we all fight," to indicate that they were at their posts and looking after the children of the women who were participating in the protest. Inside prisons, female inmates held demonstrations. To "strike" includes many degrees, actions, folds.

Debt is violence

The Feminist Economics network summarized its reasons for participating in the 2017 strike:

> We strike because we earn less than men for the same work all over the world. We strike because unpaid domestic work falls to us, affects our possibilities for studying, working, advancing; it creates a double workday for us, one at home and one outside the home. We strike because we are the majority in precarious or badly paid jobs. We strike because we are undervalued in working environments, objectified and sexually harassed in public and private spaces. We strike because we want to have control over our own bodies; in Argentina we strike for the right to legal, safe and free abortion. We strike to oppose homophobia and transphobia. We strike because gender violence kills.[17]

Exploitation has varying degrees, as does suffering; the suppression of rights does not affect everyone in equal measure. There are specific inequalities that cause unpaid work to fall to women, sapping them of time and energy. The wage gap between women and men in the 2016 labor market reached 35 percent in the unregistered economy in Argentina.[18] Means of production, market valorization and accumulation have a differential impact on women. And, even if they didn't, they should be part of the agenda of demands since they affect everyone. Labor reforms that make hiring practices more flexible and erase the protective aspects of previous laws might not impact women more severely, but they constitute a more central issue for women. It is an issue as important as retirement or healthcare, agribusiness and its environmental effects, external debt, international commerce, and the economic dominance of financial markets. Feminism is not weakened by demanding change across all conditions of life – economic, social, political, cultural – through its radical challenge of the system and willingness to construct alliances with other social movements.

The gender perspective is a critical perspective, experience of intersection and capacity to feel another's pain in one's own body. We are affirming empathy not as a political value per se but as a counterpoint to a regimen of general desensitization that constructs death or suffering of other people as something painless.[19] The Not One Less collective summarized this with the phrase "feminism or cruelty," which emphasized feminism's capacity to foster cooperation from a place of personal vulnerability and understanding of what occurs in the bodies of others, affirming that all bodies count, in contrast to a cruel regime of solipsistic, individualist, competitive life based on the destruction of others or complicit silence. Feminism stands in contrast to the cruelty that sinks the knife into the other's flesh or the cruelty that denies assistance or intervention.

The 3 June mobilization was held mainly in response to gender violence and in particular in response to the contrast between autonomy and femicide. The subsequent women's strikes emphasized the links between gender violence and socioeconomic violence. The assemblies held by the Not One Less collective sought out these articulations. In June 2017, a group of activists, under the name Non-Submissive to Corporate

Finance, organized a demonstration in front of the Central Bank of Argentina to declare that debt is violence, using the slogan "We want ourselves alive, we want to be debt-free." The document read at the demonstration was a reaction to the exorbitant external debt assumed by the Cambiemos Alliance during its first year in power, decrying debt as a key aspect of financial dominance over everyday life.[20] If the external debt of a country shackles domestic economic policies to international organizations and market pressures and financial institutions, personal debt is regulation of everyday life and restriction of autonomy.

In their published document, the Non-Submissives point out that a large part of the popular economy functions through debt. Through loans, a house is added on to, a family makes it to the end of the month, celebrates a birthday, treats illness. Loans shackle users with fees, endless payments, instalments that require more loans to pay off. They oblige women to maintain jobs or relationships that they no longer want in the name of debt. Debt is violence because "finances, through debt, constitute a form of direct exploitation of the labor force, of the vital potential and the ability of women to organize in the home, in neighborhoods, in their territories. Sexist violence is made even crueler through the feminization of poverty and the lack of economic autonomy implied by debt."[21] One form of violence cannot be separated from the other.

The document and the demonstration show another fold in which it is possible to conceive of gender violence. On the one hand, it exposes the importance of public policies and of large-scale economic regulation – taking external debt and everyday debt as dimensions of the same process. On the other hand, it points out that violence and the ways it is exerted on the bodies of women are not separate from the material conditions of existence: external debt is an issue for the feminist agenda, as is economic control of life. These issues are not generally included in the feminist agenda the way they are often woven into left-wing programs, more willing to establish general nuclei aimed at singular results. The feminist method is different: it involves considering different planes at the same time, their knots and tangles, and understanding, as a chiastic structure, the personal and the general, the private and the public, the historic and the natural.

Strike, interruption and foundation

In 1907, the French syndicalist and theorist Georges Sorel published *Reflections on Violence*.[22] Concerned with the reformist shift in socialism, he pondered the ways of producing a revolutionary change. Parliamentary action and union struggle submit the proletariat to a logic of calculation, an instrumental rationality that connects means and ends, that proposes tactics and benefits. Revolution, on the other hand, requires consideration of the immeasurable, something irreducible to calculation, remainder: the myth. Only the myth, image-force, is capable of pulling people outside the cycle in which they are condemned to reproduce a system that exploits them. The proletariat, free of any myth, may fight for partial improvements but not for an end to the plundering. The unionist's myth is that of general strike. A general strike may or may not be carried out, but it permits a re-reading of partial struggles, past strikes, demands to government. A general strike expands the revolutionary horizon beyond the narrow scope of instrumental rationality.

The myth, for Sorel, is the opposite of utopia. While utopia states what society will be like in the future and upon doing so establishes a kind of desirable subjectivity, an aim and a moral compass, the myth is the producer of events; it does not ponder what will come, it has no idea. Revolution is catastrophic rupture, extinction of what is known, not something deduced from the conditions of the present. The myth that calls to action has nothing to say of the future. The general strike fills this role because it interrupts the functioning of the world, suspending automatic social reproduction and production of wealth.

A strike can have a clear tactical plan: demands or concessions. But a strike carries with it, almost in secret, another dimension: to configure another world and another way of life. It is what led the female worker of the Wonder factory to protest, in 1968, the defeat on that other plane not related to wage.[23] The women's strikes, although they sometimes imply a specific demand, such as the strike in Poland against the criminalization of abortion, reactivate the mythical plane.[24] They mobilize images of another society, of lives redeemed, of necessary revolts, as they challenge submission to the patriarchy. The strike opens the way for questioning (what needs to be stopped?) and opens many common spaces – for better or for worse – zones of shared affirmation as well as shortcuts that avoid deeper questioning. It provides opportunity for a collective search for meaning and reason.

The creation of another temporality in the notion of the Sorelian myth is central to the women's strike, which creates a time of revolt in which to build demands and allow the emergence of a new subject. In a union strike, concessions, proposals and the subject (the union itself, the represented sector) precede the strike; in the women's strike, on the other hand, they create the very temporality in which these elements may emerge or be recognized. Walter Benjamin indicated the differences between partial strikes ("which are for the most part actually extortionate") and the general strike, characterized by a "deep moral, and genuinely revolutionary conception" against which "no objection can stand that seeks, on grounds of its possibly catastrophic consequences, to brand such a general strike as violent."[25] In Sorel, as well as in Benjamin's interpretation of Sorel, the strike plays an important role in its potential to delineate new modes of life, beyond all calculation and possibility or reality of transaction.

In the agitated months before the strikes, I participated in many assemblies and meetings, in person and virtually, on regional, local, sectorial and international levels. The conversation, unfailingly, centered on what it means to strike, whether it was a strike or a demonstration, whether it should last all day or an hour, if it should involve a pause, a mobilization, a moment of silence, a symbol placed on buildings, an identifying attire. It was all of the above. It was a halt in action that generated action: stopping in order to start, blocking one thing so that another could flow. A break from repetition that allowed for reinvention, halting competition to give way to complicity. Interruption of multitasking to think with others, playing out the utopic image of a liberated society, inscribing each act in the international women's strike. I write, and I know, as I do so, that I will re-read Sorel.

The strike is a break from everyday temporality. It revolts against it. As if it wore an angelic halo, it transcends the present. It constructs a lineage of struggles, but it is not limited to being a consequence determined by history. The series of organizations and activisms that arose after each large mobilization evidence the desire for the strike to endure: to return to the time of exception, promise for the future.

Auguste Blanqui, the tenacious French activist known as "the Incarcerated" for the number of years he spent imprisoned, wrote *Eternity by the Stars*.[26] His hypothesis is unique: time is infinite and things are finite, therefore in the universe there are many repetitions and doubles, of planets, stars and people. Even as the writer is imprisoned, many other Blanquis will be or were already locked up, on similar planets and at other times. None of them – he writes with anguish – is able to warn the others of what is to come. Nevertheless, we must not discount the notion that a battle can still be won even if all others have been lost and that Blanqui could be released from prison to become a victorious revolutionary. The theory is improbable, but what's of interest is its political basis: the revolution will be – as stated by Jacques Rancière[27] – a fortunate bifurcation, the interruption of social reproduction.

If the time of capital is endless repetition of the social order, interrupted only by natural disasters, economic collapse or war, revolutionary time is messianic, transcendental, looking to the future but also able to comprehend the past. Strike as myth, strike as interruption remits to this openness. Establishing a multiple temporality where a singular and linear one existed previously. It is a re-reading of the shared past, of enslaved ancestors – to revive one of the ghosts that haunts these paragraphs, Walter Benjamin[28] – and a genealogy of the women who invented worlds, paths to follow, recovery of the present, living memory. Consciousness of historicity does not condemn us to repetition. It is the condition for all new action. In Montevideo, on 8 March 2017, the strikers chanted "We are the granddaughters of the witches you couldn't burn." They are saying: we are all witches, our grandmothers were witches, they just went unnoticed or they fled the fire or evaded the inquisition. They construct a lineage of persecution and struggle. In Bilbao, on 8 March 2018, the collective chant put feminist lyrics to an anti-Franco resistance song.

An event is a break in time – a break that permits the past to breathe and imagine what it has not yet guessed. The international women's strike acts as this break in temporality. It is not merely a labor strike. It does not have a list of specific concessions. It is a strike in the factory, the office, the street, the bed, the house, the micro-enterprise, social media. Can we stop financial speculation or the economic interests that pursue us? Or mortgage payments? Or the judicial ruling that condemns a woman to prison? Or public transport, schools, kitchens, classes, Facebook posts, television? Striking can mean not watching TV, turning off social media, not buying products of a specific brand, boycotting certain companies. Emotions converge in the word "strike" and the term itself is disputed.

Strike, the many modes

The international women's strike occurs on different levels: local, neighborhood, national, global. None of these scales, in itself, gives sufficient credit to the force amassed in the various strains of feminism. On 8 March 2017, in different locations around Greater Buenos Aires, assemblies were held in neighborhoods, universities, workplaces. Then the activists got on trains to travel into the city. The action was called the big train ride and consisted of using the commute to hand out flyers, speak to other passengers, march up and down the train chanting. The following year, the action was repeated. The commute has become part of the repertoire of demonstrations, a spontaneous opportunity to spread the strike's message.[29] The strike implied divergence from functional roles to establish a non-instrumental moment.

The Argentine railroad network was dismantled in 1994. Some lines were eliminated, others given in concessions to private companies, forcing train repair and construction shops to close. Poverty descended on the towns along the abandoned tracks. One such place, Laguna Paiva, is proud of its nickname "Heroic Paiva." It was the last stronghold against the Larkin Plan,[30] President Frondizi's rail reform, which train workers interpreted, not without reason, as an advance of privatization. The strike against the Larkin Plan lasted more than forty days. The government decided to recruit strike-breakers – it was 1961 – and suppress the rebellion. The workers took refuge in the surrounding fields. They knew they were wanted. A train was headed toward "a group of women, very brave fighters – in reality they had never fought before but became warriors in that moment – who lived near the tracks and said 'It's not going to get past us.' They stood on the tracks. They called their neighbors to join them on the tracks, and there was a pile of sleepers and they began to pick up the heavy sleepers and place them across the tracks ... and the train had to stop"[31] – as told by a local librarian. The strike succeeded only partially: the Larkin Plan was suspended but the train repair shops never reopened.

Discovery of purpose, encounter with a kind of heroism that the women never imagined or wanted for themselves. A fork or intersection of tracks that was not avoided just because it was surprising. Fifteen years later, other women who until then had not been activists produced a political uproar by demanding the return of their detained children, alive. Female dissidents who had come before them, with their defiance, their tenacity, their iron will to cross the desert, were sometimes celebrated, sometimes drowned, sometimes feared, sometimes translated to existing logic. Maybe the women who sabotaged the train became militants or maybe not. They just thought that, in that moment and in that place, they had to say no and throw themselves on the handbrake so that the brutal destruction of living conditions could not be smuggled under the guise of modernizing progress.

In 1922, prostitutes in the town of San Julián, as narrated by Osvaldo Bayer, refused to work for the soldiers who had repressed strikers in Patagonia. They exiled these murderers from the sexual-labor pact. The prostitutes' strike showed their solidarity with the insurgent peons whose rebellion had been fiercely punished. These five women decided to withdraw their bodies from offer as merchandise, to become instead testimonies to class loyalty. They were not union workers but they went on strike. They did not have labor rights, but they created their right to say no. This act is as powerful as the women who blocked the railway with sleepers: they found in a collective action an unknown power, the unexpected ability to resist, a desire to disobey.

In 1936, a series of strikes and occupations of factories occurred in France. Simone Weil, proletariat philosopher, recorded the events in her correspondence and articles. She noted, with anguish, the fettering of labor to machinery, the subordination to the rhythm of the factory, the mechanization, the emptiness, the submission of the female worker. One scene is particularly heart-wrenching: it is cold and rainy, the female workers crowd in the open factory doorway through which they aren't allowed to pass until the specified time.[32] Managers, permitted to enter, push past them. Not one woman disobeys the order, subservient to the clock. When the strikes break out, Weil does not think they will triumph, but she knows they are necessary: "for the first and last time – I hope – other memories besides silence, subjugation and submission will surround the heavy machinery; memories that will give the heart a bit of encouragement, adding a touch of human warmth in the midst of all that cold metal."[33] The first line of the article reads: "at last one can breathe."

Disobediences

On 8 March 2017, forty-one girls were killed in a fire in Guatemala. Fifteen survived. They had been living at the Virgen de Asunción Safe House – an orphanage for some, a juvenile delinquent center for others. Beginning in 2013, the institution had been repeatedly reported for mistreatment, forced abortions, torture, contaminated food and sexual abuse. The day before the fire, the girls escaped, apparently allowed by staff to do so. The government sent 250 officers to recapture them.[34]

Through the global response launched by feminist activists to support the survivors and demand justice for the dead, details emerged:

> Fifty-six girls were locked in a classroom measuring 6.8 x 7 meters. They were given scant mattresses without sheets to sleep on and they had no access to toilets, forcing them to improvise a latrine inside the classroom. At 8:45 in the morning, after they were given breakfast, a fire was started. Some media outlets and official versions claimed that the girls themselves set fire to a mattress in protest, but this is still under investigation. For eleven minutes, the girls were exposed to temperatures over three hundred degrees centigrade and their small bodies burned. Despite their cries for help they were not released.[35]

They were left to die by fire and asphyxiation. The murdered girls were poor, imprisoned; they'd committed crimes or simply had no social support network. This happened the same day as the first international women's strike. The slaughter reminded us all of the bonfire to which rebellious women have historically been destined and the line that separates bodies that deserve to live from bodies that are disposable. They were girls and their bodies were inscribed with the severest punishment. They had indigenous and mestizo heritage, and the fire reactivated age-old oppressions. They were sexualized and had been previously punished through sex. Between the fire that killed the female workers in the New York textile factory in 1911[36] and this fire there are similarities and differences. These were not female workers fighting for rights; they were girls trying to escape endless oppression, sexual violence, devastating poverty, institutionalized cruelty. The women's strike must contemplate their lives and their deaths. What would striking look like for girls in an orphanage in Guatemala?

Unexpected coincidence connects different events on a shared date, but what happened is not arbitrary chance: these bodies had already been abused, imprisoned, neglected, stripped of rights, marginalized. These girls are the sacrificial figures of our time. They exemplified with their short lives and tragic endings what is denounced with the battle cry "not one less." It does not mean not one (valuable life) less, or not one (normative woman) less, it means not one woman less in the radical, absolute sense, that declares, every time, all lives are valuable and all bodies count, should be counted and recount their own stories. The Guatemalan collective #NosDuelen56,[37] made up of activists, journalists, artists, came up with ways to highlight the individuality of each of the girls. They highlight, as well as the number, the brutality of the collective massacre. Neglect and death unite a series of individual lives, paths, enthusiasms, interrupted desires. The #NosDuelen56 group called for artists to create portraits of the girls, which were used in the street demonstrations and online, at the memorials and in the demands for justice. Jean-Paul Sartre imagined that killing was almost impossible for anyone who could see themselves in the face of another, because that face represented the unique life that the murderer would end.[38] To construct an artistic image of each face, denouncing the indifferent criminal power that reduced their individualities to ashes, is a profoundly political act.[39]

The government response attempted to place blame on the murdered girls. They were disobedient and they put themselves at risk. This takes the pedagogy of cruelty created by gender violence to an extreme. We have all heard: "I'm going to teach you a lesson," with a hand held high or a voice that threatens punishment. Discipline may come in the form of beatings, stabbings, bullets, fire. "I'm going to teach you a lesson" is the voice of the owner, the landholder, the conqueror, the foreman, the colonizer, the master. "I'm going to teach you a lesson" is the verbal precursor to physical violence. Mariana Dopazo is the former daughter of Miguel Etchecolatz, one of the men responsible for the Argentine genocide. Along with other daughters of murderous military men, she legally changed her surname as a rejection of and de-affiliation from her father's actions. In January 2018, a judge granted Etchecolatz the benefit of house arrest. Mariana wrote a pained article: "I disobeyed him, yes, as much as it was possible to do so. And just as quickly his blows followed. He was cruel. He punished me severely and then he was concerned: 'Look at what you make me do to you,' he said. When I heard his footsteps, I smelled the scent of terror."[40] The victim is made guilty of the violence that is unleashed upon her: she is said to provoke the rapist, to seek out the corrective punishment, to make the abuser hit her. The murderer who kills to serve the nation or tortures or rapes a prisoner to gain information, in the home he uses abuse as a form of education.

The Guatemalan government, responsible for the murder of the young girls, tried to wash its hands of the matter: it was the girls' fault. Some of the survivors even internalized the narrative of guilt: I disobeyed, now I'm suffering the consequences. Feminists have tried to separate disobedience and punishment, to find the seam of the rupture; the non-conformity that will establish new ways of life, give way to freedoms, expand rights,[41] establish identities. Mariana Dopazo, despite the corrective violence of her genocidal father, reinvented her genealogy, leaving the family of a victimizer to join the family of the victims. The former daughters create this possibility for rupture. Neither family nor identity is, in the end, an issue of blood; rather, they are political affiliations, chosen communities.

To strike is to disobey; an untying of the reins of submission and control. On 8 March 2017, the women's march was repressed in the Buenos Aires city center. Some twenty people were arrested. The previous night, six activists had been detained while trying to promote the strike. On 7 March, a union demonstration devolved into outrage and violence. The police did not intervene. The first repression of a political mobilization in the capital was on 8 March. The government powers attempted once again to correlate disobedience with punishment. The joyful energy of the demonstrations frightened authorities as it exposed a collective body that had not been defeated by repression and criminalization.

Body and time

Benjamin Franklin established an equivalence: time is money[42] – measureable in savings and wealth. Measured through money and morality. Time should not be wasted. The founding logic of capitalism implies separation of men and women to allow for greater productivity. Technologies permit us to make full use of this expropriation of time. We work day and night, during office or factory hours and outside them. We are on call beyond working hours: overextending ourselves in the commute from work to home or in informal jobs or domestic chores and childcare duties. All time is subordinated to the maximization of its utility. In *Cuore* (Heart), by Edmundo De Amicis,[43] a boy secretly substitutes for his copyist father at night, so that he can earn a few more pennies. In Guy de Maupassant's story "The Necklace"[44] a woman borrows an adornment to wear to a party where she wants to impress. She loses it and in order to replace it acquires a huge amount of debt and takes on demanding jobs to pay it down. Ten years later, her body is ruined and aged.

In "The Necklace," debt functions as an expropriation of time, the chains of destitution. Time is not disposed of but is a measurement of wealth. A minute, a penny. If Franklin provides the model of the man who successfully accumulates wealth, Maupassant portrays the bitter irony of the cost of appearance, class as fraud, the brutalization of domestic work. Mrs Loisel is the opposite of Cinderella: the sad story of the working woman who sinks into debt to look like a princess for a day. How many poor families follow this path? How many quinceñera parties are princely nights that will be paid for with redoubled efforts and sad austerity over the years that follow? For others, debt begins with plastic surgery or to pay for a clandestine abortion.

Maupassant's story shows the interconnections between beauty standards, class limits, effort, time and exhaustion. Appearances are paid for in blood. The worst of the losses is the expropriation of time to rest. For this reason, the working classes fought for limits on the workday, retirement rights, sick leave, paid vacations: the right to time. "Time is money" obscures a deeper truth: time is life. It is monetized by a society that has use only for what produces wealth and value. The line that divides disposable lives and lives with value is drawn in this identification, demanding the right to life itself, just because, the women's movement, pure affirmation, offers the most radical challenge to this model.

The separation of time and the vital force with which it is measured is played out on our bodies in a singular manner. The cosmetic, pharmacological and medical industries profit by separating time from the traces it leaves on the living body. Aging is unacceptable for those held captive to beauty standards that demand thinness and youth. Just as the black power movement challenges the ways of treating hair, rebelling against models that limit beauty to straight hair and condemn kink,[45] feminism debates the demand for eternal youth, the pressure to hide one's age, the obligation to repress tiredness, changes in energy, the valorization of faces without lines and bodies without fat. These standards, as stated by fat activists, come from the neoliberal regime of thinness.

Our bodies are useful only as sites of chemical application, surfaces of an unending and unavoidable battle against time. Time was taken from us the moment it was linked to commerce, and the loss is made worse by the demand for a body as a smooth timeless surface. Separation of body and time transforms humans into profits for the industries that dole out antidepressants so we may go to work or care for our children with a smile, that spoon feed us cough syrup to maintain productivity, that slather us with creams to stave off wrinkles, that wheel us into the operating room to reverse the evidence of time, that dictate diets or workout routines so we may look ageless. A misogynist and ironic phrase that circulates in Argentina reflects reality: there are no ugly women, only poor husbands.

Pounds of flesh

Time is money, and it is counted in pounds of flesh, as we've seen from Shylock to the present. Bodies taxed, made profitable, squeezed of every last drop of value, cogs in the judicial system

– victims or perpetrators – sites of experimentation, objects of medicalization. Youth and health acquire the status of a moral mandate. A fat body is seen as sick and as a sign of ethical failure, a lack of responsibility, an inclination toward an unhealthy life. In recent years, fat activism has emerged[46] as an act of rebellion. One activist said in an assembly to organize the 8 March strike: "If you want to make the earth shake, that's what we fat girls are here for." The multiple branches of feminism accommodate a diversity of bodies and forms of dissent and numerous examples of what a body can achieve when it is freed from prescribed molds and impositions.

The medical industries produce difference as illness: obesity, sadness, the cycles of life. Time is money and money is flesh. The manual used to diagnose mental illness – DSM – turns moods (melancholy, distraction) into symptoms that should be medicated.[47] The connection between psychiatrists, laboratories and lifestyles classifies and normalizes an array of practices, dispositions and consciousness, converting the subject into a chronic consumer of medication and treatments. Who knows about the body and its processes? Not women, unless it is as guinea pigs for a new treatment. The construction of legitimate knowledge, with institutions that regulate and certify it,[48] implies the de-legitimization of everyone else. Ancestral ways of treating bodily cycles, traditionally practiced by women, were burned in the bonfires or written off as superstition. They persist, however, in widespread social practices. Thousands of women in Argentina know how to cure indigestion, rashes, warts and the evil eye with rituals and words that are passed down to them in secret. But a large part of the treatment of bodies lies in the hands of the medical industry, which does not disdain this other knowledge as blubbering or savage but, rather, lunges upon any alternative treatment in order to commercialize it. Every type of medicine will find its niche in the market and a horde of fanatical users: allopathic, synthetic, homeopathic, Chinese, new age.

In many countries, abortion is criminalized to varying degrees, but women and pregnant bodies are objects of the profitable birth control industry. Vasectomy, while less invasive than pills and less drastic than the tubal ligation which many poorer women undergo, is still uncommon. Germaine Greer chronicles the medical practices related to menopause:[49] from the development of electro-gynecology in the nineteenth century – interventions with wands connected to batteries applied to the uterus and reproductive organs, as terrifying as any torture method – to the contemporary popularity of preventative hysterectomy. A practice that is justified with the threat of cancer and the idea that the body has the potential to produce its own downfall, that the cells will go crazy and give way to illnesses that will consume it. Many notions are inscribed in this practice. Especially, that the uterus makes sense only during a woman's fertile period and after that its absence does not damage bodily integrity. Illness is business, as is the fear of illness. Current hormonal replacement therapies, which administer estrogen to avoid alterations in a woman's behavior as she goes through menopause, are based in heteronormative discipline, the institution of family and traditional sexual life.

The prohibition of abortion, the submission to normative criteria for femininity and seduction, obstetric violence, the medicalization of bodily functions, the production of health as moral regulator, position the bodies of women as subordinate to medical and pharmacological industries. Both the female body's functionality and dysfunction are profitable. This creates conformity to a regimented life and a kind of chronic fragility since these molds are unattainable and outdated. The most useful body is not the one that functions properly; it is the one that functions properly with the help of medication and supplements. In the face of this situation, the women's strike implies a politicization of health and illness. We say enough is enough to procedures that frame difference as illness and demand control over all bodily conditions, that expropriate misfortune and reproduction, that punish abortion while simultaneously stripping pregnant women of the decision over how they will give birth, converting women into mere patients and ignoring them as subjects.

The personal is political

The double affirmation "Not one less: we want ourselves alive," chanted at demonstrations and strikes across Argentina and Latin America, should be understood in the context of the existential revolution summarized in the phrase "the personal is political." The notion of life put forth by the women's movement debates all the conditions of existence and the ways in which subjectivities are created. Life is not only survival. Nor is it limited to nature or biology. "The personal is political" places all dimensions of life within the realm of public debate and collective creation. While the radical commercialization of life leads to individuation and false autonomy, ignoring that each life is lived alongside others, never self-sufficient, never wholly separated, the idea that the personal is political positions each life in relation to others and says that this cooperative narrative, this always dispossessed mode of existence, has a political nature, is cemented as historicity, is constructed as economy, is challenged through conflict. It is never natural, obvious or unilateral.

Recognition of this dispossession constitutes a break with the ideological production of individuality and with the illusion of autonomy, which supposes an intentional and solitary consciousness capable of determining its own conditions. This definition of autonomy appears in certain statements used in the women's movement, such as "my body, my choice"; but in general it is at odds and in tension with the notion of autonomy as the realization of personal desires and recognition of vulnerability. "The personal is political" implies debating the personal itself, the mode in which it is constituted by cutting the ties to its social and historical definition, in order to expose the collective nature through which all subjectivity is produced.

In certain labor conflicts the slogan "If our lives don't matter, produce without us" was chanted. It means, if our bodies don't count, don't count on them to produce wealth. The statement shows the link between the right to life and the definition of life as productive utility. Capitalism, historically, has produced this disassociation. The distinction allowed slaves, servants and the proletariat to be exploited to the point of death. Political and social movements that demanded rights created the inverse operation: life should be guaranteed as separate from productivity. The women's movement, in the face of crimes that prove our lives are disposable, takes this a step further: if we have no value (we don't deserve to be taken care of), we will not produce value. We will strike. The women's strike redefines notions of life, time, the shared and production to configure another way of life and a new social order. It is an interruption. It produces images of a time never experienced, not yet known, mythical. It is the time of carnival, revolution, party, street mobilization, occupation; a time in which the paths of the personal and political, sexuality and activism intersect. This time is the mythical nucleus of street demonstrations and strikes. The call to strike on 8 March 2017 in Argentina declared that this date would constitute the first day of the lives we want to live.

The end of the end of history (footnote)

Mark Fisher begins his book *Capitalist Realism* with the affirmation that it is easier to imagine the end of the world than to imagine the end of capitalism. A catastrophe seems more likely than redemption and the Apocalypse more likely than socialism. The Thatcherian affirmation that "there is no alternative" is articulated in the fierce capacity of capital to control everything: in post-Fordism "work and life become inseparable. Capital follows you when you sleep. Time ceases to be linear, becomes chaotic, is broken down into punctiform divisions."[50] The women's strike, nevertheless, creates an imagination more utopic than apocalyptic. It reopens a historicity that contemporary capitalism seemed to have abolished.

Paolo Virno, in *Déjà Vu and the End of History*, re-reads the Marxist thesis that capital is objectivized work which, to produce value, should be connected to living work: every time capital tries to purchase labor-power, it runs up against a living body.[51] Hence the importance of bio-politics or governance of life that, as Foucault postulated and Virno recovers, is not a repressive device but one that spreads from the contention of impulses to the most unstoppable license, of the detailed interdiction of tolerant gazes, of the ghetto for the poor to the highest Keynesian salaries, from the maximum security prisons to the welfare state.[52] The novelty of bio-politics and its capitalist function is that what is purchased are not living bodies but vital potential, labor force. That is to say, as Virno writes, "the sum of all the physical and intellectual abilities encompassed by corporality." The production process links three temporal dimensions: work objectivized as capital, labor potential and labor in action. Past-past, past-potential, and present. The appropriation of potential as labor force is the basis for the illusion of the end of history, because it obliterates the creative force that makes possible all action, even the transformative action of repetition/social accumulation. Everything is flattened in the act.

Without the difference between the potential and the real, between the actual and the virtual (to use the precise distinction proposed by Henri Bergson),[53] there is no historicity of experience:

> there is history as far as language, although we speak only through an act of words, never resolving into one or another particular emission, and neither into an infinite series of eventual emissions, but that exist as inactionable potential. There is history as far as a determined job or a determined understanding are inseparable, and also absolutely different, from respective faculties, from the labor force and the intellect.[54]

The end of history occurs when this potential is flattened in pure action or when repetition and citation prevail.

When the women's movement calls a strike it is to challenge what is understood as work and the link between work, time and life; it is producing a break in that flattening of potential. It unpacks what has been condensed by the logics of production. It uses inherited language to question what it names and how it does so. It thinks about language and about its potential. Politicized through collective action, language ceases to be citation and the labor force ceases to be merely an actualization of capital. Bodies in the streets do think. They think and they name. They name and they establish. They establish and declare the end of the end of history.

4

Power, Representation and Bodies: The Construction of a Political Subject

I demand rights for women because I am convinced that all the ills of the world come from this forgetfulness and scorn that until now have been inflicted on the natural and imprescriptible rights of the female.

Flora Tristán

Forms of feminism

Since 2011, Slutwalks have taken place across various cities in Brazil.[1] In 2015 there were enormous mobilizations in response to gender violence in Argentina, Spain, Peru, Chile and Mexico. In Brazil, female agricultural workers mobilized in the Marcha das Margaridas[2] (Daisy chain walk), and tens of thousands of women of African descent marched on Brasilia on 18 November. The following year, there were women's strikes in Poland and in Argentina. In January 2017, the women of the United States held a Women's March. On 8 March 2017 collectives and activists around the world organized the first international women's strike. During that same year feminist networks and assemblies multiplied exponentially.[3] Spurred on by the strike, activist groups proliferated (ranging from medics who assist in abortions to those involved in community radio and street art) across all of Latin America. Feminism has become the largest source of youth activism. In 2018, another international women's strike occurred. The Zapatista Army for National Liberation in Mexico held an international women's assembly in Chiapas. In Argentina, there was a coming together of activists from different unions and a massive historic march on Buenos Aires, where hundreds of thousands of persons mobilized on 8 March. This list displays the growing power of feminism and the central role of a new political subject that cannot be ignored by the prevailing order. It challenges institutions and forces them to revise hierarchies, power, practices. It also awakens opportunism and veiled attempts to appropriate or consume the movement. The force of the movement is noteworthy, as is its multiform and polyglot nature.

In this new and unique unfolding, a conglomeration of tensions and paradoxes collide. One is the issue of language economy, which condenses in the word "woman" a diversity of existences, turning signifiers into an accordion of signs. Far from a univocal relationship between biology and identity, paths lead to construction, deconstruction, self-perception, rupture. In Argentina, the National Women's Conference[4] has taken place every year since 1986, with attendance increasing each year. In 2016, 70,000 people attended, and in 2013 it included for the first time a workshop led by trans women.[5] Lesbian and *travesti* collectives refused to have their identities dissolved in the signifier "women" and demanded to be recognized for their difference. This process makes it possible to put a name to a conglomeration of existences that refuse to let their histories and diverse realities be erased. The new political subject is a heterogeneous body. And if it expands with a visibly increasing force on the streets it is, precisely, because it draws nourishment from the break with the naturalization of corporality. Lohana Berkins, a trans feminist activist, was fundamental in the deconstruction of feminism's anchoring in the naturalized female body.[6] The issue comes up when drafting documents, political manifestos, public speeches, when the necessity of naming demands a synthesis – women – that can inadvertently be taken as neo-biologism or essentialism. It requires recognition of the unity as well as the diversity of individuals who identify as women and, upon doing so, challenges the term used to name both sex and gender.

Diverse corporality also means multiracialism. Bodies are racialized and relegated to groups that occupy different places in the social hierarchy. Race determines whether one exploits others or suffers exploitation, whether one has greater or lesser chances to live. A black woman in Brazil has to fight to avoid a destiny of domestic service. The same is true for an indigenous woman in Argentina who migrates to the city. Precarious work and lack of equal access to education and health inscribe the history of colonial exploitation on modern-day bodies. Feminism surges forth in the assemblies leading up to 8 March in Argentina to denounce the structural inequality that carries the name of race. It articulates the principle of equality among all women who make up the female political subject and a consideration of the real inequality that exists between different groups of women.

On 4 June 2018 the document written in the preparatory assemblies in Buenos Aires was read by a trans woman, a woman of African descent, an indigenous woman, and a female worker who had been made redundant. Intersectionality is a decision, a constant questioning of who is left out of the dominant public presentation. Which bodies appear and which do not? To write this story, the story of feminisms, the story of women as key political subjects in the present, we must link fragments, small events, words and speeches, images. The story of that subject is also the story of their tears, the story of the unexpected mobilizations and ruptures that have come before. I often recall scenes from two documentary films that narrate the genealogy of this subject: *Las compañeras tienen grado* (1995), by María Inés Roqué, and *Piqueteras* (2002), by Malena Bystrowicz and Verónica Mastrosimone. The first details the women of the Ejército Zapatista de Liberación Nacional (EZLN; Zapatista Army for National Liberation) in Mexico and the second is about the rise of the movements of the unemployed in Argentina.

Roqué films at the height of the Zapatista rebellion. She recounts the women's law that created the movement – breaking the restrictions of political and sexual autonomy proscribed in the indigenous communities – and aided its rise to power. Twenty-four years after the public emergence of the EZLN in 1994, Zapatista women called an international assembly, on 8 March. One of them stated: "And even though we didn't have much education, we did have a lot of anger, a lot of courage derived from all the shit they do to us for being women, for being

indigenous, for being poor and now for being Zapatistas."[7]
Gender equality was a concern from the start of this indigenous
movement, but it emerged as a key issue only at the international
assembly, opening a space for dialogue between feminism and
indigenous rights.

The documentary by Mastrosimone and Bystrowicz centers
on the origin of the *piquetero* movement, named for the road
blocks used as protest measures by unemployed persons. At first,
the road blocks were linked to the closure of public companies
or the privatization of mines and drilling sites. The filmmakers
place the focus on the women who were important participants
in the organizations, although they were not the most publicly
recognized leaders. In the interviews, the issue of feminism is not
addressed, but the *piquetero* movement was fundamental to the
creation of popular feminism, which, after 2001, spread within
the movements of the unemployed and the classist parties of the
left.[8] The national conferences of women were transformed by
the incorporation of this popular activism, and political organizations were affected by their encounter with feminism.

Popular feminism found a new opportunity to take to the
public stage during the mobilizations carried out by Not One
Less. On 3 June 2015 the classist inscription of the movement was
debated. The initial organizers were a group of publicly identi-
fiable people from the media or the academic world – writers,
journalists, social scientists, designers – who used their personal
social media accounts and networks to encourage participation.
Other famous people in the media and the public sphere echoed
the call. This generated distrust among the ranks of popular
feminist activists. Nevertheless, the mobilization proved to be
something quite different: many women from working-class
backgrounds and an enormous quantity of young people took to
the streets. The space that was opened, a political achievement,
spanned diverse classes, ethnicities and generations.

Multitudes

Argentine society has a long history of street mobilization.
Political disputes are often inscribed in the urban narrative, with
comparisons over how many blocks of people can be counted
at a given demonstration. Elections and political parties cannot

contain this alternative form of politicization created through the public appearance of bodies. In 1889 José María Ramos Mejía published *Las multitudes argentinas*[9] (The Argentine multitudes), which narrated the history of the nation from the perspective of the slippery, threatening and promising subject of the masses. He was inspired by Gustave Le Bon,[10] as Freud was in his *Group Psychology and the Analysis of the Ego*.[11] A century later, Argentine intellectuals updated these readings in a collective publication that borrowed Ramos Mejía's title.[12] The work that summarized the debates of the period was not Le Bon's but *Multitude: War and Democracy in the Age of Empire*, by Michael Hardt and Antonio Negri.[13] This book impacted social science research as well as public debate, as it contemplated the subject that emerged when changes sparked by capitalism impeded the formation of a traditional working class. Neither the union nor the class-based political party imagined the battles for emancipation and its protagonists.

The updated reading was received enthusiastically in the heat of the *piquetero* conflict and the events of December 2001, when popular mobilizations railed against the double financial and leadership crisis. The transition to democracy had begun in 1983, with the fundamental decision to bring charges against those responsible for state-sponsored terrorism. One major challenge was the stabilization of the economy. In 1989, hyperinflation and looting brought a dramatic end to this first democratic government. Horacio Verbitsky, the well-known investigative journalist, describes this crisis as a kind of message to the incoming government:[14] it would be impossible to govern free from the influence of corporate power. The corporate class had been both accomplice to and beneficiary of the state-sponsored terrorism and the nationalization of external debt and saw democracy almost as an obstacle.

The government that followed carried out a wide program of reforms centered around the reduction of labor rights and the privatization of public companies. This paved the way for neoliberal accumulation, in step with the rest of Latin America. At the start of the twenty-first century, however, this neoliberal regime would be cracked wide open. The movements in support of Chavez in Venezuela and his later electoral victory, the water and gas wars in Bolivia and the 2001 crisis in Argentina were popular and massive responses to the established order.

In many countries new modes of government were attempted, focused on articulation with social movements, policies of market regulation, strategies to create equality, and modes of protectionism and reparation. Massive mobilization was part of the strategy of both the government and the opposition.

In the history of a country where crowds are capable of starting and ending processes through occupying the streets, the feminist mass was conspicuous by its absence. It had its inaugural moment with the first Not One Less mobilization. In what order should the actions of this mass be narrated? How does public demonstration relate to the construction of a new political subject? What makes it stand out in the political history of a country where issues are regularly placed on the agenda in response to public demonstrations? How were later mobilizations affected by the dramatically different political climate under Mauricio Macri's government, which was backed by corporate power and has altered the narrative on mobilization to the point of instating repressive practices against demonstrators?

Not One Less

I live in the center of Buenos Aires, seven blocks from the National Congress. There are weeks in which only a few days go by without a road being blocked by protesters. Activist movements – unions, social organizations – shout their demands on the streets. Each and every political group does it.[15] The mobilization of women in Argentina must be considered in the context of protest and occupation of public space as a characteristic of national politics. Taking to the streets to demonstrate or protest is a well-worn tactic of political practice, used by all and legal since democracy was restored in 1983. It is even carried out by conservatives, who may complain about the road blocks but who will themselves cut off street access to make their own complaints heard.

Many of the mobilizations are large, and there are often disputes over the size of the crowd and the number of participants. There was no debate on 3 June 2015, when the massive march banished any possibility of downplaying the turnout. There was surprise over its extent as well as the double novelty of a mostly female crowd and the fact that there was no link to any traditional political or social organization. It was understood by many of the participants to be something created by civil society that had occurred spontaneously, without intermediaries. This phenomenon occurred thanks largely to social media – especially Twitter and Facebook – and the call was echoed by news outlets, producing the sensation of an immediate link between the underlying message and the decision to mobilize. There were political posters, and political organizations chanted slogans related to the issues, but their presence did not overshadow the image of a turnout that went well beyond organized activism.[16]

The first demonstration was held outside of Congress.[17] As soon as the call began to circulate, protests were organized across thirty cities around the country. They called for an end to the violence of femicide, with a message that everyone could support – disagreement was defense of murder. The call was not limited to women, much less to feminists. However, the crowd was overwhelmingly female, and the posters and performances had a feminist tone. Many people said to journalists and in front of cameras that it was the first time they had participated in a demonstration. Many others were clearly familiar with the routines of occupation of public space and used well-known symbols (clothes, badges, banners) to show their political positions. The many voices of the crowd demanded the right to life. They did not ask for restrictions on the lives of others but demanded freedom of sexuality, the right to abortion, and autonomy.

The members of the Not One Less collective, which put out the call to protest, are the daughters of the mobilized mass. The mass, wrote Paolo Virno, is always ambivalent and its emergence is not in itself positive.[18] Bodies on the street may be there to denounce other bodies, to demand restrictions or the denial of rights. The massive marches in the name of public safety, for example, held in Argentina in response to bloody murders, articulated exclusionary and punitive demands: "human rights are given to criminals, and not to citizens like us," as one organizer of the first mobilization for public safety said onstage.[19] The mobilizations against femicide, as well as the documents created by the Not One Less collective and produced broadly across feminist activism, aim to understand, interpret and articulate the voice of the street and propose codes, as we tremble at the force of the bodies gathered, share stories and sing chants. The message: the problem is machismo, the cause is the patriarchy. It sets aside the demand for punishment and prison sentences to reinstate the construction of non-oppressive and equalitarian practices.[20]

In the women's marches, we chant "Now that we're together, now that they can see us, the patriarchy will fall, will fall, feminism will win, will win." This sentence summarizes various points: the strength in numbers, visibility and imminent victory. A protest song does not narrate mediation. If affirms the public emergence of the collective subject. In the plaza on 3 June there were banners identifying political parties, feminist organizations with political affiliations, organized collectives. Nevertheless, the march was recognized as autonomous. The government didn't know whether to consider the demonstration as oppositional or favorable. Among the participants were women with diverse political leanings and varying degrees of public visibility.[21] Before this first march there was no collective, just a gathering of individuals who came together to answer a call to action.

By the following year's march, a collective had formed, but one whose composition is continuously changing. Even with the many internal shifts, the demonstrations maintained autonomy from any political party. The organization's charter reads:

> Not One Less is not affiliated with any political party, but it is political, and we collaborate with other collectives that share common objectives without losing our autonomy. We are a collective that operates beyond the reach of the government and political parties, corporations and capital. Autonomy and transversal politics are necessary for a women's movement that aims to propose reforms even as it knows that everything must change.[22]

The collective statement

Not One Less was the general message behind the massive mobilizations of women. It is also the name of a collective, and, to add to the confusion, since 3 June 2016 it has been the name given to the organizational assemblies held to organize each event, which include the involvement of different types of organizations – political parties, unions, feminist collectives and cultural groups. When a statement is attributed to Not One Less, it may be original to the collective or merely supported by it. At the same time, since the term "Not one less" is key to all current feminist demands, it is referenced across multiple political agendas.

Three assemblies were held to organize the 8 March 2017 strike in the city of Buenos Aires. Activists from different organizations (around 200 collectives) participated alongside women who were not affiliated with any group. A collective document was drafted to be read at the principal demonstration. The following year there were five organizational assemblies, and attendance exceeded one thousand persons per meeting as the document was expanded, taking the previous year's version as its basis. I will pause to highlight a few of the document's key points in order to illustrate some of the decisions made and also to recount the surprising fact that a collective document, amid tensions and controversies, was able to be created at all.[23]

The document details an origin, a genealogy, an agenda of demands and a political stance. It begins:

> We are here today because together we have created a second international feminist strike. We strike against firings and government cutbacks and for legal, safe and free abortion. We strike to put an end to femicide and travesticide as well as the governmental and economic violence that nourish them. Our disobedience to the patriarchy and capitalism spreads across territories, revolutionizing homes, bedrooms, streets. We have urged all unions to participate in the strike and its organizational assemblies.

The context is defined: opposition to governmental actions, denouncement of different types of violence – sexist, economic, political – and the desired but tense relationship with the unions. Then the group's lineage is outlined:

> We strike because we are part of a shared and international history. We are here today, and we carry with us, in each of our battles, the 15,000 female textile workers, mostly migrants, who demanded an eight-hour workday at the beginning of the twentieth century in New York; we carry with us the feminists of the 1960s and 1970s, and especially the Latin American feminists, the Russian women who instigated the 1917 revolution against the tsar; the black feminists of the 1960s; the lesbians and *travestis* who paved the way for the recognition of other existences and other corporalities; the major figures and the anonymous heroines; the forcibly disappeared

and murdered women throughout the history of this struggle. We are here because we were preceded in battle by the Mothers and Grandmothers of Plaza de Mayo and by the female *piqueteras*.

This subject inherits, narrates and selects its own lineage. These women do not merely encounter a ready-made legacy, they weave it for themselves and for the women who will come after them. They do so with a consciousness that is non-identitary, knowing that each name they include is a decision. This heritage is not passed down by the history of any nation or class, by any pre-existing community. As a new subject, the women create their history and mother tongue – a legacy of both exploitation and disobedience.

The text defines the subject of the strike: "We are employed and unemployed, salaried workers and receivers of government subsidies, self-employed and employed in domestic service and childcare." Professional diversity is presented as a defining characteristic. This agenda takes on many feminist struggles: the legalization of abortion, sexual dissidence, the eradication of gender violence, denouncement of the state's responsibility as an agent of violence, demand for the separation of Church and state.

The last paragraph states: "We strike because we have created the women's movement as a political subject. #Desire moves us. Desire for an international feminist movement that will revolutionize the world. Desire for inclusive, radical and intersectional feminism that invites everyone to unite in the resistance to racism and capitalist exploitation." The political subject is defined as part of an international movement, a strand of feminism that is inclusive and intersectional, anti-patriarchal and anti-capitalist, that "emerges as an alternative, the world over, to the advance of repression, racism and conservativism."

The document outlines an agenda of demands, illustrates the diversity of the subject that it creates, publicly displays what it conceives of as its own past, and explains its future aims. The strike is born of a unique moment in which what has been traditionally ignored is now exposed. It is the fruit of past organizational effort and seed for harvests that have yet to be reaped. No subject may endure without historicity. The unprecedented and earth-shattering mobilizations of women are furthered through these words and actions. A collective narration reminds us what has already been achieved and does not hold back on promises for what is yet to come. The life of a movement pulses through its stories, its loving remembrance of the past, and its mapping of the present. Words are a folding of events, a tapestry of meaning.

This political document, drafted through great collective effort, exposes how a subject, a narrative and an historic moment are constructed. None of these elements existed before the women's strike. Nothing could have predicted, within the Argentine political context, such a broad transversal politics, capable of producing a text that accommodates internal tensions and opposing traditions. Its texture is the roughness of the multiple. We may call this desire to create common ground "frontism," less evident in the organizational program than in the tone of the language utilized. Frontism, built up at the assemblies, breaks down in the disputes over who will speak on stage and the order in which the groups will march. The problem of visibility restores divisionary logic.

New waves of mobilized women emerge at each of the international strikes. Activists were shaken out of confinement to their small groups and invigorated by a new vitality that did not belong to us but that was transferred to us, modifying our sensibilities. On 8 March an alliance between feminism and social antagonism played out, shaping a radically democratic political subject. Argentine feminism, with its amassed experience, poses many questions regarding power, representation and rights, as well as classist interpellations and popular experiences, cutting across the entire political spectrum. At the same time, its collaboration with labor syndicates, social movements, popular neighborhood organizations and disputed labor sectors allows for a deepening of the feminist proposal itself. The subject begins to take shape, with new characteristics that complicate its classification and summarization.[24]

Dubious victories

In *The True Life*, Alain Badiou[25] imagines that the triumph of liberal feminism is possible – not as an end to repression but as the necessary updating of contemporary capitalism. Women as an army for accumulation of capital, capable of creating a new directorial elite, efficient and executive. The elevation of the feminine from a subordinate position to a place of power would be possible through a deep transformation of subjectivity, emerging from the differentiated production of the passage to adulthood. According to Badiou, in traditional societies, daughters accessed adulthood through marriage (through the mediation of man) and sons through military service (mediated by the law). Neither rite of initiation exists in most contemporary societies, among other reasons, on account of the democratization of the struggles against traditional hierarchies. Without the military initiation rite, the son never exits adolescence; his body is given over to consumption, sacrifice or merit, but he is unable to leave behind his infantile attachment to toys. The daughter, on the other hand, is a woman from the start. No waiting period. No putting it off. Hers is a premature womanhood. For the philosopher, this early becoming may transform the oppressed of today into the dominant group within a new but still unequal order. An alienated triumph. Because if woman has been historically constructed as the evil part, as a position and non-place, in the new order she will be the one who will govern, hyper-adapted, pragmatic organizer of existence. Badiou separates capitalism from the patriarchy and imagines the future as a dystopia of successful women surrounded by listless men.

Badiou's concern is an interesting one, although it ignores a series of tensions central to feminist theories and movements and ignores other, non-European theoretical and political production. There is always a risk that an insurrection will triumph only in its most conservative form, producing new elites and a partial shift in hierarchies. Badiou worries that feminism will displace communism as a construction myth and horizon for a non-capitalist society. Nancy Fraser is no less angry in her view: a certain brand of feminism has become the handmaiden of capitalism as it turns sexism into justification for new forms of inequality and exploitation.[26] For Fraser, some brands of feminism were convenient and easily translated by neoliberalism: criticizing the notion of the family wage provided a varnish of empowerment to the incorporation of women into the workforce under flexible conditions; the denunciation of economicism postponed the criticism of the political economy in name of the debate on sexism; and critique of the welfare state as paternalist laid the groundwork for the capture of popular lives by NGOs and microcredit companies.

All social movements produce messages that can be resignified and appropriated, put to the service of new restrictions. And, if anything characterizes capitalism, it's the ability to assimilate, the capacity to convert criticism into legitimization and funnel counterculture into the market dynamic. If the criticism of the family salary positioned the female wage as its objective, lessening the pressure to earn for all workers (by building families whose earnings come from two salaries), at the same time it produced greater autonomy for women who, through personal income, gained access to the monetized economy and were granted the autonomy to choose, construct and denounce.

Both Fraser's and Badiou's interpretation warn of the same threat: the neoliberal appropriation of any elements that would challenge the dominance of its regime, achieved through stripping the critique of the patriarchy from the criticism of social inequality. The Argentine women's movement has this dilemma in its sights. It is conscious of the risk and of the fact that every act – demonstration or strike – demands reflection on these connections. When it does so, many voices, especially from media outlets with closer links to those in power, will ask what one issue could possibly have to do with the other: what women's rights have to do with land disputes or with aquifers or with the closing of factories or the repression of protesters. When feminism presents a list of causes it supports, the spokespeople for neoliberal common sense call for a pure form of feminism, easily explained, reduced to a "gender" agenda. Efforts to avoid a dramatic destiny as handmaiden of capitalism or emerging as a new elite are already underway. The experience of popular strands of feminism allows us to pose – but not answer – the question of whether women are the point of articulation of demands, as the proletariat was in classic capitalism.

Life in question

Contemporary social struggles deal with the right to life. In many cases, they no longer deal with civil, political or social rights but are involved with the right to inhabit a space and survive on existing resources without being appropriated or codified by the market. The struggles of indigenous peoples, the battles over mineral rights and extractions that cause irreversible damage to the environment, the agricultural movements or the occupation of land take the idea of life head on. In poorer neighborhoods of Argentina, social organizations implement strategies to feed and protect the vulnerable: soup kitchens and meal vans, defense measures against the violent logic that the black market for drugs and corrupt security forces establish in the area. These struggles were renewed by the massive mobilizations against gender violence which constructed a complex conception of violence, not hand-to-hand combat between the female victim and her murderer, but something inscribed in the prevailing logic that produces disposable lives. When bodies are exploited to the point of death, or denied access to water, or displaced by the advance of agroindustry; when health services are driven by a commercial function, or governmental institutions act as another armed band that fights with bullets, or poor neighborhoods become ghettos; when capital casts its shadow over lands, leaving behind deserts – what is at stake is the right to life. Can the growth of the violence of femicide be contemplated outside a context which on a daily basis produces the inhibition of empathy toward suffering? If the value of life is at stake, as central to the market appropriation as to the conflict itself, shouldn't the individuals at the center of that spiral of violence have something fundamental to say?

When the women's movement states "We want ourselves alive," it does not mean only surviving and preserving biological life. "Life" implies autonomy, creativity, connection, desire, strength in numbers. The distinct modes in which the chant is continued indicate this. Some women chant "We want to be alive and free," others "alive, free and desiring" or "alive, free and debt free." In this way, "life" is linked to other qualities that reinforce a meaning that has always been present in the feminist affirmation.

The notion of life as more than mere survival, although survival is a condition of life, puts at the center of political subjectivity an issue that has always sparked debate. At the start of the twentieth century, philosophers of life who had been working since the previous century provided arguments for public mobilization and the aesthetic debate. José Carlos Mariátegui was able to appropriate Friedrich Nietzsche's vitalist conception and at the same time foster the combination between this philosophy and Marxism.[27] Two decades earlier, Georges Sorel had translated the Bergsonian consideration of life from a political perspective. These appropriations hinged more on the affirmative dimension of vitalism and on the conception of life as a vital force or creative energy than on something already given. For Henri Bergson, in Gilles Deleuze's keen interpretation, "life" is difference that interrupts repetition – not merely repetitive dynamics but duration and vital impulse.[28]

During the twentieth century the notion of life was the subject of controversy.[29] The rationalist operation of certain Marxist theories exiled it from the field of analysis, to the point that its very formulation was seen as suspicious: in *The Destruction of Reason*, György Lukács postulated that the philosophical and political affirmation of life as an impulse had paved the way for the destruction of rational principles, making Nazism possible.[30] In doing so, Lukács posited a limited and Manichean notion of reason that would place life on the side of the unthinkable and dangerous.

While political philosophy avoided contemplation of life, the regime of accumulation increasingly interweaves with life. Michel Foucault developed the critical notion of biopolitics to analyze the logics of power directed toward fundamental biological aspects of the human species.[31] Could "life" also be the topic of social struggles against power?[32] Would it carry the risks of an uncritical affirmation, of a polarization between passion and reason, a counterpoint between will and rationality? Carla Lonzi, Rivolta Fimmenile feminist activist in the 1970s, postulated a difference between men and women that centered on the consideration of life: "The masculine species has expressed itself by killing, the feminine by working to protect life."[33] She considers life as survival, from which meaning emerges. Whereas "man has sought the meaning of life beyond life and against life itself, for woman, life and the meaning of life are continuously overlapping."[34]

While difference may be affirmed, there is still the profound risk of unilaterization and of defining life as mere survival. Since the emergence of Not One Less, the women's movement in Argentina has deliberated over two types of statement. On the one hand are those who refer to a series of concrete preventative measures – judiciary actions with a gender perspective, economic resources and shelters for women at risk, a public register of femicide – and on the other are those who maintain that, to guarantee life, it is necessary to transform society, to alter the regimes of exploitation of labor and natural resources, the ownership of territories.

During 2017, one of the slogans used by the movement was "Our bodies, our territory," coined in order to link feminist struggles with the demands of the Mapuche communities in Patagonia. Some of these communities are made up of young people who come from families that migrated to cities and who live in precarious conditions. The new generation wants to reclaim their indigenous identities and recover their ancestral lands. The state represses them in defense of the rights of large landholders. The Not One Less collective held a feminist assembly in support of the indigenous people's claim to the lands and to denounce government repression of their protests. It was an unexpected alliance, one that displays the overlap between contemporary struggles: none of the movements emerge from naturalization of life, even though they may appear to do so. It is not about blood or traditional belonging to a specific ethnicity or sex. Just as someone can be a woman without being so biologically, a person can be a Mapuche born in an urban setting, formally educated, and fluent in the colonial language. Identity is a political decision. Life is creation, distance from or reinvention of the biological, even though it appeals strategically to an essence: radical politics require – Athena Athanasiou states – "a certain tension between the 'affirmative' and the 'deconstructive.'"[35]

Women play a fundamental role in many of the contemporary struggles over territory and living conditions as agents of community ties and organizers of resources, able to raise awareness of the importance of care for what is shared. Verónica Gago points out some characteristics common to popular economies: "the ability to work at microscales, confidence in the value of the affective as a productive moment, experience of the minoritarian as a specific *potencia*. The historical character of these features has to do with a dense history of subjectivities associated with reproductive labor."[36] If the unequal distribution of social tasks charged women with the domestic tasks of childcare and reproduction, it also created a knowledge that is useful in situations of crisis and conflict. This knowledge is part of the social surplus value, unpaid work par excellence, but at the same time it makes it possible to build communities and resistance to the forms of power that put populations at risk. The historical production of experience allows for an understanding of women as fundamental agents of community, producers of connections, and builders of strategies to avoid poverty, constantly forced to think about their own fragility[37] and historically constructed as nurturing, attentive to the vulnerability of others.

The affective appeal

The right wing in Argentina appeals to people's emotions. Collecting endless data on the preferences, affections and sensibilities displayed on social networking sites or quantified by consumption, new restrictions are created. Each individual is constantly providing information on what they like, what they think, what they choose. These data can be processed and turned into statistics that marketing experts translate into strategies to help sway public opinion. Political arguments hold less clout than the affective appeal, and shared passion is the defining trait of collective identity. Politicians address crowds like evangelical preachers to produce emotional speeches. Hate becomes a force of cohesion; its circulation constructs an "us" built on aggression toward "them." Leaders no longer limit themselves to inciting these passions in public debate but aim to create a generalized sense of agitation and urgency.

In 2015, two artists/sociologists, Roberto Jacoby and Syd Krochmalny, held an exhibition constructed from the online forums of newspaper readers: *The Hate Chronicles*. It involved a collection of poems and a visual art installation, where phrases extracted from the dregs of newspaper comment sections were presented as graffiti, bestowing on the messages a power that had been diluted by the digital format. "We should kill them all," "Black pieces of shit," "A bullet in your brain," "They're all fags and yet they complain," "The scarf the Mothers wear is a diaper because their heads are full of shit," were some of the phrases collected in the chronicles and books and plastered across the walls. Two years later, Silvio Lang and the ORGIE collective wrote a play based on the work.[38] Actors danced, ran around, behaved like a herd of animals, a pack of wild dogs, voraciously aggressive, while a chorus sang the words of the poems in a kind of evangelical-pop spectacle. This work, in its various incarnations, is a critique on the times: it names and works with – as Gabriel Giorgi writes – "hate as a central political emotion in modern-day democracy."[39] The series of works created under the title *The Hate Chronicles* insinuate that the reaction to the conversion of hate into politics cannot be rational progressive argumentation; rather, it is a response that challenges passions and emotionality.

In the 1960s in Argentina, as in many parts of the world, a profound rebellion took place. While it borrowed its politics from the Cuban Revolution, it also incorporated elements from countercultural movements such as new ways of viewing desire, the body, emotions. Feminism represented the most radical rebellion in this confluence of new ideas, as it linked the personal and the political.[40] Different strands of feminism's clash with other theories of emancipation, such as Marxism, emerged not only from the hierarchy of elements (which contradiction should be considered most important, which struggle should be prioritized and which would be secondary) but also from the feminist central focus on the body and sensitivity. Pilar Calveiro recalls that, "of the numerous forms of disobedience that were carried out in society, the most radical and confrontational was that of the armed guerrilla groups."[41] Some of these groups harshly rejected other forms of disobedience and upheld traditional values of sexual morality, inciting militants to practice monogamy under the threat of sanction. The Frente de Liberación Homosexual (Homosexual Liberation Front), aligned with the militant leftist Peronist Montonero movement, were forced to listen to chants such as "We're not fags, we're not cokeheads, we're the soldiers of Perón and we're Montoneros." María Moreno maintains that revolutionary organizations' repression of sexuality, desire and the body was related to the militants' perception of their own sacrifice, a denial of the body's vulnerability and a heroic conception of the political.[42]

Feminism is not sacrificial. It is in opposition to sacrifice. It is not heroic; it is quotidian. It gleans politics from questioning everyday life, entangling the public with the private. "The personal is political" means that there is no such thing as impersonal politics or redemption without understanding of the concrete bodies involved. When the body appears – writes Judith Butler – it imposes its principle of humility.[43] The body cannot be in all places (as a statement, a speech, a message on social media may be); it can suffer injury and its condition is finite, it can die and disappear. Militant forms of feminism are set against the background of vitalist materialism: the affirmation of the body, its powers and its vulnerability, reflection on emotions as object of politicization, sorority as mutual care, ideological mainstreaming and festive reciprocity. Feminist theories permit configuring emancipation along these lines. Perhaps for this reason feminism tends to flourish and spread in times of breakdown of other ideologies and has the power to question, in a subversive and transformative way, what the new right wing questions in a reactionary way. It is the new specter haunting the world: the Brazilian edition of *Le Monde diplomatique* in January 2018 ran the headline "The revolution will be feminist."[44]

What will the revolution look like?

Horacio González takes an anecdote from *Red Virgin: Memoirs of Louise Michel* to contemplate revolution: it is something that is handed down and is always only partially transmitted, never equal to its whole; it is a gift and an inheritance.[45] Louise Michel, a militant in the Paris Commune, twice cut her red band to give it to others. The first time, in combat in France, she gave half of her band to a group of prostitutes. She recognized them as equals and included them in the revolution that was underway, despite her comrades' reluctance. The second time, exiled in New Caledonia, she witnessed the rebellion of the Canacos people. As her fellow exiles supported the side of the colony, Louise recognized the continuity between one struggle and the other, ripped her scarf in half, and gave a piece of red fabric to one of the rebels. Revolution, says González, is this part that is passed on. It is also the decision to see the connection others might have to the revolution: prostitutes and indigenous peoples. Michel foresaw the languages and subjects of the feminist revolution.

The twentieth century saw rebellions of farm workers, nationalists, anti-colonialists, but the most anticipated revolution had as its subject the proletariat. International socialism produced texts,

assemblies, strategies and battles that centered on this antici-
pation. Why was the proletariat the subject of the revolution and
not the farm worker, not lower classes in general or women? On
the one hand, as taken from Marx's writings, it was the class
that emerged from the highest development of productive forces
and the one that had nothing to lose because it had already lost
everything. Workers are free in two senses: in the juridical sense
(they can be hired) and in the material sense (they are lacking
any means of production; to reproduce their life they must
work for others). The proletariat, to become liberated from
these chains, must disrupt the social order on the whole, bury
capitalism completely. Lukács expounded on this hypothesis: the
proletariat is objectivized through the productive process, is left
in a passive state: "The objectification of their labor-power into
something opposed to their total personality (a process already
accomplished with the sale of that labor-power as a commodity)
is not made into the permanent ineluctable reality of their daily
life."[46] There could be no partial emancipation, no sectorial
struggle, no halfway redemption: the destiny of the proletariat
is tied to the revolution. Under this interpretation of communist
objectives, all existing revolutions – except the Soviet one – failed
in their production of a new subject and settled for a diminished
plan for redemption.

In recent decades, productive shifts in capitalist logic have
produced a subject more closely linked to immaterial work,
now focused not on the factory but on collective intelligence.
To contemplate this new political subject, Italian autonomism
brought forward the category of multitude, which Ernesto
Laclau thought of more as the effect of a hegemonic articulation
than as resulting from social relationships.[47] The political subject
would emerge less from a shared social condition than from the
connection between heterogeneous ways of life recognized as
common through the hegemonic link itself.

The revolutionary subject "woman" does not necessarily
imply feminine nature or biology, which would be dangerously
limiting. The subject emerges from the historic construction of
social practices and their association with sexual and gender
norms. If action is always citation, if the body is assigned to
and molded by a specific space – like the proletariat in chained
submission to the machine – the body can also produce its own
means of deviation and rebellion, creating difference and dissent.

It is clear – evident in the shift in social logic and also in the feminist critique – that wealth is accumulated not only through appropriation of what labor produces but also by hoarding the surplus produced through community knowledge and action and the work of domestic reproduction. Community-based knowledge and domestic activity are centrally driven by the efforts of women. As Silvia Federici writes, the patriarchy's plundering has its origins in capitalism, and the development of the productive workforce is incomprehensible without relying on unpaid work.[48] Would questioning the relationship between genders, the sexual division of labor and patriarchal control, pull a fundamental pillar out from under the social order and cause the very conditions for its reproduction to topple? We don't dare remove the question mark, because it is a well-known fact that cunning capitalism has managed to survive all prophesies of its demise. The yet unwritten and unenacted agreements of international feminism aim to establish a new subject and a new type of revolution.

The neoconservative offensive

A network of feminist collectives designated 2018 as the year of women who fight, the year that what has been achieved in each individual territory would be taken to the global level. The neoconservative offensive is international: it combats "gender ideology," a term which condenses the knowledge gained through gender theory and feminist and LGBTQIA[49] activism and public policies that strive for the recognition of diversity. The contemporary witch hunt is led by fundamentalist men. Social networks are flooded with the opinions of fake users – trolls – who spread a unified message. In November 2017, Judith Butler's visit to São Paulo was preceded by a fierce campaign on social networks and personal attacks as she arrived at the airport. Witch, lesbian, slut: invectives displayed online and on posters.[50] These messages are emitted by political, religious and economic powers growing across many sectors.[51]

The notion of "gender ideology" carried out the operation of presenting the conservative discourse as non-ideological, an unblemished exteriority, in opposition to the ideas and discourses that are supposedly ideological. This discourse can be presented as non-ideological to the extent that it claims to be identical to reality, a tautological discourse with respect to the facts, without distance or mediation: things are the way they are, a woman is a woman, a man a man, they were born that way, women should give birth, men should govern. The most extreme arguments invoke divine decision, but common sense is satisfied with the appeal to biology and the affirmation of reproduction as the purpose of life. To state that there is an ideology of gender is to claim the naturalization of sex and to configure the presumably natural as normal and moral. The tautology has a repressive, normalizing dimension. The language of gender ideology operates to deny historicity and contingency; it creates unambiguous speech which it projects into reality.[52] The construction of sedimented practices socially assigned to women as traits that supposedly define the feminine essence implies the abolition of their contingency.

At different times in history, social mobilization has been able to undermine this naturalization and challenge the naturalized association of a signifier to a single signified formed as a result of social sedimentation. Street-level feminism produces this dissemination of knowledge on the historical nature of genders. Part of the political right wing is willing to accept this rupture and convert it into a defense of diversity, as long as the tautological affirmation of the capitalist order is preserved. Class inequality and private property are considered off limits. In Argentina's capital, the past government's defense of sexual diversity – even trying to attract tourists as a gay-friendly city – contrasted with the naturalization of homelessness that left thousands of persons living in precarious conditions.[53] Political repression is directed mainly toward crime, or codified political activism as a crime against property, and only secondarily against disobedience to the heteronormative order.[54]

In January 2016, soon after the government of Mauricio Macri took power, Milagro Sala and a group of other activists from the Tupac Amaru organization were imprisoned. Sala is an indigenous woman from the province of Jujuy who built through strong leadership a popular movement and had close links to the ruling political party that lost power in 2015.[55] The Tupac Amaru group began with a food van – called Glass of Milk – and ended up building entire neighborhoods, hospitals, schools, pools and parks. They organized the first ever LGBTQ pride march in the province and held memorable Three Kings parties for local children. The organization challenged the most stratified structures of the province, as it launched a popular and indigenous powerhouse onto the public stage. The local government was forced to negotiate with the demands and pressures of the organized and combative lower class.

Since 1985, many of the persons considered responsible for the state-sponsored terrorism that occurred during the Argentine dictatorship have been brought to trial. The cases were not unified, so the trials took place across various provinces. Jujuy was the last province to bring charges against any offender, despite the fact that the region had seen major repressions such as the Ledesma Blackout, where an intentional power outage provided the conditions for the kidnapping and forced disappearance of hundreds of workers, including the doctor who had been treating people in the town. The Ledesma sugar mill is owned by a longstanding oligarchic family that utilized state military power to stamp out union resistance. Nevertheless, the company's owner remains part of the provincial elite of Jujuy. Formal accusations against him as a civil accomplice were brought only after an enormous mobilization that attracted tens of thousands and Tupac Amaru activists put pressure on local judges. And he was absolved of the crime when the Tupac Amaru organization was weakened by the imprisonment of its leader and many members. The provincial government that took control of Jujuy in 2015 made the decision to put an end to Tupac Amaru's influence. It initiated a series of arrests on the grounds of threats, pressure, slander and corruption and imprisoned the group's leader, Milagro Sala, as a preventative measure for a minor offence. A fierce media campaign was launched against her, aiming to cast her as a symbol of the illegal use of public funds.[56] Nothing has been proven, but the denigration of her character permeated public opinion and the organization has now almost totally dissolved.

The new right wing abuses judicial processes and media strategies to destroy popular adversaries, be they in government or leaders of civil society. Political repression includes this campaign of defamation that links activism to corruption. Jailing activists does not need to be justifiable punishment; judicial charges are simply handed down by government-appointed judges.[57] The efficiency with which this was carried out in the case of Milagro

Sala and the debate over how she led the organization made it difficult to put the demand to free her at the center of the feminist agenda. Not until the government began to repress and eliminate the right to social protest and international organizations began to demand her release was her case supported by all organizations that took part in the 2017 international women's strike.

Milagro is the witch of the moment: small and strong, with a formidable will to fight, far from the normative model of the feminine, willing to be disobediently violent, capable of connecting issues and demands that are generally thought of separately – housing and health, work and social models, sexual diversity, human rights, indigenous rights. The group's name, Tupac Amaru, is tragically apt in that both leaders were captured and their rebellions quashed. Neocolonial power – with its sugar barons, servile politicians, accommodating judges – restored and resplendent. The neoconservative offensive has many faces, but wherever it appears it refreshes the memory of a hierarchical, racist, colonial order. Elizabeth Gómez Alcorta narrates one such scene:

> A few days after Milagro was arrested ... a reporter from TN interviewed members of the cooperatives camping in protest in the Plaza Belgrano, outside Jujuy's capitol. He approached a man of about forty, who had clearly led a life of labor and he asked the man "Sir, why are you here?" "To make sure that my daughter, one day, won't have to work as a maid cleaning your house."[58]

When reactionary violence is employed by government institutions and their interpretative machines, it activates reactive nuclei, transforms the levels of accepted and explicit violence among people and social groups. It doesn't invent them, but it raises the threshold of what can be stated without sanction. The attacks on gay and lesbian couples, police repression as civil control, the denunciation of political and cultural activists by their neighbors, are all results of the authorization to manifest the passion that guides them, to the degree that they see themselves reflected or protected by the public discourse. Misogynist and homophobic prejudices are nothing new. For a period of time these sentiments couldn't be shared openly without fear of a backlash. Today cultivators of hate are free to express themselves with provocative pride.

Power and collective logic: dichotomies and ruptures

Judith Butler writes: "Perhaps, paradoxically, 'representation' will be shown to make sense for feminism only when the subject of 'women' is nowhere present."[59] Deconstruction and affirmation are two poles of the women's movement created through its actions and writings. The various strands of feminism all risk falling into the same traps. The first of these traps lies in the paradoxical representation of a subject constructed as subaltern as it simultaneously seeks to break with its subaltern status. It constructs a political subject on the basis of configurations (the sex–gender subjectivation) that can (and should) be retraced by their very politicization, already underway. Another trap is the temptation to remain locked safely behind a series of Manicheisms, which are preserved even when valorization is inverted. The separation of the body and spirit, passion and reason, emotion and argumentation, reappears as a dichotomy in some of the feminist movement's writings. Their response to the Cartesian and Christian West, which hierarchically divides the high from the low, the spirit from the material, often falls victim to the same scheme: it takes for granted the poles of that duality and limits itself to inverting its valorization.

Simone de Beauvoir[60] analyzes the conformation of the abstract masculine subject, who does not assume his socially marked embodiment, and relegates the embodied condition to the feminine sphere. The woman is converted into pure body and the man into a disembodied universal, freed in transcendence. The emergence of spiritualized reason implied the shift of women to material and domestic corporality, devalued and repressed. Silvia Federici writes that,

> In this process, not only did the body lose all naturalist connotations, but a *body-function* began to emerge, in the sense that the body became a purely relational term, no longer signifying any specific reality, but identifying instead any impediment to the domination of Reason. This means that while the proletariat became a "body," the body became "the proletariat," and in particular the weak, irrational female (the "woman in us," as Hamlet was to say) or the "wild" African ...[61]

In Latin America, as in all colonized lands – another series of dichotomies overlaps, placing reason, the spirit and science on the side of the colonial metropolises and, on the side of the New World, experience, lack of reason, magic, the desirous body, the savage, the opposite of civilization. Against the deterioration of rationality in the Old World, the New World exalted experience and passion.

Some practical strands of feminism, with as much need as Latin Americanism to dispute valorizations that legitimized hierarchies, constructed a materialism of connections, a defense of the body to body, a vindication of desire. It reaffirms what was previously devalued: language is attached to emotions; corporality demands the center stage in the political arena. In the assemblies and marches a politics of the body is at play: modes of exhibition, shows, protest rituals, caresses. Hugging and dancing intersect other modes of political presentation. They surge beyond the confines of party lines. They do not follow the discipline of the social movement; they construct a new one. The habitual modes of greeting are substituted by an effusive hug, between friends or strangers. Caresses, normally displaced by modes of urban courtesy, are prevalent. A popular street festival signs a new treaty with the shared body.

On the streets of Argentina the women's movement invents plebeian ceremonies and rituals. It produces images of the future society that it aims to build. During the first months of 2018, mobilizations were held to demand the legalization of abortion. On 13 June the measure was approved by half of the Chamber of Deputies, but on 8 August it was rejected by the Senate. On the night of the first vote, something unique happened: the occupation of the street that held vigil overnight as the law was being debated saw new friendships, unexpected cooperation, deep solidarity, nurturing care. Warmth against the winter cold, protection in the unfamiliar surroundings, parties around improvised bonfires, a glimpse of the narrative that feminism has set as its goal: a coming together that establishes, empowers, connects. Are these merely passing connections, arising from the demands of political combat, or are they threads that will persist and go on to weave new ways of life? On 8 August the scene was repeated, but the insistent rain and the finalization of the vote at midnight meant there was no need to camp overnight.

In the documents of the Not One Less collective the statement "Desire moves us" is a battle cry. We understand it as the recovery of the fully logical notion that women should be able to articulate freely our own desire without repercussion. This militant statement presents "body" and "desire" as facts, omitting the winding and complex paths drawn by norms, discourse and power. It must be remembered, each time, that a body is created through those intersections and not by biological materiality, that neither obedience nor capacity for resistance should be taken as a given. Feminist politics speaks to the body produced by social norms, not to an existence that precedes it. It considers desire more as perseverance toward transformation than as affirmation of completeness. Gabriela Rodriguez Rial and Cecilia Abdo Ferez contemplate the public demonstrations of the Not One Less movement:

> But awareness of the challenge of taking the unconcerned existence of the body as the *basis* of a feminist theory does not exclude the possibility of accepting the proposal of this Butlerian genealogy and at the same time prioritizing, now no longer solely within feminist theory, the notion of a feminized body as an item of popular communication, democratizing potential, and indicator of shared and legitimizing experience for participation in street demonstrations. Bodies, we believe (just like "women" or "machismo"), are impure concepts, straddled across the popular and the academic. This impurity communicates, facilitates, permits – although it also, we must accept, poses obstacles.[62]

Maurice Merleau-Ponty, from *Phenomenology of Perception*[63] to *The Visible and the Invisible*,[64] conceptualized the corporality that winds through the world, never fully individualized, because it encounters meaning in openness, in dispossession, in common belonging. The successful myth of Robinson Crusoe – shut away inside a sovereign and self-sufficient ego – obscures the reality of mutual care, the construction of common sensibilities, the need for others. While the body is always disposed toward the collective, reason is not immaterial. Reason, from the Merleau-Pontian phenomenology, is sensorial. To think is to use sounds and signs. It is material, audible, visible thought. The dichotomy between body and reason devalues the body (it is lower, subordinate, controlled) and implies the emptying out of reason, its conversion into abstract rationality, instrumental logic, blind to meaning. Merleau-Ponty postulates the ideas of chiasmus and flesh to contemplate the duality between body and world, body and spirit, not as oppositional but as overlapping folds, unshakable bonds, where none of the dimensions may exist without the other, because they conform to a general mode of being.[65]

Western societies invented abstract rationality, and then critical theory took on the task of picking it apart by showing that the dichotomy on which rationality relied impeded thinking of its other – passion or myth – to the point of leaving it defenseless against what it wanted to deny or combat. In the face of this lifeless scarecrow, opposing the notion of complete corporality runs the risk of positing a body molded by the same logics of power. Enclosed within unquestioned models of production of desire and regimentation of sexuality, such a body is vulnerable to coercion in the guise of liberation. Publicity and marketing convert this body into a fetish and its emancipatory promises into slogans.[66]

Can feminism avoid the trap of fervent belonging to an existing space, which implies ignoring the critique of how this space was constructed? Can it produce a revision of the dichotomy, in its own practices and texts, in its theories and forms of organization, as a way to give center stage to the body as it truly exists, dispossessed, in connection with others, historicized, feeling and thinking? Can we, in the politics we are inventing, affirm that our experience is not the other of reason but sensorial reason conjugated in experience? Will we ever stop dreaming the dream passed down to us, a corporality that is free, full, desiring and illogical?

A certain affirmative vitalism, emitted from positions of power, takes the notion of life as a characteristic of the prescribed order, and defense of it is taken as a command to avoid change. Neoliberal discursivity tells us that we should live and how we should do so: healthy, young, sexually active. A transformative moment cannot take as its own supposition the new hegemonic idea of the normal and desirable. It should interrupt it, shatter it, turn it inside out like a glove, find its true nucleus and its revulsive potential, extract it and make it grow. Feminism needs critical thought and the teachings of deconstruction in order to avoid taking for granted the position from which speech is emitted, the body on which it is inscribed, the truth it harbors.

Can the subaltern speak?[67] Maintaining doubt, the questioning state, awareness of the problematic nature of every enunciation, avoids internalizing the same classifying logic that we have set out to challenge. Rationalizing, normative discourse reduces and subordinates desire, the body and the domestic. We defy this logic as a criticism of its social configuration. Only from this critical view, conscious that there is no point to be literally affirmed, may we establish any alternative rationality or politics, new ways of configuring collective agency and power. We must contemplate from the chiasmus and not from the pole, from where ideas intersect and not from where they diverge.

Micropolitics and organization

Upon calling into question the system of daily life, the distribution of chores, the socially necessary division of labor, feminism affects sexuality, child-rearing and caregiving. Nothing can be attributed to the natural, as politics and controversies have revealed. Contempt of established hierarchies between the sexes/genders shakes the foundations of the practices in which they are materialized. Popular and street-level feminism as it is articulated in the Argentine context is micropolitical in a dual sense: it surges from a transformation of life – intolerance, dissidence, rupture – and constructs collectives that, in many cases, are formed by a group of friends or neighbors, small and horizontal.[68]

For decades, catcalling on the streets was a common practice, an idiosyncrasy of Argentine customs. It ranged from the supposed gallantry of the compliment to the crude declaration of the sexual practices to which the woman in question would be subjected. The varying degrees of aggression were reinforced by male groups. The comment made to the passing woman was not directed solely at her, as a threat or a warning, but was common currency among men, proof of virility, a search for belonging. Any debate over this practice went only as far as a distinction between gallantry and obscenity. Only recently, in 2015, did a rebellion against catcalling get to the root of the problem. A young woman began a campaign on social media against verbal harassment on the streets. She challenged its traditional classification as flattery, based in the *machista* perspective of the practice in public spaces. Young women began to declare that no one had the right to comment on their body or attire unless the opinion was asked for; that a comment by a stranger shouted as they walked by was violence. Months later, the city of Buenos Aires penalized harassment on the streets. The rebellion challenged the codes that organized modes of street transit.

Many of the interventions by contemporary Argentine feminists have a similar tone, taking approaches that are more practical than theoretical, emerging from dissidence against both private and public social customs. A youth rebellion is underway, which involves intergenerational education – daughters urging their mothers to refuse to accept control, inequality and violence. In the same sense, campaigns such as A mí también (Me Too) or No nos callamos más (We will not remain silent) break the silence that naturalizes abuse and victim blaming. The transformation is profound and vast; it spans bodies and ways of life, and it changes us.

Some of us say that we are the daughters of 3 June 2015. Others call themselves daughters of the strike and cite their collective's founding date as the day of the national women's strike, 19 October 2016. Several groups recognize their date of establishment as 8 March 2017, the international women's strike. Each new event creates new collectives, produces a catharsis that converts non-activists into activists and lays the groundwork for collective construction. No one is the same after the experience of belonging to this powerful common force.[69] A thousand clusters of different flowers will have more blooms than a forest of a single species. The public demonstrations modify those who go out onto the streets as well as those who are merely spectators, those who remain in their homes and those who leave them. It incites a willingness toward activism; it is an act of sowing and, at the same time, of reaping. On 8 March 2018, the cameras of a university television station filmed an elderly woman on a balcony. First she is seen crying, then waving her arms to the song being chanted on the streets below. The image went viral. A team from the television station sought her out and interviewed her. She told them about the violence she'd suffered, her life in a boarding house, her eighty-four years lived, and the emotion of seeing so many women. She said: "There are so many of us, there should be more. And we're going to triumph."

Within the women's movement diverse perspectives live side by side, from demands for equal representation in government and cries to break the glass ceiling so women may ascend to hierarchic positions or to political power to challenges to the very notion of power, which classifies feminism as other in a male-dominated world. They may seem to be contradictory positions, but the movement underway does not feed into Manicheism. All strands are connected by the question of what power would look like from a feminist perspective.

Feminism is in dialogue with a complex and vast historicity which includes the popular strands of feminism that emerged in the *piquetero* movement and the 2001 rebellion, as well as the brand of feminism emerging from the organizational rigor of the National Women's Conference. Knowledge shared between the organizations involved in the national campaign for the right to abortion is added to the experience of human rights movements and union activism, as well as feminist activists who during the twentieth century tried to break down the exclusionary and hierarchical organization of society.

The conditions for the emergence of popular feminism in Argentina were created within political parties and social movements that furthered gender issues. Leftist political and social groups gained crucial experience in poorer neighborhoods, in alliance with female community leaders who had their own agendas, such as the right to abortion.[70] The relationship between these smaller fronts and the larger organization involves different degrees of conflict, and there have been complaints made by activists over attempts to subordinate them. But nevertheless the pooling of experience produces capillary transformations. The event that is often referred to as foundational is the 2001 rebellion.[71] The demands that emerged from this crisis overlap with those of the national women's conferences, and both in turn overlap with the national campaign for legal, safe and free abortion, which gained enormous support during the first half of 2018 when it was debated in parliament for the first time ever. Hundreds of voices from civil society rose up to argue in favor or against it. Demonstrations took place on the streets every Tuesday, a kind of fair and festival, where thousands of activists met, performed, listened to music, danced. The relationship between what went on in parliament and what occurred on the street outside shows the power of contemporary popular feminism. It has objectives beyond the passing of one law but will show support through the public demonstration of bodies demanding rights and producing language and performance. The Senate rejected the law for legalization of abortion by 38 to 31 votes. The contrast between what occurred inside parliament and what went on outside was brutal. The representatives of traditional power – in this chamber the majority of the population enjoys the smallest proportional representation – sat comfortably inside while outside a mostly young crowd waited in the rain, hugging, dancing and singing. Under debate was the autonomy of women, their full citizenship. This, at the forefront. In the background, the construction of a political subject.

Political *conventillos* and friendships

What kinds of political practices do contemporary feminists re-create? In what ways of constructing the present do they configure their own politicalness? The Not One Less collective was built around demonstrations. And in 2017 it finally drafted its charter,[72] which defines its mode of organization as a search for political friendships and collective intelligence:

> We need to foster the practice of trust and mutual care among ourselves: a political friendship. To create links and alliances, shared phrases, agreed-upon modes of processing, collectively, our misfortunes and the violence we've suffered. To share in order to disarm what has tried to destroy this friendship, this intelligence that can only be collective. In each of our biographical backgrounds this suffering and the traces of pain are present. We recognize them, we recognize ourselves in them, but they will not be justification for tactics that are non-consolidating and oppositional to the feminist ethic that we have built. We are willing to invent new ways of life, based in care and not in competition, through friendly conversations and not factious insults, guarding our vulnerabilities and not allocating our injuries to others. No one says that it will be easy. We say that it is a political task. The most important one.

Conversation becomes a strategy for collective organization. An intervention by activists in Villa Soldati borrowed from the historic *conventillos*, boarding houses where in the late nineteenth and early twentieth century immigrants recently arrived to Buenos Aires rented rooms. In these low-income residences, families crowded together, creating a linguistic and cultural melting pot. The immigrants spoke diverse languages and dialects, depending on their country of origin. In 1907 renters held a strike against a rise in rent. It was called the "broom strike" because it was led by women, or the "*conventillo* strike."[73] "To *conventillear*," as a verb in Argentine slang, is to circulate rumors, gossip, to be observant of what is going on.

If violence happens in the home, protection against it happens in public. It requires exchange of knowledge, circulation of information. "To *conventillear*" is to talk to your neighbors, to tell them what's going on and what others are going through. To spread information that will break down the domestic prison. Pedro Lemebel, the extraordinary Chilean journalist and queer activist, baroque cultivator of writing as performance and performance as politics, writes an ode to autumn: the leaves that fall, incessant, from the trees are excuses for the women to go out and sweep the pavement every day: "The rain of sad leaves that requires them to sweep the pavement again and again, to establish their gossipy politics, their brief space camouflaged as order and cleanliness where they, all together, all autumn's accomplices, pretend to pile up dry leaves concocting the chatty politics of their domestic conspiracy."[74] In Pasto, Colombia, to organize the 8 March strike, some activists called for women to "patch" the plazas. To "patch" is to get together to chat. Breaking silence and isolation is a militant practice and a means of self-defense.

José María Arguedas, in *Los ríos profundos*,[75] imagines a rebellion that grows in the *chicha* bars, spreads among the women who run the shops, circulates even as the protesters seem defeated and the natives on the haciendas drip with servility. The *chicha* bars are places of meeting, of rumor, conversation, conspiracy. The deep rivers referred to in the book's title are those of the indigenous resistance against colonial power and the tireless plotting, spread by word of mouth, through gossip and rumor. Traditionally feminine spaces, such as the kitchen, are resignified as sites of practical thought – "the scientific practice of the singular," as Michel de Certeau writes.[76] The popular feminism of the Southern Cone aims to recover what was achieved by our female ancestors, stuck in traditional roles, seeking in those historic practices specificity and power and the deconstruction of those assigned roles. Can we extract from the *conventillo*, the sweeping of the pavement, the *chicha* bar, the grocery store or the kitchen, a nucleus of resistance, a mutual recognition, to expand our contemporary rebellion? It would demand not mythologizing these actions, not converting them into the object of an affirmation that avoids challenging the sexual division of labor. The modes in which practices attributed to women were used as resistance tactics must not ignore consideration of their ambivalence. This implies not inheriting without criticizing but acknowledging and, at the same time, deconstructing.

Assembly

The assemblies held by the Not One Less collective to organize the women's strikes were an extraordinary process of mutual recognition and construction of a shared agenda. The horizontal conversation required precision, agreement, restraint; decisions over how long each person could speak and how to evaluate whether speech favored a specific party. The assemblies constructed practices, rhetoric, modes of intervention and definitions. Through conflicts, rows, tensions, common ground was gained, accommodating to difference. If large mobilizations are hospitable to the verbal expression of pain, humiliation and rage, the assemblies are the setting for processing dissidences. The meetings in Buenos Aires were attended by organizations that considered prostitution sex work – sex workers' groups, the organization called Feminist Whores among them – as well as abolitionists who consider all prostitution to be almost slave-like exploitation. The *conventillo* is a place of shouting and arguments, and the assemblies saw this as well, but a collective document was nevertheless drafted in which the condemnation of sex trafficking coexists with the defense of rights for sex workers. The push for abolition of prostitution is very much alive within contemporary feminism, but acceptance of the subaltern group's self-definition prevailed. An assembly must presuppose that political truth emerges from the confluence of heterogeneous positions, that justice cannot be validated by an external program or ideological argument considered untouchable or immune to confrontation. Assembly requires every statement to work out its contextual truth.

The truth of the assembly is the truth of the bodies that form part of it. Social networks allow for ubiquity, being present while not, adhesion through a quick opinion; assembly imposes a different temporality, active patience, listening to the point of exhaustion, affirmation of the body's humility, euphoric or exhausted, attentive to the tone of a speech, moved by an idea, restless in the line for the bathroom, uncomfortable in the hard chairs. After so many assemblies, a kind of political friendship keeps difference from creating distrust.

The assemblies accommodated the possibility of building alliances but not unanimity or identification. Activists from opposing political parties voiced adverse positions; some were hesitant to participate alongside activists from other unions or confederations, people of diverse religions, collectives with specific demands. Each group, and especially the political parties, pushed to inscribe their demands in the collective document. Among the most disputed points were the expansion of work beyond jobs compensated with wages and the decision to consider prostitution work or slavery. In the assemblies, each person may speak for a number of minutes decided on in that meeting – which varies between three and five – and political groups often register several of their activists in the list of speakers so that their positions will have greater resonance. The assemblies aim to be democratic and horizontal and to take on the challenges that this implies, but it is a difficult process.[77] Differences between people and antagonisms among political programs are not diluted. They create an atmosphere, demand participation in discussions, submit the program to the repeated scrutiny of the watching, listening bodies of others.

During 2017, the assemblies went beyond meetings to organize strikes and marches. Meetings took place in zones of conflict: in a tent outside parliament set up by workers made redundant by the multinational PepsiCo.;[78] in El Bolsón, in the midst of furious denunciations of the forced disappearance of activist Santiago Maldonado;[79] in Jujuy to demand freedom for Milagro Sala and other female political prisoners.[80] There were assemblies in poor neighborhoods, similar to the assemblies for the organization of the 8 March 2018 strike. The assembly changes location and upon doing so its physiognomy changes: other bodies are incorporated, new words circulate. It is never the same assembly. Woven anew each time by the bodies present, its dynamic and tone shifts. Upon moving to different territories, statements and intonations that do not fall within the codified political language are given center stage.

The Not One Less collective uses assembly as a tool, an egalitarian device that circulates words and aims to shake up traditional representation, because the voice of each individual stands on its own, even if their speech is influenced by a pre-existing organization. Each body counts and can recount its experience. A meeting implies the selection of speakers. An assembly means opening up and knowing how to support this opening up, to foster it, converting multiplicity into efficiency. For 8 March 2018, the assemblies organized demonstrations, agreed on documents, gathered funds, rented stages and sound equipment, defined the list of those who would take the stage. Without delegation to a directorial elite or a managerial logic. To say "the assembly" is to name a process of tremendous complexity, slow, difficult, confrontational, with advances and setbacks, partial failures and tenacious militancy. The assemblies tackled the dilemmas presented by a horizontal process of self-organization while maintaining the energy needed to accomplish its goals.

Will it be able to continue doing so? Or will it fall victim to internal corrosion, militant sectorial forces that merely paused to marvel at the novelty? In the series of assemblies carried out to organize the 3 June mobilization, the process was more limited in vitality. In the larger assemblies, the collective power breaks any one political party's focus on its bottom line, avoiding the creation of an almost idyllic scene where there are no oppositional forces. When that does not happen, words and controversies remain corseted inside previously assigned roles. And the unique space created by the bodies gathered dissolves. Feminists find themselves faced with the challenge of honing their strategies of articulation, creating spaces for gathering together and for collective construction capable of going beyond the more traditional points of political life.

Leadership and power

The Royal Spanish Academy, which mans the toll booths of the roads that transform the Spanish language, even the varieties spoken in Latin American countries, as if they were its colonies, objects to the use of the word *"presidenta."* It maintains that *"presidente"* is sufficient to include both genders, feminine and masculine. It does not have the same objection to the accepted word *"sirvienta,"* despite the fact that, by its own criteria, *"sirviente"* should suffice to include both genders. Perhaps this is because serving is a traditionally feminine profession and it is uncommon for a woman to govern a country. An institution with origins in the monarchy and as ostensibly conservative as the Royal Spanish Academy resists the linguistic modifications created by the women's movements against sexism in the language. In this instance it combines with the European Spanish disdain for Latin American political innovation.

In the twenty-first century three Latin American *presidentas* governed simultaneously: in Brazil, Argentina and Chile.[81] In other countries female presidential candidates and many young female leaders have emerged from social activism.[82] In some countries, parliamentary quotas led to legislative seats filled by women. After the coup against Dilma Rousseff, the new Brazilian government not only eliminated ministries and weakened policies but restored a cabinet of all white males to power.[83] On 15 March 2018, Marielle Franco, a legislator in Rio de Janeiro, was murdered. She was black, raised in a favela, a lesbian, a feminist activist, and an outspoken critic against police brutality in poor neighborhoods. Barely a week had passed since the largest 8 March demonstration ever seen. Her death was the culmination of misogynist revenge on the lower class and an attempt at discipline, sentiments that spurred support for the government coup as well.

Dilma Rousseff, Cristina Fernández and Michelle Bachelet are not leaders that emerged from feminism. Nor are many of the female members of parliament. Yet, under their respective governments, mixed cabinets emerged, legislative changes took place, and strategies to increase the autonomy of women were developed. In Chile, the depenalization of abortion was approved in 2017 for certain circumstances (risk to the mother's life, rape, unviability of the fetus). In Argentina, marriage equality and gender identity laws were passed – allowing self-reporting of gender on national identity documents and guaranteeing access to the healthcare system – as well as the law for prevention and eradication of violence against women.[84] In Brazil, Rousseff implemented key policies, creating the Ministry for Women, Racial Equality and Human Rights in 2015.[85] Policies for social reparation and distribution of income increased female autonomy. The "Zero Hunger" campaign in Brazil[86] and the Universal Allowance per Child[87] program in Argentina distributed economic resources among women who held jobs in the informal economy. In Argentina, programs such as "Women Do"[88] financed community modes of production and included training with a gender perspective; and the Integrated Sexual Education program influenced the school system by educating children and young adults across all social sectors. While some of these programs were left in place under Macri's rule, with greatly reduced funding, their critical and valuative aspects were stripped away. The "Women Do" program still awards money to beneficiaries, but funds are allocated to each woman individually, dissolving the cooperatives. The neoconservative offensive separates the reproduction of life and the conditions needed for female autonomy.

The new right wing in Argentina, unlike the leaders of the Brazilian coup, does not declare itself opposed to "gender ideology." To the contrary, it flirts with feminism while it purges it of any combativeness. For the first time, a well-known feminist activist was placed in charge of the National Women's Institute. Women are appointed to positions of power as, simultaneously, acceptable feminine models linked to traditional roles are constructed: from the dedicated female social activist who fights hunger in poor neighborhoods[89] to the female governor who respects religion and handles her public affairs without neglecting her family.[90] The new right wing creates its programs around information taken from focus groups and Big Data. It appeals to a logic that includes gender equality among its widely accepted beliefs but maintains naturalized gender roles: women can act in the public sphere and are recognized for doing so, as long as their discourses and actions reaffirm the traditional values assigned to women by sex and gender norms.

Without the feminist struggle, common sense would never have changed. The majority of the population voted a woman as president and other majorities elected women to parliament and provincial governments. Nevertheless, misogynist arguments are trotted out in the criticism of these female leaders. The former president Cristina Fernández de Kirchner was nicknamed "the nag,"[91] and during her government magazine covers depicted her having an orgasm (from the pleasure power gave her) or burning on a bonfire like a witch.[92] She was portrayed not as a rational statesperson but as a pleasure-hungry madwoman, not as an opponent to be defeated but as a heretic to be burned. The history of Argentine politics has seen many offenses against men who governed, but these specific insults could only be launched at a woman. The relationship between power, female leaders and feminist struggles is complex. Power and governance from a feminist perspective remain almost uncontemplated. Not only what kinds of policies and programs could be implemented, although that is part of the agenda that the social movement itself puts into play, through petitions and demands. Organized feminism, heterogeneous and enshrined as a political subject, places demands on institutions, political parties and the state. The practical micropolitics employed by a large part of the movement and the persistence of the conservative logic of accumulation within political parties fail to address the issue of what it means to exercise power in a feminist way. Many activists would respond that it is less about a complex articulation than about an irrefutable antagonism. Others, that it is about imposing a feminist agenda even within politics that are not feminist.

The push for parity in elections and political representation forces the political system to acknowledge that the current structure lacks gender, racial or class equality. In response, those in power employ tried and true tactics, going into damage control: smoothing down the more radical aspects and preserving the status quo. In the lists of female elected officials, wives and sisters of well-known leaders abound; women granted visibility thanks to their lineage are implicitly trusted because of the family to which they belong. Often, these women are political activists in their own right. The fact that their work is overshadowed by their surname is another symptom of the dominant logic.

Laws for equality oblige us to revise the rules of the game, widen the margins, break the automatism by which white males are chosen to fill seats and positions. These laws do not generate feminist politics but construct conditions for equal opportunity so that the right to vote fought for by suffragists may be accompanied by the right to be voted for. At the beginning of the twentieth century in Argentina, and in sync with international feminism, there were women – Julieta Lantieri – who attempted to register their candidacy and showed up to vote. The female vote was not prohibited; it didn't even seem necessary to specify this, because the electoral register was built from the lists of citizens enrolled in obligatory military service. Argentine males, in a society whose majority population were immigrants. In 1947, the women's vote was finally passed, under the first Peronist government. And seventy years later the law of equality in the lists was voted in through an alliance between female legislators across several political parties, who decided to ignore the parliamentary order of the day and debate this law without consulting their own parties ahead of time.[93]

Feminist power

There's a protest song that begins "Power, power, power to the people ..." and continues with "Now that we're together, now that they see us." "Power" is hard to define, but what's being criticized is the greater visibility given to masculinized modes of conceiving it. The chant challenges the distance between private experiences and public rhetoric. In September 2017, I attended a conference in a city that had been thrown into tumult by the conflict between the national government and the Mapuche people. At the end of my talk, audience members were given the floor. There was a notable difference in the comments depending on the participant's gender. Women tended to narrate their own experiences: as teachers in indigenous communities, as feminist activists, as neighbors of women living in violent circumstances. The majority of the men who spoke appealed instead to more classically political rhetoric, explaining their positions using generalized statements and well-worn phrases. This may be an extreme case, but the differences are not coincidental. Different formalized molds for public discourse had been internalized by the speakers.[94]

Feminisms challenge the division between private and public, which relegates an entire category of experiences to obscurity. They support the power to recount the lifeworld in the public sphere – a world where temporality is multiple and functions as an assemblage. Judith Butler debates the difference established by Hannah Arendt, in *The Human Condition*, between the valuation of the private and public spheres[95] because, if political discourse emerged in the latter sphere as free speech, it did so by rejecting the former. In the private sphere, silent women and slaves; in the public, speaking – monolingual – men. In ancient Greece, a barbarian was any person who did not speak Greek, the foreigner whose orality was taken as senseless noise. The public sphere did not recognize any kind of heterogeneity, neither of languages nor of bodies.

If women were traditionally relegated to the private material and polyglot sphere, now, as female bodies clamor together in public, we can see the potency of our materiality. I continue paraphrasing Butler: while the word may be univocal, identitary, monological, subject to order, the body is, at once, singular and plural, because its interdependence is evident and it is always part of some alliance or ensemble. It is less an entity than "a living set of relations."[96] It requires others in order to express itself fully and to survive. The feminist discourse, which translates this lived experience, is always intertwined with others; it recognizes corporality and interdependence more than claiming autonomous awareness.

Sharing mourning as a public experience and publicly reflecting on sexuality or maternity allows us to rethink government policies in unique ways, not only to construct discourses or ideas from civil society. It also imagines healthcare practices, modes of conceiving public safety or distribution of resources.[97] One mode of reconceiving power from the feminist perspective implies considering all public issues from a gendered perspective. Not the creation of one government ministry or secretariat dedicated to women's issues and dissident bodies, but for the critical eye of the gender perspective to traverse the entire government, all areas, all budget proposals, all programs. Feminism runs the risk of being satisfied with a quota or reduced to a sectorial issue. Mainstreaming issues is a necessity because the patriarchy as a system is furthered by relationships: it affects social distribution and production; it is a part of the collective imagination, of language and rites.

Can we imagine and create a micropolitical and horizontal form of feminism that could be articulated with a feminism in power, capable of modifying modes of government, legitimacy and obedience? Perhaps the deepest change in feminism will come in a distancing from its separatist tradition and its proclaimed rejection of leadership. Not abandoning its tenets but attempting to understand their failings. At times, horizontality as a premise has resulted in obvious sectarianism, with female leaders of small groups tending to divide into factions by the multiplication of implicit leaderships. The lack of structures capable of creating a clear division of work and representation within collectives left space for only very few voices to be heard.

In 1917, the peasants' revolt seemed to have triumphed in Mexico. Forces led by Emiliano Zapata and Pancho Villa took the nation's capital. A magnificent scene occurred. Villa sat in the presidential chair, Zapata beside him. They discussed what they should do next. They held up each option, like taking corn off the cob. Their consensus: this isn't for us: let's call someone who knows how to govern. They both decided to return to their territories, leaving power to a supposedly friendly government who promptly betrayed them and started a war to defeat the rural generals. The refusal of power gives power over to others.[98]

I read this last sentence and I know it expresses a fundamental controversy within the Not One Less collective, where the production of radical actions and concepts that cannot be appropriated by a neoliberal translation is prioritized over the construction of a new hegemony. I don't think it's enough: if women constitute the political subject of our times, if we make up an international force that aims for radical transformation, we must think about the relationship between micropolitics and government policy. Nancy Fraser maintains that domination by financial capital requires consent. To get this consent, neoliberalism varnishes its designs with rights and rhetoric in support of women and dissident bodies. Just as happened to the Mexican farm workers, they rule in our name, channel the power of our assembled bodies, show solidarity with certain demands, while they simultaneously carry out policies that deepen exploitation and inequality.

5

Modes of Appearing: Language and Theatricality

... but finding that my own language must break up and yield if I am to know you. You are what I gain through this disorientation and loss.

Judith Butler, *Precarious Life*

Languages

In a group chat to define international communication strategies for 8 March 2018,[1] one debate concerned how to describe this common subject and, at the same time, acknowledge the multiplicity of its composition. Identity is construction, a result of the same activism that searches for and accumulates definitions. The debate exposed the range of diversity: cis women, trans women, lesbians, bisexuals, asexual women, black and indigenous women, disabled women, fat women. These are just some of the political subjectivities produced around corporality. Finally, it was decided to use the general term "feminists" – a move from the focus on the diverse corporality and sexuality toward an identity that presents itself as a political affirmation and position in the public space.

"Feminists" shape a common zone in which diversity is negotiated, as opposed to "women," which carries with it the naïve supposition of a shared experience beyond political identification – something like the presumption of the existence of a class in itself (supposedly biological). Gayatri Spivak warns of the risks when appealing to "the positivist inclusion of a monolithic collectivity of 'women' in the list of the oppressed whose unfractured subjectivity allows them to speak for themselves."[2] The instability of names, the plurality of self-definitions and the becoming of non-heternormative corporalities interfere with inclusion in a conglomerate whose contours have been previously defined by the biological inscription of bodies and their gendered adaptation. The question reappears in the debates on the assignment of quotas in arts, sciences, politics and literature or is configured in terms of "visibility." These discussions underscore historical exclusions in the construction of canons formed on masculine values, in every field. There is now a push to give visibility to women who were participants of public events, or produced works that were omitted from specific histories, and to find ways to guarantee the presence of women on the artistic scene. The feminist struggle is here, in part, to point out both past and present exclusions. But, in this dimension of the struggle, we must take care to not erase the deconstructive revolution in the push to recover "women."[3]

Cecilia Abdo Ferez writes that "'all bodies count' also because each body can study its own wounds and find new ways to narrate, always and necessarily incomplete, these wounds suffered, taking them as signs in dispute as a means to reconstruct biographies and make connections that question sexual division and a framework that ascribes binary value."[4] The narrative on exclusion and violence, on power and difference, always runs the risk of becoming binary, of taking for granted a specific corporality, a sexual preference, a pattern of behavior. The women's movement is this shift from identity assigned by a normative order in a binary way to an appearance in the public space that breaks down the very order that names women as such and poses the question of how to name what has been broken down. That's why the recognition of racial or corporal attributes that expose a body to vulnerability or discrimination is intermingled with sexual orientations and sensibilities outside the hegemonic models. These are often listed as modes of diversity and demand the inclusion of new parts into the sequence, new links of signification. Subjects appear and speak in their own name, to demand recognition. The acronym for sexual diversity – LGBTQIA

(Lesbian, Gay, Bisexual, Transgender, Queer, Intersex, Asexual) – accommodates new signifiers because, if the subaltern can speak, its words are self-identification and differentiation.

Not One Less, as a massive event, emerges from the questioning of common ground, not from merely mobilizing our specific deconstructed and constructed identities. In its initial communications it debated the term "women" as defined within the binary regime. The definition is a cultural-discursive construction that, because of its repetitive sedimentation, appears bestowed with naturalness. Who is the "regular everyday woman" often described in mass media? Is it the woman who believes her selection of a male partner is something natural, or is it the woman who carries out unexpected modes of solidarity? The woman who teaches her daughters to do domestic chores as she sends her sons outside to play ball? The woman who teaches respect for diversity and shares her doubts with her children, or the woman who reproduces the notion of normality? The woman who worries about conforming to established beauty norms or the woman who feels guilty for her unexpected desires? The woman who wants to advance in her professional career or the woman who agrees with the hierarchical order of her working life? The woman who belongs to a religion, who votes for traditional parties, a union activist, the woman who opens new worlds as she denounces the conditions in which she lives? Women who fight and women who rest, hedonist pleasure-seekers and stoics, women in poor neighborhoods and in rural areas, those who define "women" beyond hegemonic sexual and gender norms, women who assume divergent sexualities as well as serial monogamists. When we use the term "women" we are speaking to this conglomeration: those who recognize as diverse and those who act under the presumption of naturalness, because the definition of "woman" in a heterogeneous society cannot be limited to what has been dictated by the dominant normative pattern. It is also the conglomeration of practices that are recurrent and possible, although they are not hegemonic.

Not One Less was the message of the largest mobilization of women in Argentina's history. The initial call reinforced the traditionally feminine, using the color magenta – one of the colors most closely associated with the female gender.[5] The message allowed for massive appeal and the logo included the iconic representation of woman, binary logic par excellence, the image used to mark public toilets and dressing rooms. The call took the well-trod path, the path laid by the prevailing ideological consensus. And the bodies that turned out on the street ripped this representation to shreds by showing the real diversity behind the icon and upon doing so challenging forms of representation.

The problem is communicational and political because an iconic image or a representation can function as an exclusionary device. Monique Wittig recalls that woman and man are political categories produced by a group of concepts, categories and abstractions that are linked to material violence on bodies with the excuse of organizing and interpreting.[6] The identification of the masculine as the universal is a form of violence that is repeated daily, and the feminist movement should not reproduce this violence it stands against by erasing the diversity of its identity. How do we build a shared identity that does not hide the things we do not have in common? And how do we overcome the obstacles that enclose feminism within a series of impressions? Language and ways of naming are central in one way or another. If the first demands recognition of diverse identities that shout to be heard in the public sphere, the second demands that the statements be recognizable in order for the interpellation to be effective. When we use the term "feminists" instead of "women" to name the political subject, to avoid forming the subject on the basis of sex–gender categorization, we run the risk of narrowing the category to those who have already defined themselves as feminists. In a context in which many people practice autonomy and dissidence in ways that could be considered feminist although they don't consider themselves as such, calling them feminists can be limiting. All discourse implies a negotiation between limits and risks.

In the Argentine public sphere a clarification is still heard: I'm not a feminist, I'm feminine. It is said by famous women, by politicians, by neighbors. It's a reaction against the stereotype of the feminist who hates men, rejects the masculine world and hegemonic femininity. These women declare themselves lovers of men – not lesbians – modern mothers fond of cosmetics and appearances. These declarations are not uncommon but they have the feel of another time. The massive mobilizations are in this sense pedagogical: they show that the multiplicity of bodies encompasses those who respond to the attributes traditionally associated with the feminine gender and those who express very diverse modes of constructing corporality.

The call put out for the first Not One Less march was scripted from gender stereotypes. The street blew these stereotypes to pieces. The political experience of feminism that came later demanded thinking on this double plane, which implied repeated calls to those who still didn't consider themselves feminists (and who felt left out of the exclusively feminist statement), and, at the same time, it showed, through discourse and action, through rituality and performance, that demanding autonomy and freedom is feminist. Many people carry out feminist practices, although they do not call themselves feminists. The social movement that unfolded between 3 June 2015 and 8 March 2018 carried out a formidable process of reconstruction and education in which massiveness has become linked, increasingly, with the radical break from prescribed molds.

Words meant to challenge must go beyond readability within a discursive and normative order. They must contain the power to move people. Political manifestos tend to seek poetic and political effectiveness more than communicational logic and conceptual precision. They must use words in ways that will touch bodies and mobilize emotions and, at the same time, create more just conditions. One manifesto begins by stating: "The women of the world find ourselves in a process of existential revolution." This sentence constructs a shared sense of self that is later explained to include women, lesbians, trans, feminized bodies.[7] The initial synthesis seeks emotional connection; the explanation that follows gives a detailed description of the individuals housed within the term.

Politics of language

In an assembly before the strike on 8 March 2017, one of the participants proposed using the term "heteropatriarchy." Other attendees disagreed, arguing that it would alienate non-activists who were unfamiliar with the specific language of militant feminism or gender studies. Does this mean we have to renounce precision? Or avoid politicization of the language we utilize? These discussions expose the political nature of each linguistic and communicational decision and highlight the fact

that language is not merely an instrument but a fundamental
political practice.

Antonio Gramsci, philologist and incarcerated activist, said
that all words had a metaphorical origin. Language consists of
such a large accumulation of metaphors that their metaphorical
condition is obscured.[8] As a word is used, its meaning is
cemented and we stop perceiving its arbitrary metaphorical
nature. When a new word appears – resulting from generational
invention, media creativity, activism or technological innovation,
borrowing or contamination between languages – speakers are
able to judge the word's pertinence, its relevance, its sonority.
But we are unable to judge words that are part of the heritage of
the language in which we were socialized.

The process of naturalizing a word obscures its origin
and erases its historicity. It turns language into a plane of
conformity. It ignores other ways of thinking, interpreting,
looking at the world. Dictionaries aim to be descriptive but they
are formidable ideological catalogues. Until a short while ago,
the Royal Spanish Academy's dictionary included under the
entry "woman" the definition "the weaker sex." Lexicographers
might say: if the word is used in this way we should register
that usage. But the register, obviously, is never complete or
total; it implies a selection that has more than a little ideology
behind it. By choosing a definition, a certain nuclei of meaning is
ratified, legitimized as real data and bestowed with a normative
meaning. Being in the dictionary becomes synonymous with
validity and legality. Under the guise of description, prescription
is smuggled.[9]

Common sense materializes in words and grammatical structures. Literature operates on the tension between invention and
inheritance, between the sedimented (which permits the readers'
comprehension) and the work that innovates new meanings.
Politics as rupture also implies emergence, the revision of
language, a reminder of its historicity, the breakdown of its
tautological appearance. Pervasive in the media and transmitted
by common sense, tautology flattens the signifying operation
to one dimension, which is taken as truth. "Sophia Loren is
beautiful because she's all woman," for example. Or "That story
by Borges is serious literature." Each of these affirmations is built
on the denial of the subjective nature of words – beauty, woman,
literature; by situating words in relationship to an example

that is presented as tautological, they crystallize meaning. It's a celebration of naturalized identity.

The functionality of this naturalization remits, in part, to the fact that the speaker cannot advance in a state of doubt, at least in the world of objects. "Hand me a plate" does not imply the same problems as affirming that a painting is not art. Everyday speech is characterized by pragmatism and objectivity.[10] Conservative political discourse proceeds systematically to the mythic tautological operation, because its aim is to reinforce the established order. For dissident movements, the road to be traveled is the inverse: shed light on the obscurity of origins, restore the metaphorical nature of words, free the signifiers locked inside ideological nuclei, problematize them. Quite recently, in 2014, the Royal Spanish Academy removed the definition "the weaker sex" under the entry "woman" thanks to the efforts of feminist struggles.[11]

Broadening the field of possibilities implies rethinking modes of naming. A debate rages across different languages with respect to the universal masculine. In some Latin American countries, where the local languages are gendered, the governments implemented the use of both the masculine and feminine for official use – for example, "todas y todos," "ciudadanas y ciudadanos," "maestras y maestros." This was objected to as anti-economical by conservative sectors of the linguistic field and as binarizing by movements for sexual diversity. On social networks other attempts are ventured: the replacement of the o that usually denotes the male noun or pronoun used as default with an x (ciudadanxs, amigxs), or with an e (ciudadanes, amigues), because the x is impossible to pronounce orally. The Royal Spanish Academy responded that a language derived from Latin should respect the universal masculine. It ignores, with this suggestion, the fact that a language is above all living history, something that changes, that is constantly influenced by social norms and that is used to express both the conditions of life and the struggle for those conditions. Reverence for Latin heritage hides the close relationship between modes of naming everyone under the (pseudo) universal masculine "todos" and a system of social relationships that implies hierarchic inequality among the genders.

Horacio González warns that "language is only truly modified in the slow march of days as millions of speakers use it in different ways. Not by bandages or artifices of quick justice, although it is certain that they play a role in warning of a problem."[12] To disrupt the language so that it does not continue to reproduce the relationships of domination is not a small task, but social movements highlight overlooked problems and demand the creation of political solutions. Inventing words, duplicating, alternating feminine and masculine as universal disrupts the automatic use of the dominant and at the same time preserves the economy of discourse and legibility. Cristina Burneo Salazar conceives of gender-inclusive language as shifting the norm, "as a vehicle for transformation of a system and not an inorganic group of recommendations."[13] That is to say, not only as the register of a need for the breakdown of binary logic but as a comprehensive reflection on language.

Confronted with transformations of ways of life and patterns of behavior and the democratic impulse provoked by the public appearance of non-heteronormative bodies, some institutions have been absolutely reactive to proposed changes in the language. The reluctance to change cannot hide behind linguistic legitimacy for very long. Nor can conservative mocking defense of idiomatic elegance which is seen to be at risk. Science and beauty act as guardians of a legitimacy under suspicion.

The fight for translation

The challenge of politics interrupts the established order. It recognizes it in an attempt to transform it. It speaks in a certain language so it can be understood. At the same time, it offers images of another way of life, of a time to come; it introduces new words, expressions, connections. In the documents written by the Not One Less collective, different writing strategies are employed: widely accepted language, as well as new expressions, uses or meanings – through the process of internal translation, narrating the meaning of a word as it is put into use – poetic images that create meaning beyond the argumentative composition of the text. The objective is to be understood without shying away from the linguistic innovation that the appearance of these words and bodies demands.

The innovations produced through academic investigations and gender studies in universities or feminist collectives were translated to a broader public. A document read on 3 June 2015 at the demonstration in Buenos Aires denounced machista[14] culture. "Machista" is a widely used adjective, part of colloquial speech. In the 2016 documents, the term "patriarchy" was used instead to indicate that machismo results from a system of social relationships that implies hierarchies, gender inequality, invisible labor, differential rights.[15] In the document read on 8 March 2018 the movement was declared to be made up of "sons and daughters of this anti-patriarchal and anti-capitalist history."[16] Emphasizing the connection between the patriarchy and capitalism is an attempt to impede the neoliberal appropriation of the feminist struggle, sexual dissidence, and the movements against gender violence.

I'd like to focus on one document to highlight the rhetorical processes employed. In the manifesto written before the first national women's strike, on 19 October 2016, women were called to march: "So that they cannot stop us with their criminal pedagogy. To create the pedagogy ourselves, because together we are going to build a society free of machismo. Because freedom implies definitively dismantling the patriarchy."[17] The notion of pedagogical crime was introduced here, taken from the writings of Rita Segato, to produce an interpretation: "We strike against femicide, the culmination of a pattern of violence, that ties exploitation, cruelty and hate to the most diverse forms of autonomy and feminine vitality, that takes our bodies as things to be used and disposed of, to be violated and looted." All the documents demand recognition of the political subject, described as:

> Housewives, participants in both the formal and informal economies, teachers, members of cooperatives, academics, laborers, the unemployed, journalists, activists, artists, mothers and daughters, domestic workers, women you pass on the street, who leave their homes, who live in your neighborhood, who went to a party, who have a meeting, who walk alone or accompanied, those who chose to have an abortion, those who didn't, women who decide for ourselves how and with whom to express our sexuality. We are women, trans, *travestis*, lesbians. We are many and, in response to the fear they want to impose on us, and with the fury that they rip out of us with violent force, we cry out, we protest, we shout together: Not One Less! We want ourselves alive.[18]

The issue of translation has multiple layers. On the one hand, the movement seeks efficient ways of making its demands heard, and this requires translation. On the other hand, various actors are simultaneously attempting to appropriate and resignify the statements that the movement places in the public sphere. The conversion of the feminist demand into punitive puritanism,[19] the neoliberal feminist construction of a corporate agenda based in gender issues – which proposes the inclusion of "empowered" women into the very order that worsens conditions of life for women[20] – the use of feminist struggles as legitimization of institutional violence or repressive government policies, are all appropriations of the value created on the streets. Further appropriation appears in the media's distortion of the movement as well as the utilization of feminist strategies in publicity campaigns across different markets.[21] Translation is a political intervention. And, as Mikhail Bakhtin[22] knew, social antagonism implies the dispute over the appropriation of the other's language, the incorporation of its terms into the hegemonic worldview. Rebellious movements produce images, ideas, languages, that can be integrated – resignified – into the very ideology that reinforces its subaltern status. Appropriation is a strategy used by companies, political parties, institutions and governments, which protect their dominant positions by appealing to the discourse of gender.

The transnational company Benetton, in November 2017, launched a campaign in Argentina centered on the color purple, a color often identified with the feminist struggle. A major conflict emerged that included the company as the silent protagonist. In August of that year, security forces had repressed the members of a Mapuche community who occupied lands that belong to Benetton. During the repression, a young activist named Santiago Maldonado disappeared. The government attempted to cover up the crime committed by the national guard, and only after much pressure from the public did it demand a search for the young man. A feminist assembly was attended by dozens of organizations. Feminism took on the struggle for lands, adopting the phrase "Our bodies, our territories." Benetton responded with its purple campaign in the same month as the march against violence toward women.[23] A series of artists organized an intervention on the company's posters and billboards, showing that the color was being used as an attempt to hide the disgrace of the activist's forced disappearance.[24]

The conflict involved diverse actors: indigenous peoples, feminists, anarchists, artists, activists from different political parties and human rights organizations, security forces, the government, a transnational corporation, the media. Those who attempted to hide the truth were not able to impose their version in a monolithic way thanks to social media campaigns and street demonstrations. Images, symbols, political narrations and interpretations were disputed. Stories on the conflict over lands and identity in the south of Argentina[25] emerged as troll factories set up a virtual campaign to minimize the activist's forced disappearance and defame the young man's family.[26] The Not One Less collective participated in actions to give the issue greater visibility.[27] A year later, the filmmaker Tristán Bauer released the documentary *El camino de Santiago*, and during the premiere a group attacked the theatre with stones. The media and factories of fake users on social networks linked to the government built a version that defended the actions of the repressive forces, but a huge and heterogeneous effort in civil society and a strong nuclei of political activists managed to counteract it.

The feminist perspective connected the activist's forced disappearance, the company lands claimed by indigenous communities, and the appeal for a non-individualist conception of autonomy of bodies and desires – a clear dispute over translation. One translation was attempted by the corporate–government coalition, and another was achieved through a social movement which, despite internal conflicts, showed a lucid vitality under grave circumstances. The struggle over feminist translation plays out in a context fraught with multiple public controversies – which produce diverse social actors, on a jumbled and multilingual scene – and in a society with a long history of street demonstrations. The recent emergence of feminism allows for a more radical intersection of these diverse conflicts.

Alliances, intersectionality, the transversality of agendas materialize as languages, modes of speaking, discourses, incorporation of words or names proposed by social actors. In other countries, the street protests against gender violence did not lead to involvement in any struggles that followed and did not create a lens from which social conflict could be viewed. Not One Less persisted in Argentina as the name of the feminist mobilization beyond the first demonstration. The collective that uses this name as it continues to organize mobilizations reflects not only on gender violence but also on its relationship to social, racial and economic inequality. Can feminism achieve this articulation? Can it expose common goals and shared logic where they are not evident between diverse actors, disputes and languages? In the contemporary experience of the feminist movement this transversality is strategically plotted and sustained.

Media and networks: disputes over meaning

The first call to protest with the slogan "Not one less" circulated widely in the media and across social networks. Even in a divisive political climate marked by fierce opposition or fervent support of the government, the call was universal. Journalists, actresses and politicians snapped photos holding signs that read "Not One Less" and invited others to take to the streets. Increased awareness of gender violence and the attention given to the murder victims did the rest: thousands of people posted the call on social media, becoming agents of a multiplying force without center or direction. The hegemonic system of mass communication converged with media activism and social networks to spread the summons. This could be one of the reasons for the initial massive turnout.

This is not what usually happens. Rossana Reguillo analyzes the use of digital resources such as streaming, memes, the human microphone and the hashtag to infiltrate the media with "disobedient images that, in addition to generating visibility, force conventional media to modify their routines of silencing or criminalizing in order to avoid being widely discredited."[28] These are activism's means of auto-narration, of presenting its own debates and images. Social movements dispute the translation of their statements by media corporations that work to dilute radical content. Movements must construct their own representation in order to avoid being only partially read and interpreted. Within the Argentine feminist movement there are two positions that are not contradictory: the call for more journalists to write from a gender perspective within communication companies and the creation of independent digital media – agencies, journals, radio stations.[29] The demand for representation without distortion in the traditional press[30] coexists with the production of alternative communication strategies.

Critics of the virtual world tend to oppose social networks and street demonstrations, keyboards and bodies. For digital enthusiasts, social networks produce political outcomes, subverting traditional forms of political commitment or adhesion by allowing opinions to be expressed from the safety of the home. The Argentine women's movement, like other movements – Occupy Wall Street,[31] the French Up All Night,[32] the demand for information on the murder of the forty-three grad students in Ayotzinapa, Mexico[33] – sees more overlap than opposition between the virtual and material planes. Social networks are fundamental to the diffusion of the calls to action and to the production of autonomy, essential to street mobilization and assembly, in-person meetings, and the construction of collective politics. They make action possible for people who cannot mobilize because of disability, age or fear. Re-tweeting or posting become tools of politicization and not mere substitutes for assembly, mobilization, strike. Social media campaigns accompany the mobilizations and incentivize them, generating a state of alarm or shared consciousness.[34] The occupation of spaces – the streets of New York City, or the plazas of Paris, or outside the National Congress in Buenos Aires – produces, from that very spatiality, images, hashtags, statements, discourses. They are internationalized through this same dynamic and situated in a materially defined location.

Between 2016 and 2018, the mobilizations and street demonstrations carried out by the Not One Less collective emerged from assemblies held by different collectives, parties and syndicates to define the content of the political actions. The non-hegemonic character of feminism was affirmed. The media outlets owned by concentrated communication groups tried to limit its visibility. Posts on social networks attacked the supposed politicization of the movement.[35] The offensive has several lines: obscuring facts, making accusations of misappropriation,[36] reducing and limiting representation. The attack is launched from different sectors, but all aim to counter the street-level power of the women's movement, its capacity to accommodate diversity and to construct mobilization as political pedagogy.

One media tactic is to avoid covering the press conferences or large mobilizations unless there are incidents that involve clashes with security forces. The image of a small group confronting the police displaces and substitutes the images of the masses on screens and the front pages of newspapers.[37] This is not only an attempt to stir up scandal and attract the spectator's attention; it also constructs meaning as the image of the masses is obliterated. The political construction of this mass is ignored in the name of making a larger impact. It omits any consideration of documents and manifestos: words are silenced in the plan to remove mobilized feminism from the plane of visibility. Connecting the notion of mass protest with images of violent acts seeks to create a fear both of the demonstrators and of the repressive power of the security forces. Mobilization is an invitation to take part – one chant repeated in the marches is directed at spectators, to those watching from their homes or on the pavements: "Women, hear us, join the battle." The celebratory and empowered crowd extends an invitation. Yet the media produces its pedagogical opposition: inciting fear in order to create feelings of paralysis, separation and isolation.

During the dictatorship, when almost all modes of communication were complicit with state-sponsored terrorism, either through coercion or by conviction,[38] a group of militants created ANCLA, a clandestine news agency. In its call to spread information on forced disappearances, murders and kidnappings, it stated: "Break the isolation. Feel once again the moral satisfaction of an act of freedom. Defeat terror. Circulate information."[39] It was as relevant to circulate what the regime hid as it was to break the terrified complicity each person was forced into, producing a resistant subjectivity. The current dispute over the representation of events does not compare because it does not have the ultimate threat of death for the person that spreads the oppositional message. Nevertheless, it remains necessary to question the control of information by large media machines and to circulate data and images that incite collective action.

In the outrage over the murder of Lucía Pérez in 2016 – a horror show played out across screens – followed immediately and unexpectedly by the call for a women's strike, the press coverage was broader. Members of the Not One Less collective circulated through editorial departments, television news sets and radio stations, appeared on gossip and news programs, before serious journalists and opportunists alike. They did it right up to the start of the protest. Then they stepped away from the programs and interviews to which they had committed. This had not been planned in advance: it occurred as a shared intuition, manifested as exhaustion and loss of enthusiasm. This silence can be taken as a dispute over the conditions of communication, the urgency of the need to question when and why one should appear, viewing the media from the needs of the movement – to put the disruptive statement center stage – and not the other way around.

Accusations of misrepresentation put two images at odds: the first spontaneous mobilization, created "by the people" with a specific and valid agenda (the struggle against femicide), is placed in contrast to the series of actions that occurred afterwards constructed by activists, covering a wide range of issues – capitalism and sexism, political repression and lack of public resources to prevent violence, sexual abuse and the access to natural resources, employment and land. The criticism that circulates on social networks and some media outlets is that the initial demand was distorted by politicization.[40] The conservative offensive denigrates activism and presents its own actions as apolitical: government institutions are managed like corporations and social commitments made viable by NGOs. Being political is construed as something partisan, partial and self-interested.

This narration tells the story of a legitimate mobilization, massive and spontaneous, that had its street-level value appropriated by a small group who redirected its intentions. The heterogeneous makeup of the first mobilization – which included political parties, social organizations, feminist collectives, and many individuals who did not identify as activists – is erased in allusions to the "self-summoned crowd." This is as theoretical as the "regular everyday woman" or "natural speech." The appearance of bodies on the street, collective actions, are always political acts. The denial of this characteristic, defining the political as partisan, is not an honest mistake. It is an effort to limit the constructive and foundational power of the mass, to lower it to ground zero of the confrontation: a group of angry citizens, gathered only to protest. To conceive of it as a political mass allows for suspicion of the cooperative force that summoned the people, that inspired them to mobilize and directed their march. We do not know what a body can do, Spinoza wrote. Much less do we know what a collective body can do when the fragile and vulnerable individuals who form part of it combine their powers.

The first reason to question the ideological notion that sets self-summoned individuals against the mass of political activists is that any collective action is always political and its apparent spontaneity belies the organizational efforts that make it possible. The second is that the idea of a mass composed solely of activists is no less false. Even in a mobilization called by political representatives, with classic partisan identifications and modes of occupying the street defined by organizational belonging, the decision and will of the demonstrators is never called into question. The party or organization that drags docile bodies into the street, alienated by obedience, is an ideological illusion. In media discourses, this illusion is constructed around the accusation that payments were made or benefits offered to the participants in a demonstration. Self-summoned protesters are supposed to act out of legitimate desire or necessity, whereas militants act out of spurious interest.[41]

The construction of these opposing images is used in interpretations of all mobilizations in Argentina. The media treatment of Not One Less followed the classic pattern: a story of appropriation and distortion of the movement, which fell victim to the sin of becoming political.[42] This attack circulates in mainstream media outlets and on social networks; offensives have even been launched from message factories – call centers of false users – against some interventions of the collective. This occurred in cases where the government decided to take the disputes to social networks: the imprisonment of social activist Milagro Sala and the forced disappearance of Santiago Maldonado. These instances produce a condensation and reiteration of the argument, showing evidence of a centralized decision.[43]

After the strike on 8 March 2018, the mass media began to circulate a narrative of events: the crowd of women had been tricked by leftist groups who control the stage and the speeches, distorting the true meaning of the mobilization. The movement's stated autonomy was ignored to create a more digestible narrative. It is another form of translation appropriation: debating the meaning of what Not One Less is, refuting statements made by the collective itself as it utilizes political and communicational strategies.[44] This line of attack encompasses and rises above the previous one. It denies the meanings that the collective known as Not One Less puts into play; it declares them spurious and political and substitutes them for other representations that it deems legitimate. María Eugenia Vidal, governor of the largest province in Argentina, leader of a right-wing political party, presented a program of gender policies that claimed to make Not One Less unnecessary. This statement channels the power from the streets to declare itself opposed to femicide. The stated goal is to ensure that there is not one less. But it could be read another way: to ensure that no feminist movement can occupy the streets and dispute neoliberal governability. The conflict is reduced to a single demand which is configured as legitimate and assimilated into conservative political-ideological contexts in an attempt to dilute the force of popular feminism. The denial of any connection between femicide and other forms of social and economic violence (from the wage gap to the raising of the retirement age, from the growth of external debt with its effects on public policy to the criminalization of protest) is to say that this form of violence is isolated and can be solved with specific and limited policies.[45]

Not One Less, through this appropriation, becomes a general expression that can be used to endorse any plan; its mere mention ennobles the speaker. The ideal is at odds with the movement's reality, more controversial and specific, which seeks to become not a general symbol but to construct an antagonistic logic that, if it redraws social partitions, it is not to deny or forget them. The conservative attempt to recodify the movement constantly attacks statements and actions in order to neutralize their revolutionary power. The very statement "Not one less" has a transversal power and is very widely accepted. This allows the cause to be taken up by actors from a diversity of political backgrounds, even those who hold views in opposition to the proposals of the feminist collective.

The differences between the very first massive mobilization of women and the subsequent marches are a source of interpretative and political controversy. Communicational and organizational needs emerged from concrete alliances; they overlap with different groups, agendas and demands. What is denounced as politicization is a concerted effort to create a unified body in assemblies, to develop strategies for street-level mobilization, and to permit the collective production of statements – or, rather, effective political materiality.

Narration

No political subject can control all the ways it will be interpreted. Less still when these interpretations are produced by centralized powers which have a huge reach such as mass media. The representation of a movement is disputed territory. Every demonstration implies the production of images, texts, statements, modes of representation. The rise of partisan press, new communication technology and social networks multiplies the ways in which interpretations are formulated and circulated. Destined for other people in principle, it simultaneously proposes a discursive narrative to the participants themselves. The narration of a collective event is not univocal. It is multilingual, biased, conflictive, a kaleidoscope of viewpoints, contradictory, paradoxical; it can be at once an epic tale and a list of criminal records. This book is one possible narration, a glimpse inside the movement, an attempt to tease out conflicts, solutions, promises and obstacles. The reader will surely be able to identify overlooked areas. It is not a chronicle, although chronicling is one of its internal folds.

To narrate what a polyglot and massive movement does is part of the same task. It is a specific consideration of words, their value, their deterioration. The discussion on the lexicon of public interventions poses the question of efficiency: is it understandable, does it elicit emotion, will it cause a stir, awaken consciousness, get people heated? It also attempts to avoid shortcuts and jargon, empty words. In *The Jargon of Authenticity*, what Adorno[46] calls "jargon" is words abstracted from the vital flow of language and presented as symbols of value, hierarchical labels. Validation more than thought.

This does not only happen with erudite words that aim to ennoble a speech or the speaker who enunciates them. All words, writes John Berger, can be "mere labels": "Most mainstream political discourse today is composed of words which, separated from any creature of language, are inert and dead. And such dead 'word-mongering' wipes out memory and breeds a ruthless complacency."[47] Words are situated at the intersection of a certain historicity – memory – and empathy with others. The inert word implies a breakup of collective belonging, erasing empathy. Language is historical sedimentation. Speakers access through language the memory of the community. They do so, although they are unaware. They speak and understand because their life is intertwined with the lives of others, because language is other, even when it puts forward individual speech. It is not familiar. It is foreign. Against this background of foreignness, we undertake singular, creative, ludic navigations.

Empathy is more than emotional openness, more than the apologies offered by neoliberal governance, more than a name given to the ignorance of drastic and concrete inequities of race and class. Berger defines empathy as the ability to recognize the shared existence of humanity. The social production of disposable lives cuts these ties, interrupts the commonality of experience as it introduces in each person not the illusion of the competitive individual but the effective fabrication of this subjectivity. The women's movement affirms among its protest songs: "If they touch one of us, we'll all come out." At the center of the politics it constructs is the recognition of the shared: shared fragility as well as shared power.

In this recognition, language and the mode of narrating the movement are central; they invent a genealogy, re-create singularities of the language of women, transmit experiences. The narratives are not different from, or posterior to, appearance on the streets. They are modes of describing this appearance. The narration is more on the side of poetic images than the side of word-labels that have already been flattened. The Not One Less collective's charter specifies: "Handing down words between generations is also part of women's speech, our inheritance of protection tactics used by the supposedly weak. We tell stories, we tell our own stories, we speak about ourselves, and together we build memories of wounds, daily heroisms, mutual protection. In this weaving, we create ourselves; we are also present in the word."[48]

The narration of this subject is constructed in praxis – like all praxis, it is also linguistic – and at the same time deconstructs and reaffirms. It deconstructs as it aims to politicize what is usually taken for granted, to question the molding of its own sensibilities, to historicize its own conditions, to challenge the common logic that legitimizes its exclusion or its subaltern status, to lose the innocence that leads it to say "I" or "we" without hesitation. It reaffirms as it constructs a language in tension with existing languages, without demanding coherence or homogeneity, as it simultaneously appears in the streets and builds networks and territorial organizations. To narrate itself is to recognize that the subject must be de-constructed in order to construct itself, that it must withdraw itself to invent itself, that it must pass judgment on the judicial and linguistic order that produces and names women as subaltern to construct emancipated subjects, which we call "women" with the condition that the word must reverberate with multiplicity, with disobedience and anomaly;[49] no longer one individual left outside the masculine universal but a heterogeneous mass of singularities.

"Women" is what the binary order has constructed as "other," as incomprehensible or insignificant; for this reason, "women" can include all marginalized identities. This writing is my hypothesis or my desire. This is the reason for the emphasis on what the movement "should" do. Am I a naïve writer or a desperate activist? Both things, both nourished by the way in which the movement has unfolded in recent years. Knowing that history is open-ended and there is not one truth. What I write today as a hope may be read in a few years as a failure or defeat, because the movement may be limited to feminist activism or become trapped within pre-existing party lines, or the neoliberal translation of it may triumph. The statements and images collectively constructed may be used to legitimize exclusionary policies; the enormous push for equality that sustains feminism may be erased and a new meritocratic logic established. The idea of gender inequality, presented as an isolated issue, accepting the lines of social and racial inequality in which it is inscribed, without questioning existing logics of exploitation, may ultimately settle for the individual autonomy of women, now with freedom to lead, govern and enjoy pleasure. That would be no small victory against the history of patriarchal submission, but popular feminism aims and hopes for more.

The street and bodies: rituality and performance

We read the uses of the street like a text. We interpret what the bodies say with their public appearance, their clothing and their rituals of march and movement. We trace a genealogy of those appearances, following the lines that lead to the birth of new creations. The appearance on the street implies dramatization and inscription in the language. All mobilization is a setting of scene, and this expression has to be stripped of all falsehood or fiction. It is an exhibition of mobilized bodies, a demonstration of strength in numbers, a choreographed dance of the subject that speaks to others.

The mobilizations of women in Buenos Aires between 2015 and 2018 exposed a paradox. The collective subject is motivated by pain – it comes out, initially, to say it will not accept femicide and gender violence – but mourning does not manifest as sadness and the mobilizations are combative yet festive. The demonstrations display the celebratory tone of the movement. Women were shocked by the turnout, the euphoria of the massive crowd – the majority not resulting from government interpellation;[50] we knew we were experiencing something unprecedented. This is not a mass of spectators seeing themselves represented on a cinema screen, as occurred in the fascist aestheticization of politics.[51] In the feminist mobilizations, women witness themselves forming the multitude first-hand, as they see the bodies gathered alongside them on the street. Not because there are no images to serve as register, later analyzed and circulated, but because these images are produced not by the media industries but by the demonstrators themselves, curating their own aesthetic and narration: aesthetics are politicized as part of the demonstration. Photographic and audio-visual coverage by collectives such as MAFIA[52] or Emergentes,[53] with wide reach on social media, inform the representation of activists. From one mobilization to another, aesthetics, styling, uses of symbols, ways of acting are established. The visual register combines, mainly, two types of images: close-up shots of faces (often shouting or chanting) and panoramic crowd shots.

On 3 June 2015, during the demonstration outside Argentina's National Congress, an infinite crowd of bodies established a movement to which many today remain loyal – working to sustain that initial momentum and what it has given way to; the outpouring of emotion was palpable. I wasn't able to cry while the demonstration was underway. I had to get home, be alone for a while, and process my emotions. The surprise left me breathless, tearless, wordless. A month later, one participant published a summary of the event. It said the atmosphere that day on the street was created by feminism and its purpose was to welcome:

The mobilization on 3 June was for many people baptismal and its tone was welcoming. The crowd moved slowly as women looked out for each other, the public sphere becoming an accommodating space protected from the elements. The space outside Congress was one of listening and sharing: the things women tell each other in secret were freed from the realm of the personal and private to be openly expressed through public and political speech. For those who have suffered machista violence, it created a place where their stories could be told.[54]

The written and audio-visual chronicles, the documents drafted, all reflect the surprise over the turnout and attempt to interpret the phenomenon. From 3 June 2015 to 8 March 2018, the movement constructed rituals, styles, modes of circulation, words, identifying characteristics. Increasingly accentuated is the celebratory nature: the celebration of the occurrence itself, its massiveness, its persistence as a movement without owners, leaders or bosses. During the overnight vigil on 13 June, as the legalization of abortion was debated by lawmakers, the collective and insomniac street occupation saw these diverse aspects converge. The mother of a young woman recounted her daughter's preparations: each of the girls carried in her backpack lemon, vinegar, a handkerchief, glitter and paint. They were prepared for teargas and to decorate themselves for battle. Glitter and lemon, carnival aesthetics and practical knowledge gained in previous confrontational mobilizations. The feminist rituality connects elements that were once separate, creating a bellicose yet festive corporality. The street was so welcoming that it felt like home.

This new subject is in its beginning, incipient, dawning. It is a subject built through a celebration of bodies brushing past each other, embracing, dancing.

Inherited knowledge

Two other massive mobilizations in Argentina have influenced the feminist demonstrations: the yearly gatherings on the anniversary of the 1976 military coup and the Gay Pride marches. The "Never Again" marches for memory and justice have been held every 24 March since 1986 with the number of attendees, as well as the internal conflicts, growing annually.

There are generally various calls to the same march put out by opposing political parties and human rights organizations with divergent positions. This poses obstacles to building a unified panel for planning and decision-making. One group of organizations calls people to march at one time and another three hours later, so that the Plaza de Mayo[55] and the surrounding streets have time to empty out after the first speech and the bodies can be substituted by those who support the second, according to the plan of the organizers.

In recent years, the reality has been quite different.[56] The two mobilizations have become practically interchangeable: the participants make up an almost indistinguishable multitude, excerpts of the speeches are heard, groups of street artists, theatre troupes and percussion bands perform, people take selfies and post them on social media, like vacation photos only with a demonstration in the background. On social media, personal photos – small groups of people who went to march together or met by chance – are alternated with large aerial views.

The demonstrations of the Never Again movement stand against state-sponsored terrorism and in defense of memory, truth and justice. But beyond these demands, which establish the protests in relationship to the past, the tone is festive:[57] each 24 March, we celebrate the fact that we are alive, that we collectively say "no" to state-sponsored terrorism, that we are proud of the activists who managed to put an end to the terror, proud of the fact that there are many of us and that our numbers grow as each year new young people join, girls and boys who grew up under democracy yet nevertheless feel committed to memory and justice. Participation, collective coming together, is moving. This joyful feeling of belonging manifests itself in the women's marches as well. Both mobilizations have a dual nature: the denouncement of mourning and the celebration of existence and vitality.

The women's marches also share a common thread with the marches for LGBTQIA Pride,[58] seen in the aesthetic production of the bodies who make up the scenery. Participants wear badges, clothes, adornments. Vests or shirts indicate belonging to a specific group; banners head up each column. The Pride marches combine carnival aesthetics with elements of parody and costume, exaggerated makeup, high heels, partial nudity, sequins. Daytime marches with nocturnal staging, like a street party where each person may celebrate the uniqueness of their body with affirmative joy and defiance.

Queer staging and carnival

Unlike Brazil, Argentina doesn't have a festive and street-level carnival celebration to manifest a utopian ideal of a society free from hierarchies and suffering. In Brazil, as analyzed by the anthropologist Roberto DaMatta,[59] carnival implies a rupture from the separation between private and public space and dissolves class differences. Some divisions, however, are restored through cover charges, assigned seats and bracelets handed out to allow or deny access. But these practices don't occur in every city: in Olinda, home to one of the biggest carnival celebrations in Brazil, the party consists of long street parades, marching behind bands of musicians, bodies packed together, brushing against each other in the ecstasy of community belonging, love and sensuality on display, without distinction between protagonists and spectators. Carnival acts out (as indicated by Mikhail Bakhtin in a study of popular carnivals in the Middle Ages and the Renaissance)[60] the utopian notion of equalitarianism, the inversion of high and low, and corporality as pleasure.

In Argentina, this carnival-like atmosphere is present in political demonstrations. Pride marches channel it through parodies of the feminine and masculine, defense of the queer, and baroque aesthetics. These same practices of organization and styling of public appearance are re-created in the women's marches: from glitter dusted over bodies to partial nudity,[61] clothes with inscriptions or that are part of a specific attire considered to be representative. During the mobilizations for the legalization of abortion, many demonstrators wore green and painted their nails and hair this color. The impact of the campaign is so strong that, every day on the streets of Buenos Aires and its suburbs, young men and women are seen wearing the color green, in addition to the green handkerchief that symbolizes this struggle tied around backpacks, purses, arms, necks. In the marches, many wear vests and shirts that express belonging to an organization or that highlight queer identification. A group of Not One Less activists from the Villa Fiorito neighborhood took it to an extreme and organized a fashion show. The models wore backpacks, patches,

T-shirts, body paint. These girls, from a very poor neighborhood, plebeian bodies destined for sacrifice, occupy the public space to display themselves as warriors, powerful, beautiful. They parody traditional fashion shows, restricted to bodies that fit established beauty standards, and instead place themselves center stage as subjects ready for combat and pleasure. The object of the parody is not the army of demonstrators but the fashion show. They mock what is considered worthy of exhibition and public display. They challenge, with their appearance, which bodies deserve to be seen and how. They demand to be seen/represented beyond a report on crime or the social assistance payroll.

The painted body, adorned, written on, asks to be read. In some cases, the naked torso offers the skin as surface to display a message: "Ni yuta ni tuya,"[62] "We want ourselves alive," "Legal abortion now," "My body didn't ask your opinion," "Organize your rage." These are signs of belonging to the collective and, at the same time, of marking dissidence, forming part while demanding recognition of singularity. The mobilizations of women display the deconstruction of assigned identities, bodily norms, rules that regulate the use of public space. They question the differences between political demands and personal desires. The ritual of going topless is revolutionary in a society that allows men but never women to show their naked torso, and at the same time it systematically constructs valuations on the fullness, beauty and size of female breasts. If in the public space the feminine body is always threatened with harassment or violence, if it must be protected and covered to reduce its risk of harm, the mobilizations show support of nudity: they establish a zone of protection where it is possible collectively to live out freedoms that are denied individually. The act of setting clothes aside is both denouncement and affirmation, a break with social conventions and a conversion of vulnerability into power.

The unknown in question

Less evident but not insignificant is a third lineage of this festive and non-submissive force. On 17 October 1945 a popular mobilization established Peronism as a massive fact and central actor in Argentine politics. Several newspapers and magazines published the same images: the demonstration seemed more like a street party, the protesters – a communist writer wrote that they did not look like the laborers we know, they were dressed up – like members of a parade. The festive mass contrasted with the crowd of correct laborers, the serious workers, members of an organization, knowledgeable of the proper ways of moving through the city. The October demonstration upended traditional representations of the laborer. Individuals with no affiliation to political parties or unions turned out. A new sector of the working class mobilized, migrants from rural zones who had come to the large cities, workers in expanding industries, union members as well as others new to public demonstration.

The media references at the time to carnival, parades or costumes were an attempt to negate the relevance of the event, to ignore its condition of class and reduce the mobilization to a farcical stage show. The historian Daniel James affirms that what stands out in the memory of the actors of that mobilization are the carnival elements such as parody of power, dance and music, laughter and mockery: "This proletarian crowd did not sing the workers' chants typical of the rallies, such as the ones held on 1 May; they didn't march in tidy columns or obey the tacit rules of decency and civil restraint. In place of that, they sang popular songs, danced in the middle of the street, whistled and shouted, and they were often directed by men on horseback dressed as gauchos."[63] Parody is a strategy commonly used by the marginal: challenging what normalizes its subaltern status not with open opposition but with mocking displacement, sarcasm, expressing suspicion of dominant norms.

Currently, explicit corporal performance as part of public demonstration is read as a display of the subject's political opinion, which organizes their strategies and modes of public appearance. It is seen not as a deplorable fictionalization of a presumably real corporality but as evidence of the fictional nature of all public construction of bodies. It is taken as a real body whose presentation is not arbitrary but more real the more explicit the construction of its appearance.

Identity is a signifying practice: it is configured with the advent of a subject of enunciation, through the narration of its own historicity and conditions of its appearance and the regulation of its visibility. The modes of appearing on the streets and speaking to the press are practices of identity construction. In the mobilizations of women there are representations, the bodies are exposed and the verbs conjugated are heterogeneous. A person cultivating queer aesthetics marches alongside someone wearing a T-shirt for a political party alongside an organized activist. Groups of women in costumes as part of a group dramatization coexist with the casual attire of women who just got off work or left school. In all cases self-representation is consciously political.

Roberto DaMatta[64] analyzes different aspects of carnival that are useful for contemplating the feminist mobilizations, which include not only marches across cities, but assemblies and workshops:

a) The production of a "kind of special time, empty, without work, like a holiday." Absence of routine, of organized and prescribed time, of obligations, establishing another time that is not dictated by the calendar (whether of carnival or of national holidays), but produced by the mobilizations themselves.

b) The division between home and street is broken and the street becomes "a safe and humanitarian place."[65] This experience, which DaMatta attributes to carnival and which goes against rationality (since the street and not the home is the place where we feel comfortable and protected), is fundamental to the feminist mobilizations that have occurred in recent years. If the home is the place where gender violence often materializes, the street is a welcoming space.

c) The street is a multiple and ownerless space, where people may represent themselves. Even though there are political organizations which employ the conventional logic of representation, the power of the mobilizations comes from the bodies present, which attempt not to speak in the name of others but to express their own singular statement, which, if it surges from a collective, is one that did not exist before the movement.

Bodies on stage

One debate repeatedly emerges before every women's march or strike. How can cis men participate? Should they go out on the streets? Do they have the right to join the strike? The feminist movement is asked to worry about including a group of the population that has no historical problems with public visibility. The debate implies the question of whether feminist political identity can be assumed only by women or dissident, non-heteronormative bodies.

At the National Women's Conference the decision was made that men would not participate in the workshops but that they could show support by joining the mobilizations. In the majority of public spaces, even in leftist organizations and assemblies of students or laborers, the male voice is more audible than the female. Traditional sex–gender constructions mark some bodies for the public sphere and others for domestic reproduction. This means that men often speak more and feel more comfortable with public speech and political argumentation, since rhetoric is one legitimate means for demonstration of virility. A successful man can and should know how to speak in public. The dominant traditional construction of the feminine does not imply this skill or disposition. Women must empower themselves, deviate from the attributes assigned to them, find spaces in which to raise their voices. While the Me Too movement travels the world, in Argentina we shout "We will not be silent any longer," and in various spheres – theatre, art and science – reports emerge from women who have been abused, harassed, mistreated by colleagues or misogynist practices and whose accusations were doubted or silenced. Only the acceptance offered by the feminist movement and the rebellion that takes fragility as common ground can make these voices heard. One expression that many women paint on their bodies and signs is: "Sister, I believe you."

The women's workshops and feminist assemblies held to plan the mobilizations and strikes exclude masculine participation to avoid reproducing the male pre-eminence dictated by gender norms. The voice that feminism tries to build requires its own spaces, active patience in the face of missteps or contradictions. It is a voice that can be easily drowned out by rhetorical molds that validate certain modes of discourse and diminish or silence others.

This restriction was not established in the mobilizations, and many men did march. An attempt was made, not always successfully, to keep men from occupying managerial roles or heading the columns and dictating modes of marching. In some organizations, the task of security for the columns reinforced traditional gender roles. Many men also marched in support of the movement without trying to overshadow, with their public presence, the power of this other subject that gathers, that takes the streets, that shows that its body cannot be contained within an assigned mold, interrupting the traditional construction of the female subject by being political.

In the assemblies held to organize the women's strikes (19 October 2016 and 8 March 2017 and 2018) the debate over male presence re-emerged. Meetings in workplaces defined modes of participation: quitting time, agenda and alliance. Male workers demanded the right to adhere to the measure. This minimized the very argument upheld by the strike: if our bodies don't matter – because the number of murdered women grows – produce without us. The strike required that the tasks usually carried out by women should be done by others: domestic work and childcare, as well as commercial and industrial activities, work in public institutions and transportation. A general strike implies the cessation of all these activities; a women's strike attempted to expose the magnitude of feminine participation in all social roles. The debate was clear with respect to tasks that could not be suspended, such as childcare. The women's movement said: we strike, but you'll have to figure out a way to do the work without us.

The demand for participation by men reproduces assigned patterns of behavior that destine men to public life and assign to them the privileges of representation, the authorized voice and visible participant. Their request to adhere to the strike or participate in the mobilization was configured as a desire to fight in solidarity with the women's movement and feminist activism. But this argument ignored the movement's request: to show support by remaining in the background and carrying out the tasks that women had suspended. Or, rather, the demand for equal participation in the women's movement denies the movement's specific needs and, at the same time, furthers masculine visibility. In the debate, a collective called Anti-Patriarchal Men[67] emerged, proposing a series of actions to support the mobilizations and strikes without disputing the female primacy or overshadowing the power of this insurgent feminist subject. On 8 March 2018 there were unique interventions such as the creation of childcare spaces in cultural centers, so that mothers could attend the march. Spaces run by male workers.

The male demand to participate in the actions – strike, march – to the same extent as the women is an attempt to maintain privileged access to public space. In an unequal society, the interruption of the practices that further inequality often require positive discrimination, the establishment of quotas or restrictions. In a similar way, the construction of the woman as a political subject and feminist identity demands certain separatism, regulation of conditions, disputed alliances, measures to ensure these intersections do not result in the limitation of its emerging potential.

Public art

On 30 September 2017 the Arte Urgente (Urgent Art) assembly brought together over sixty artistic collectives in a space that had been used as a clandestine detention center during Argentina's military dictatorship.[68] At the close of this meeting, Ana Longoni outlined the different periods in the public art movement in Argentina. Since the transition to democracy there have been three large waves of artistic activism, understood as the practices of

> persons or collectives (defined as artists or not) that use creative practices to influence their conditions or produce change (denouncement or invention of logics of existence). Art as a vector that can be a part of the transformation of our lives, of the lives of others. Artistic activism stems from an idea completely different to the notion of autonomous art, locked in a closed circuit, linked to the market, a public of elites.

The first wave of art activism was linked to the struggles for memory, truth and justice. One central action was the Siluetazo,[69] first carried out in the third resistance march called by the Mothers of Plaza de Mayo in September 1983, still under the dictatorship. Since then, the Siluetazo has been reproduced in countless marches up to the present. It consists of outlining human silhouettes, drawn to scale, and hanging these images in public places. The empty space of the outline alluded to the absence of bodies, the forcibly disappeared persons. The letters NN, from the Latin *nomen nescio* (name unknown), were inscribed on each image to indicate that their identity was unknown. Longoni and Bruzzone write that the Siluetazo

> signals one of those exceptional moments of history in which an artistic initiative coincides with the demands of a social movement and takes shape through the impulse of a multitude. It implied participation, in an improvised and immense outdoor workshop that lasted until midnight, from hundreds of protesters who laid down their bodies to be outlined as silhouettes and then displayed on the walls of buildings, monuments and trees in spite of the ominous police presence.[70]

The Mothers had asked that the silhouettes be pasted vertically and not on the ground, to avoid their being associated with the police procedure of making chalk outlines of dead bodies. In this way, the artistic representation did not collide with the demand for return of the forcibly disappeared persons.

Artistic-political practices form part of the social archive. In early 2015, a group of activists carried out a Siluetazo to denounce femicide, and the artistic intervention was re-created at several other demonstrations. In this case, the silhouettes were left on the ground and were intended to refer to the chalk outline. It was a denouncement of the harvesting of women, their murdered bodies disposed of like rubbish, and the media and judiciary discourse that revictimizes the victims by destroying their privacy or suggesting a connection between their behavior and their suffering. The practice has spread, and Siluetazos are now carried out by many groups. Sometimes passers-by are invited to lie down on a strip of paper, to put themselves in the place of the victim, while an activist draws their outline. Others add the name and age of a murdered woman. It is artistic invention and appropriation of a legacy, updating inherited forms of represen-tation, aesthetic-political symbols, and practices recovered from different contexts.

The second wave of art activism emerged in the late 1990s around the rebellion that took place on 19 and 20 December 2001.[71] It linked issues of human rights with the conflict embodied by the *piquetero* movement. The Grupo de Arte Callejero (GAC; Street art group)[72] was central to this process. On 18 December 2001, this collective created an artistic intervention on the street outside the Stock Exchange to denounce the articulation between financial power and repression by throwing out little toy soldiers attached to parachutes. The action was called *Invasion*.[73] Social conflict was growing increasingly tense, and the city center – where the Stock Exchange is located – was the scene of protests and desperate attempts to extract funds. The city felt like a pressure cooker. The day following the GAC's intervention, the conflict came to a head. Shops and supermarkets were looted: groups of people entered stores and took merchandise. The government declared martial law, so that repressive forces could control the situation. In the city of Buenos Aires, a street rebellion aimed to resist military control.[74] The police murdered twenty people but were unable to stop the conflict on the streets. The president resigned in the midst of a political crisis derived from the impossibility of controlling the financial market. The GAC's artistic intervention, which connected economy and repression, anticipated the implementation of martial law. It highlighted the threat in order to denounce it in support of the popular rebellion. Many of the collectives that first inspired the political imagination around 2001 continue to produce artwork and political performances.[75]

The third wave that links social movements and artistic practices coincides with the emergence of Not One Less in 2015. Through the process of mobilization and the subsequent women's strikes, several art collectives were established across several cities: Mujeres de Artes Tomar,[76] Aúlla,[77] Las Mariposas – A.U.Ge,[78] Nombre en Construcción,[79] Cien Volando,[80] Resquicio Colectivo.[81] These collectives perform musical acts or plays during demonstrations or political mobilizations. Some are open groups that encourage participation from protesters; others, such as the musical ones, imply previous experience. Each group has a repertoire of interventions. Mujeres de Artes Tomar[82] carries out an action called "Whisperers." They move around with tubes, place them to the ear of a person and tell them something. Gossip, overhearing, camaraderie, sharing of information, are incorporated into the demonstration. Not all the collectives that emerged from or are active in this context are composed exclusively of women, but those that recognize as their founding date 3 June 2015 or 8 March 2017 are entirely female. In 2018, certain groups made up of men and women decided to perform without men during the 8 March strike.

Visual arts have also had an impact on the women's movement. In 2017 many well-known artists published a manifesto called "Nosotras proponemos"[83] which challenged the criteria of art curation and criticism that disguised misogynist positions behind the valorizations of good and bad in art.[84] That same year, Fernanda Laguna and Cecilia Palmeiro held an exposition called Mareadas en la marea,[85] displaying works created for feminist protests: banners, signs, photos, manifestos. In the first months of 2018, a group of artists formed a Cuadrilla of female painters to carry out collective actions. The Cuadrilla created a series of murals and paintings in public spaces as part of the publicity leading up to the strike on 8 March. They worked in groups and painted only walls where they had been given permission, since the previous year several activists had been detained for vandalism.

Artistic collectives are spaces of activism, political practices in themselves. They participate in organizational assemblies but have their own dynamic of participation, not different from other feminist groups. Feminism as political identity brings together collectives that propose diverse strategies: from the medics who help make abortions safer to those who provide support for women living in violent situations, from neighborhood activists to cultural and artistic collectives, from gender studies scholars in universities to specialized lawyers.

Artistic collectives do not fall outside feminist activism but are part of the same process of creation of the subject around several nuclei more than a center of alliances and adhesions. This third wave of artistic activism is related to the women's movement in a way that is unlike the previous links between artistic collectives and human rights. In the public denouncement of the forced disappearance of citizens, led, for example, by groups such as the Mothers and Grandmothers and HIJOS,[86] some activists held more prominence within the movement because of their family relationship to the forcibly disappeared. The feminist movement has no center. The artistic groups create representations and discourses as much as the explicitly political groups do. Confluence and horizontality prevail. This may be on account of the singularity of the feminist subject or for reasons related to our times. Contemporary activism – not only feminist activism – creates very close relationships between aesthetics and politics. Marcela Fuentes states that, even though, historically, there have been many examples of tacit use of the body within civil disobedience and protest – for example, Ghandi's peaceful sit-ins, Rosa Parks's refusal to obey segregationist laws, and the marches of the Mothers of the disappeared in Argentina and other countries, contemporary protests frequently resort to the use of symbolic elements and utilize the body to communicate messages beyond geographic and idiomatic barriers.[87]

Today's proliferation of technologies for image capture and reproduction and the possibility of global diffusion are not overlooked by contemporary activists, who combine aesthetics with political reflection on its meaning using techniques of duplication and massification of images. Artists are not merely road companions; media activists are more than amplifiers. All become producers of the event.

Theatricality of the street

During public demonstrations, artistic collectives, female percussion groups and dance troupes accompany the protesters, at once a public presentation and a representation. All political groups, in fact, make use of performance as they occupy the street. Members of the national campaign for the right to abortion march with green scarves around their necks. Paramedics march wearing fuchsia wigs. They throw colorful smoke bombs and run away at certain points in the march, letting out a battle cry. Some union activists set up their own percussion groups and divide their preparations between assembly and rehearsal.[88] All mobilization implies some dramatization, staging, styling, decisions over identifying attire and the use of recognized symbols. The novelty of the women's movement is the degree of self-awareness and the ways in which celebration and ceremony are interwoven. Carnival rituality and pagan religiosity; this is neither a deployment of combatant bodies nor a crowd gathered for a stroll.

In 2010, Argentina commemorated the bicentenary of independence from colonial power. There were huge shows and celebrations across the country's capital. Millions went out into the streets. Vanguard public art combined with popular music, political action and national ritual. The massive turnout was surprising, in an unprecedented atmosphere of cordiality, free of any violence or hostility. It was a festive multitude, summoned for a government ritual that occupied the center of the city to affirm its national belonging. If there was any conflict, it was secondary, on the plane of interpretation, because participation in the festivities could be read as support of the government. The feminist mobilizations have a celebratory air; euphoria surges from the female mass, but the sense of belonging is created in the moment (it is not the pre-existing belonging to a nation commemorated with a ritual). It commemorates itself. At the same time, it is presented as the subject of a conflict: it appears publicly to say that it demands change and that its rage results from mourning.

Diana Taylor understands performance not only as an ephemeral vanguard act; it is also an "act of transference that permits identity and collective memory to be transmitted through shared ceremonies."[89] The mobilizations of women are ceremonies of creation and transmission; they affirm belonging to an identity in construction, something new that would not have been possible in the past. They seek reaffirmation through ritual. No one was born into this community (as one is born into rites and liturgies of national identity), because the community is built through the very act of public appearance. Every action may live on as citation, as a ritual. Henri Bergson[90] affirms that every concrete act produces at the same time something virtual: a memory. The phenomenon of dèja vu occurs when the memory reappears stripped of its vital force, in a disincarnated present and an interrupted time. Political movements tend to produce rituals and at the same time fear them. Rituals assure that a notion will be repeated, its symbols reaffirmed; rituals are also dangerous because they may remain static. A movement dies from too much repetition, when its citation is recycled without being updated, when it remains immobile and unconnected to life.

Guadalupe Treibel states that feminist demonstrations have had an artistic nature since their beginnings: "Wasn't it, in a sense, a performance the way the women marched on Washington in March 1913 to demand the women's vote? On a shining horse the suffragist Inez Mulholland opened the way for thousands of suffragettes, followed by brigades of mounted women, nine all-female orchestras, twenty-six floats."[91] From this legacy we saw the splendid proliferation of costumes, curated aesthetics, choreographies and performances that traversed the globe on 8 March 2018. Countless female photographers and videographers, organized in collectives or allied with activists, converted each ritual into an image, exponentially multiplying the dramatization into something international, exemplary, quotable.

The feminist street ceremonies proliferate, amplify, reinvent. They toy with the logic of the spectacle[92] and gather from it tools for battle. Like any underlying debate dealing with a subject in construction, we can't say much about its future. Just this: that if there is anything we can call future and not apocalypse, if there is anything that may awaken our political imagination and not our fear of catastrophe, it is the feminist movement. An infinite sea of heterogeneous feminisms; a linguistic chaos that sets us free; a tide that washes everything out and levels the ground for reconstruction; a space that welcomes the silenced and makes room for their words; a collective contemplation of cruelty, so that we may avoid cruelty ourselves; shared creation; a desire to convert bodily fragility into power; invention that constructs its own heritage and lineage; a tremble (of fear) in the face of what we do not know and what is demanded of us. Infinite richness.

Provisional Epilogue

A book about a movement underway doesn't have an end; it cannot draw conclusions. A short while before 8 March 2018, while the massive assemblies were already in full swing, the Argentine government declared that it would not impede the parliamentary review of a law making abortion legal, safe and free, even though it declared itself to be against its passing. With this official decision, the debate made it to Congress.[1] The National Campaign for the Right to Abortion was at the forefront of the women's strike on 8 March, and hundreds of activists and experts spoke before congressional committees. The streets outside Congress were filled, every Tuesday, with activists and activities; requests to health service providers to provide legal abortions increased, and a rebellion occurred within the medical schools. In many religious institutions, students attended class wearing green scarves – the symbol of the campaign to legalize abortion – and the Church's position was debated.

As all this was happening, the streets were increasingly monopolized by green scarves and the country was sinking into a financial crisis. This is not something new, but our familiarity with it makes it no less destructive. The multicolored women's movement is now charged with keeping its most important demands from being ripped from the battlefield, usurped by a regime of control that destroys lives and existences. But aren't political movements always disputed territories, fraught with controversies over the connection between one demand and another? The debate over the legalization of abortion is about more than merely placing abortion on one side of the law or the other. It implies a transformation of life through social depenalization (abortion is no longer something to be shamefully hidden; we can publicly recognize and speak about it) and the flourishing of youth activism. The so-called Green Tuesdays (the days on which activists, artists and curious spectators gathered outside Congress to support the legalization of abortion) saw huge turnout among young adults and teenagers who found in feminism a path to a militant subjectivity.[2]

The criticisms that emerged after the first massive mobilization under the slogan "Not one less" reappeared in the debate over the legalization of abortion: objections to supposed classism in the prioritization of this demand, to shifting the focus away from activism that emerged from poorer neighborhoods, to the possibility that putting gender violence in the spotlight obscured other modes of social inequality. What happened was quite different, and it is what we have tried to examine through this narration of events: the movement began to support other struggles, to set aside its agenda, to construct new dialogues. It did not accept the limits of the gender agenda. When what's at stake is a profound[3] transformation of relationships, sensibility, sexuality, when many paths lead to disruption, then the discussion of law is merely one dimension of the collective experience.

Female university students in Chile in May 2018 held a series of protests against gender violence and institutional sexism.[4] The female law students of the Catholic University spoke out against sexist phrases repeated by their professors: "Young lady, why are you showing so much cleavage? Did you come here to take your exam or to get milked?" "We must demand more of ugly women because the pretty ones, even if they're dumb, will find a husband anyway. An ugly and dumb woman, on the other hand, won't be tolerated by anyone." "Young lady, do me a favor and take the four big ones this degree costs [4 million Chilean pesos] and go to the mall instead." "When a man sees a woman and has the desire to rape her, it's nothing more than a distortion of his natural inclination." At Catholic schools in Argentina, students rebelled by vandalizing the anti-abortion signs that covered the walls of these institutions. The feminist rebellion, like a deep river, does not always surface at the same time in all places.

It silently modifies the landscape. What was once naturalized becomes intolerable, the exploitation behind the habit revealed. I use natural metaphors such as tide, river, earthquake, tsunami to express the magnitude of these transformations. These analogies are not meant to minimize the importance of militant, political and intellectual activism. The metaphor also implies that, even when activism goes silent, it is still waiting in the depths; it is not dispersed or exhausted, it grows.

For this reason, the focus of this book has been the construction of the feminist political subject, with all the challenges, unexpected turns and missteps that this implies. Multiple, disjointed, polyphonic. Each person is a small part, tiny, minuscule, of a process that is international and territorial. In my case, as one member of a collective that takes the name of a massive and foundational mobilization. During the time I spent writing this book, the collective had arguments and ruptures, and a large part of its makeup changed. As did its debates, agendas, political proposals. We remain in search of new theories on political construction and feminist practices. It is not easy and we're feeling our way. We have failed, many times, but we have never avoided facing the obstacles and conflicts that impact each group as well as the movement as a whole. Because, beyond each collective, feminist activism is broad and far reaching, vibrantly heterogeneous, multifaceted in its diversity.

There are two challenges fundamental to the construction and unfolding of the political subject "woman" or "feminist." One, the challenge of intersectionality. Carrying out what Angela Davis[5] calls feminist methodology: the search for intersections, affinities, connections, between issues that appear separate. Discovery of common ground where it is not apparent implies constructing alliances. To this end, popular feminism goes beyond the gender agenda to question the entire social order of systematic inequalities and exploitation. The second challenge arises from the construction of these alliances. If the objective is intersectionality, achieving it demands a decided transversality with respect to the partitions of the political system and union organization, the ability to take the heterogeneous nature of reality as a jumping-off point, an impure politics that can recognize in each political nucleus the Trojan horse that will allow the feminist perspective to infiltrate and invade.

A mass of people are betting on a world in which all

differences have a place, in which lives are not disposable, in which the regime of control can't jeopardize existences, in which women and *travestis* are not taken as hunting trophies. The multitude stammers, because it does not yet know how to demand, in a precise way, this autonomy, this desire, this right, this equality. Multiple strands of feminism crisscross the contemporary scene to lay the foundation for collective construction. We continue to create a new political subject, but some battles are lost as a political and economic counteroffensive is launched: after the defeat in parliament of the legalization of abortion, an attack occurred against professionals who practice non-criminalized abortions. Mobilized feminism's growing show of force is met with new forms of persecution and sanction, attempts to undermine our power and deny our rights.

Meanwhile, the fight does not cease, organizations grow, activism multiplies. Feminism is a land of great political experimentation, where the most radical questions are posed and the most innovative modes of organization are established. There will be stumbles, missteps, surprises, contradictions. We stand at the edge of an abyss: aware that our lives are at stake – both biological life and life as the ability to create. The deep river stops the desertification produced by neoliberalism, surfacing in specifically feminist organizations as well as in feminist practices in other struggles. The expansion and multiplication of these practices keeps us going, gives us hope, sparks our passion. The story is not over and our bodies are committed to writing it.

Notes

Foreword

1 See, for example, Banet-Weiser, S., Gill, R., and Rottemberg, C., "Postfeminism, Popular Feminism, and Neoliberal Feminism?" *Feminist Theory* 21/1 (2020), pp. 3–24; Aruzza, C., Bhattacharya, T., and Fraser, N., *Feminism for the 99%: A Manifesto*. London: Verso, 2019; Wiegman, R. (ed.), "Sexual Politics, Sexual Panics," *Differences: A Journal of Feminist Cultural Studies* 30/1 (2019) [special issue]; Farris, S., and Rottemberg, C., "Righting Feminism," *New Formations* 91 (2017) [special issue].

2 See Bahndar, B., and Ferreira Da Silva, D., "White Feminist Fatigue Syndrome," *Critical Legal Thinking*, 21 October 2013, http://criticallegalthinking.com/2013/10/21/white-feminist-fatigue-syndrome/; Sabsay, L., (2014) "Nancy Fraser: *Fortunes of Feminism: From State-Managed Capitalism to Neoliberal Crisis*," *Feminist Legal Studies* 22/3 (2014), pp. 323–9 [book review]; Brenner, J., and Fraser, N., "What is Progressive Neoliberalism? A Debate," *Dissent* 64/2 (2017), pp. 130–40.

3 About the notion of femicide, see Russell, D., and Harmes, R. A. (eds), *Feminicidio: una perspectiva global*. Mexico City: UNAM Press.

4 See Introduction, pp. 3–4.

5 We evoke here the idea of singularity considered by Gilles Deleuze: see Deleuze, *Difference and Repetition*. London: Continuum, 1994, pp. 251–2.

6 Among a number of publications on the recent feminist revolt

released in Argentina in the last years, see, Peker, L., *La revolución de las mujeres: no era sólo la píldora*. Córdoba: Eduvim, 2017; and *La revolución de las hijas*. Buenos Aires: Paidós, 2019; Gago, V., et al., *8M constelación feminista: ¿Cuál es tu lucha? ¿Cuál es tu huelga?* Buenos Aires: Tinta Limón, 2018; Cavallero, L., and Gago, V., *Una lectura feminista de la deuda*. Buenos Aires: Tinta Limón, 2019; Gago, V., *La potencia feminista o el deseo de cambiarlo todo*. Madrid: Traficantes de Sueños, 2019; Nijensohn, M. (ed.), *Los feminismos ante el neoliberalismo*. Buenos Aires: La Cebra, 2018; Nijensohn, M., *La razón feminista: políticas de la calle, pluralismo y articulación*. Buenos Aires: Cuarenta Ríos, 2019.

7 Cano, V., and Fernández Cordero, L., "Prologo" to Butler, J., Cano, J., and Fernández Cordero, L., *Vidas en lucha: conversaciones*. Buenos Aires: Katz Editores, 2019, p. 10 (the translation is ours).

8 See chapter 5, p. 144.

9 See Mbembe, A., "Necropolitics," *Public Culture* 15/1 (2003), p. 11.

10 See chapter 1, pp. 8–9.

11 Powell, K. J., "Making #BlackLivesMatter: Michael Brown, Eric Garner, and the specters of black life – toward a hauntology of blackness," *Cultural Studies – Critical Methodologies* 16/3 (2016), pp. 253–60.

12 See chapter 2, p. 36.

13 Mbembe, "Necropolitics," p. 11.

14 Dillon, M., "La amistad, nuestra victoria," *Página 12*, 14 October 2017.

15 Gago, V., *La razón neoliberal: economías barrocas y pragmáticas populares*. Madrid: Traficante de Sueños, 2015, p. 23.

Introduction

1 Adorno, T., *Minima Moralia: Reflections on a Damaged Life*, trans. E. F. N. Jephcott. London: Verso Books, 2005.

Chapter 1 Mourning

1 Moreno, M., "Elogio de la furia," *Página 12*, 10 June 2016, www.pagina12.com.ar/diario/contratapa/13-301412-2016-06-10.html.

2 Zambrano, A. M., "Observatorio de femicidios en Argentina," *Informe de femicidios*. Buenos Aires: Casa del Encuentro, 2015.

3 Segato, R., *La guerra contra las mujeres*. Madrid: Traficantes de sueños, 2017.

4 "Comisión Nacional sobre la desaparición de personas," *Nunca más*. Buenos Aires: Eudeba, 1984.
5 Badiou, A., *The True Life*, trans. S. Spitzer. Cambridge: Polity, 2017.
6 On 20 April 2017, members of the Not One Less collective read before the Senate a document in which they opposed the tightening of penal laws:

> The solutions such as the one now sought by the Legislative Power will not change in any way the violence we experience. As you all well know, penal rights arrive too late: they are activated after we are already dead. The Senate's reforms seek to increase the time a person must spend incarcerated before seeking parole, early or conditional release, and in some cases seek to prohibit it entirely. We ask for policies that will prevent murder: that reinforce education with the perspective of gender, the training of judicial and security forces, a speedier government response to reports. Increased penalization and prolonged sentences will not deter crimes against life. It is punitive demagoguery in response to social outrage.

The document was entitled "Not in Our Name" and was an attempt to avoid the reactionary appropriation of the social movement. The majority of legislators voted for harsher sentencing.

7 The document was read in the plaza outside Congress in the city of Buenos Aires:

> In the year 2008 one woman was killed every 40 hours; in 2014, every 30. In those seven years, the media published news about 1,808 femicides. How many women will be murdered just for being women in 2015? We don't know. But we do know that we have to say enough is enough. In these years, femicides orphaned almost 1,500 little girls and boys, and some are obligated to live with their mother's murderer. The problem belongs to all of us. We must construct the solution together. We need to commit ourselves to changing a culture that tends to think of a woman as a consumable and disposable object and not as an independent person. Femicide is the most extreme form of that violence, and it affects all social classes, creeds and ideologies.

8 Butler, J., *Precarious Life: The Powers of Mourning and Violence*. London: Verso, 2004.
9 Canetti, E., *Crowds and Power*. New York: Viking Press, 1962.
10 Freud, S., "Mourning and Melancholia," in *The Standard Edition of the Complete Psychological Works of Sigmund Freud*, Vol. XIV. London: Hogarth Press, 1986, p. 244.
11 It also includes many people who do have direct ties to the victims, family members and friends, who add their own individual

mourning to that of society. On the first 3 June marches (2015 and 2016) the victims' family members had a central and visible position, though the construction of more warlike and festive modes of occupying the street later displaced their centrality.

12 Spinoza, B., *Theological-Political Treatise*, trans. S. Shirley and S. Feldman. Indianapolis: Hackett, 2001.

13 Despentes, V., *King Kong Theory*, trans. S. Benson. London: Profile Books, 2009.

14 Tatián, D., *Baruch*. Buenos Aires: Ediciones La Cebra, 2012, p. 42.

15 Marielle Franco was a sociologist and a congresswoman in Rio de Janeiro. Born in a favela, she was a social activist, feminist lesbian, and she was shot to death, along with a driver, on 14 March 2018.

16 Butler, J., *Notes Toward a Performative Theory of Assembly*. Cambridge, MA: Harvard University Press, 2015.

17 Catanzaro, G., "Teoría (y) crítica del presente: paradojas de la autonomía en la época del neoliberalismo post-utópico," in *II Congreso Latinoamericano de Teoría Social y Teoría Política: Horizontes y dilemas del pensamiento contemporáneo en el sur global*. Buenos Aires: UBA, Facultad de Ciencias Sociales, 2017.

18 Jablonka, I., *Laëtitia, ou, La fin des hommes*. Paris: Seuil, 2016.

Chapter 2 Violence

1 Santoro, S., "Radiografía judicial de los crímenes de odio," *Página 12*, 18 February 2018, www.pagina12.com.ar/96457-radiografia-judicial-de-crimenes-de-odio.

2 Peker, L., *La revolución de las mujeres: No era sólo una píldora*. Villa María: Eduvim, 2017.

3 Segato, R., *La guerra contra las mujeres*. Madrid: Traficantes de sueños, 2017.

4 González Rodríguez, S., *Huesos en el desierto*. Barcelona: Anagrama, 2010.

5 Segato, *La guerra contra las mujeres*, p. 47.

6 Ibid.

7 Jean Pierre Faye, in *Langages totalitaires: critique de la raison narrative, critique de l'économie narrative* (Paris: Hermann, 1972), lays out a complex analysis of the processes that made the annihilation of a part of the population utterable.

8 Las Casas, B. de, *Fray Bartolomé de Las Casas, disputa o controversia con Ginés de Sepúlveda contendiendo acerca de la licitud de las conquistas de las Indias*. Alicante: Biblioteca Virtual Miguel de Cervantes, 2007, www.cervantesvirtual.com/obra/

fray-bartolome-de-las-casas-disputa-o-controversia-con-gines-de-sepulveda-contendiendo-acerca-de-la-licitud-de-las-conquistas-de-las-indias--0/.

9 Ortiz, F., *Contrapunteo cubano del tabaco y el azúcar.* Sucre: Biblioteca Ayacucho, 1978.

10 Segato, *La guerra contra las mujeres.*

11 Ibid., p. 22.

12 Canelo, P., "Si el ejército tira, mata," *Anfibia,* 2015, www.revistaanfibia.com/ensayo/si-ejercito-tira-mata/.

13 Ballón, A. (ed.), *Memorias del caso peruano de esterilización forzada.* Lima: Biblioteca Nacional del Perú, 2014.

14 Boesten, J., Prologue to Ballón, *Memorias del caso peruano de esterilización forzada,* p. 23.

15 Gloria Anzaldúa, in *Borderlands/La Frontera* (Madrid: Capitán Swing, 2016), angrily pondered the link between women and their communities to keep appeals to the community from omitting the acknowledgment of its coercive and sacrificial dimensions.

16 Horacio González follows the trail of narrations on captive women and the way they entwine with the "national consciousness." Among many works, the poem "La cautiva" by Esteban Echeverría stands out, as well as the painting *Return from the Indian Camp* by Della Valle. In both, on one side is the fragile white woman and on the other a mob of violent masculine bodies that would condemn her to domestic and sexual slavery. González, *La Argentina manuscrita.* Buenos Aires: Colihue, 2018.

17 Actis, M., Aldini, C., Gardella, L., Lewin, M., and Tokar, E., *Ese infierno: Conversaciones de cinco mujeres sobrevivientes de la ESMA.* Buenos Aires: Sudamericana, 2001, p. 178.

18 This narrative is recovered by María Moreno, framed as a funny story when it was told to her. And she recalls that Pilar Calveiro dedicated her book *Poder y desaparición* to Lila with this sentence: "For Lila Pastoriza, dear friend, expert in the art of finding weak spots and shooting at power with two weapons of extreme fire power: laughter and mocking." Moreno, *Oración: Carta a Vicki y otras elegías políticas.* Buenos Aires: Sudamericana, 2018, p. 171.

19 Calveiro, P., *Poder y desaparición: Los campos de concentración en Argentina.* Buenos Aires: Colihue, 1998, p. 94.

20 Ana Longoni (*Traiciones.* Buenos Aires: Grupo Editorial Norma, 2007) analyzes a series of novels which depict a romantic link between the detained women and their captors in the context of betrayal – novels in which sexual relationships are portrayed as a clearer sign of betrayal than speaking during torture. In the end: the demand that the victim of a sexual attack self-immolate to preserve her honor or, more than her own honour, that of her partner-owner.

María Sondereguer asks who the bodies of these women belong to: the notion of property is silently established in the notion of rape as a crime against honor and in the repudiation of the woman as tainted by her contact with her torturer. For each woman, her body is not her own; she is dispossessed of it in her relationship to others. The bodies of women are declared the property of others: fathers, husbands, torturers, judges that can send them to prison for having an abortion. Sonderegger, "Violencia y silencio de género," in *Memorias en tensión, 1: Silencios y violencias de género*, ed. G. Yoel, forthcoming.

21 Yoel, *Memorias en tensión, 1: Silencios y violencias de género*.
22 Lizey Tornay describes the dilemma of hearing victims on three levels: encouraging them to speak, recognizing the diversity of the experiences across different concentration camps, and thinking of the women not as passive victims but as strategic agents. This notion is fundamental: not as agents who can give consent or as purely passive. Their strategies are the tactics employed by the weak, aware of their slim chances of survival. "Nuevas fronteras," ibid.
23 "Manifiesto 8F: es tiempo de desobediencia al patriarcado," *Ni una menos*, 6 February 2018, www.niunamenos.org.ar/ manifiestos/8f-es-tiempo-de-desobediencia-al-patriarcado/.
24 Oscar Terán states that repressive policies produce an initially unthinkable approach between counterculture and insurgency: "the 1966 coup and its attack on progressive sectors and progressive aspects of Argentine culture constructed new connections between intellectuals, politics and violence, by which the armed path created alliances that were never dreamed of up to that moment." Terán, *Nuestros años sesentas*. Buenos Aires: Puntosur, 1991, p. 144.
25 Segato, *La guerra contra las mujeres*, p. 101.
26 Simón Rodríguez, the revolutionary pedagogue, thought that there could only be a republic (the overcoming of colonial power) through the recovery of sensitivity, the capacity for compassion, of feeling the suffering of others as one's own. But this implies practices, concrete connections, community life. Rozitchner, L., *Filosofía y emancipación: Simón Rodríguez: el triunfo de un fracaso ejemplar*. Buenos Aires: Ediciones Biblioteca Nacional, 2012.
27 Brazão, A. *Violência contra as mulheres*. Recife: Sos corpo, 2007, p. 70.
28 Ibid., p. 72.
29 Brazão, *Violência contra as mulheres*.
30 Federici, S., *Caliban and the Witch: Women, the Body and Primitive Accumulation*. Brooklyn, NY: Autonomedia, 2004, p. 64.
31 Ibid.

32 Ibid., p. 187.
33 Rozitchner, L., *La cosa y la cruz*. Buenos Aires: Losada, 1997.
34 Rozitchner, L., *Materialismo ensoñado*. Buenos Aires: Tinta Limón, 2011.
35 Freyre, G., *The Masters and the Slaves [Casa grande & Senzala]: A Study in the Development of Brazilian Civilization*, trans. S. Putnam. Berkeley: University of California Press, 1977. Flora Tristán travels to Peru in 1835 in search of her (denied) paternal inheritance. On a sugar plantation, she meets two female slaves locked in cells as punishment. They'd allowed their children to die of hunger. Far from judging them with the European prejudice that disguises racism as humanism, Flora understands the decision of not wanting to give birth to children destined for slavery. In Ouro Preto, then called Vila Rica, female slaves were selected as birthers. The women with the shortest statures and widest hips were forced to mate with black men who were also short (because the tunnels of the mines were small). The women were condemned to constant reproduction. Their productive work was giving birth. The children born through this process worked in the mines from the age of six.
36 Fredrich Engels, in *The Condition of the Working Class in England*, narrates a scene that he considers horrifying: an unemployed worker darns his wife's stockings. When a friend arrives, he isn't able to hide the mending in time and cries bitterly. While his wife has paying work, he's unemployed and takes over the domestic chores: "I have to mind the children, sweep and wash, bake and mend." And the writer states: "Can anyone imagine a more insane state of things than the one described in this letter! And yet this condition, which unsexes the man and takes from the woman all woman-liness" (Engels, *The Condition of the Working-Class in England in 1844, with Preface Written in 1892*. London: Allen & Unwin, 1926). A decade later, Marx would value "the dissolution of the old family ties within the capitalist system," even when he finds it shocking and repugnant, as part of the creation of "new economical foundation for a higher form of the family and of relations between the sexes" (Marx, *Capital*. New York: International, 1967).
37 Federici, S., *Revolution at Point Zero: Housework, Reproduction, and Feminist Struggle*. Oakland, CA: PM Press, 2012, p. 66.
38 Trímboli, J., *Sublunar: Entre el kirchnerismo y la revolución*. Buenos Aires: Cuarenta ríos, 2017.
39 On 14 and 18 December 2017 there were enormous mobilizations in the city of Buenos Aires against the social security reform proposed by the Argentine government, which, among other things, raised the retirement age and changed the formula used to adjust pensions for inflation. The demonstrations ended in police repression. During the

14 December mobilization, a young woman was detained on her way home from work and fondled by the arresting police officer. A video of the event quickly went viral as proof of police injustice (www.minutouno.com/notas/3053748-en-la-represion-gendarmes-detuvieron-y-manosearon-una-joven-que-salia-trabajar). In the repression of the march on 18 December, a woman being dragged away by an officer was asked: "What are you doing here? Tell me, you little slut."

40 "Historic materialism forgets the key emotional element that has determined the path to private property. This is what we want to emphasize so that the archetype of property is recognized, to show that man's first concept of object was the sexual object." Lonzi, C., *Sputiamo su Hegel*. Rome: Editoriale grafica, 1970.

41 Uruguay legalized abortion in 2012. In Cuba the practice has been decriminalized since 1965. In Brazil, Bolivia, Colombia and Chile abortion is not punishable in cases of rape or risk to the mother's life. In Mexico it is legal in some states (such as Mexico City) and in others it is illegal. In Ecuador, Venezuela, Guatemala, the Dominican Republic, Panama, Puerto Rico, Honduras, Paraguay, Costa Rica and Peru, it is punishable with jail time for the woman who has the abortion. In El Salvador and Nicaragua, abortion is illegal even in cases of rape or risk to the mother's life.

42 In El Salvador, dozens of women are imprisoned for abortion. In February 2018 Teodora Vásquez, whose case had been taken up by international organizations, was freed after almost eleven years. She had been sentenced to thirty years' imprisonment. Dalton, J. J., and Sahuquillo, M. R., "El Salvador libera a una mujer condenada a 30 años por aborto," *El país*, 16 February 2018, www.elpais.com/internacional/2018/02/15/actualidad/1518705362_091423.html.

43 One week after the 3 June 2015 march, an article was published summarizing the increase in reported abuses. The 144 telephone helpline that received the reports went from an average of 1,000 calls per day to 13,700. In the city of Buenos Aires, calls to domestic violence helplines doubled. Vallejos, S., "El impacto del #NiUnaMenos," *Página 12*, 7 June 2015, www.pagina12.com.ar/diario/sociedad/3-274376-2015-06-07.html.

44 The law for prevention and eradication of violence against women, sanctioned in 2011, was not enacted until after the June 2015 march. Its implementation remains only partial as the National Institute of Women, responsible for its application, has seen dramatic budget cuts. The women answering the telephone helplines in the province of Buenos Aires work under temporary contracts, and shelters for the relocation of at-risk women and children are scarce.

45 "The victims, across the country, are reporting it more and more.

This is shown in the numbers of the latest results gathered by the Public Prosecutor's Office presented by barrister Julio Conte Grand: 1,110 cases of rape in 2015, 1,242 in 2016. Other crimes against sexual integrity, such as simple or gravely injurious abuses: 9,900 in 2015, 10,989 in 2016" (www.infobae.com/sociedad/policiales/2017/10/05/los-numeros-de-los-abusos-sexuales-y-violaciones-en-el-pais-mas-de-la-mitad-de-las-victimas-son-menores/).

46 Alcaraz, M. F., "Todas somos fanáticas de los boliches (sin violencia)," *Latfem*, 15 September 2017, www.latfem.org/todas-somos-fanaticas-de-los-boliches-sin-violencias/.

47 Frontera, A., and Zanellatto, R., "Memoria feminista para las fanáticas de los boliches," *Latfem*, 27 December 2017, www.latfem.org/memoria-feminista-para-las-fanaticas-de-los-boliches/. The digital publication *Latfem* compiled a report with the title "Fanáticas de los boliches." Several journalists analyzed the crimes against young women who had been abducted after going out (to nightclubs, out dancing, in the taxi on their way home) and the media criticism of the behavior that construed them as agents of their own misfortune through their use of drugs or alcohol, indulging in sex, or even partying itself. The pedagogy of femicide is spread through media diffusion of common sense: it attempts to normalize and moralize. The report ventures interpretations on this type of femicide and also proposes a feminist revindication of pleasure, distancing itself from the puritan modes of thinking about activism.

48 Data taken from the Gender Equality Observatory for Latin America and the Caribbean, https://oig.cepal.org/es/indicadores/feminicidio.

49 Roxana Sandá wrote a fundamental article from which I take the data summarized here: "¿Qué onda las pibas?," *Las 12*, feminist supplement of *Página 12*, 1 September 2017, www.pagina12.com.ar/60033-que-onda-las-pibas.

50 Guy, D., *El sexo peligroso: La prostitución legal en Buenos Aires, 1875–1955*. Buenos Aires: Sudamericana, 1994.

51 Cited in Sandá, "¿Qué onda las pibas?"

Chapter 3 Strike

1 Tristán, F., *The Workers' Union*, trans. B. Livingston. Urbana: University of Illinois Press, [1843] 2007.

2 Mary Wollstonecraft and Flora Tristán are often remembered for their offspring. Wollstonecraft was the mother of Mary Shelley, the author of *Frankenstein*, and Tristán was the grandmother of Paul Gauguin.

3 Marx, K., and Engels, F., *The Communist Manifesto*. Auckland: Floating Press, [1848] 2008.

4 In the first pages of the digital edition of Tristán's *The Workers' Union*.

5 Tristán, *The Workers' Union*.

6 Bellucci, M., *Historia de una desobediencia: Aborto y feminismo*. Buenos Aires: Capital Intelectual, 2014.

7 The space was made up of women from UEPC, AGEPJ, SUOEM, UOGC, Sindicato de Luz y Fuerza de Córdoba, ADIUC, Asociación La Bancaria, SEP, CISPREN, SURRBaC, SINPECOR, APOPS, APA Córdoba, SMATA Córdoba, STIA Córdoba, SADEM, SIMPECAF, SUTAT, UOLRA Córdoba, AMMAR Córdoba, APINTA, ATE Córdoba, SATSAID Córdoba, SECASFPI, FEPUC, Colegio de Profesionales en Servicio Social, Colegio de Psicólogos, Foro Sindical de la Mesa de Trabajo por los DDHH Córdoba, CGT Regional Córdoba, CGT Rodríguez Peña, CTA de los Trabajadores and CTA Autónoma. The unprecedented confluence bridged differences among the union centers in attendance which, up to that point, had never been involved in a shared show of force.

8 An estimate of the number is difficult, since this economy is inherently unregistered, but the IMF, in 2017, affirmed that 46.8 percent of jobs were informal. Casabón, C., "La economía informal de América Latina supera por primera vez la de África Subsahariana," *World Economic Forum*, 15 May 2017, https://es.weforum.org/agenda/2017/05/la-economia-informal-de-africa-esta-retrocediendo-mas-rapido-que-la-economia-latinoamericana.

9 Gago, V., *Neoliberalism from Below: Popular Pragmatics and Baroque Economies*. Durham, NC: Duke University Press, 2017.

10 Natsumi Shokida analyzes Argentina's 2017 census from a gender perspective. I'd like to summarize some data from her work: 75 percent of unpaid domestic work is carried out by women and 98 percent of domestic service jobs (paid) are held by women. Domestic service constitutes 17 percent of the female labor force and has high rates of informality. Additionally, 36.7 percent of workers are unregistered (whereas among male workers this figure drops to 32.3 percent). Shokida, N., "La desigualdad de género se puede medir," *Economíafeminita*, 2018, https://economiafeminita.com/la-desigualdad-de-genero-se-puede-medir/. In Brazil the rates of informal work varied greatly depending on public policies in effect, reaching numbers similar to Argentina's in 2012, but having started from 54 percent in 2002. Alejo, J., and Parada, C., "Desigualdad e informalidad en América Latina: el caso de Brasil," *Revista Desarrollo y Sociedad* no. 78, 2017, pp. 149–99, www.scielo.org.co/pdf/dys/n78/n78a05.pdf.

11 Sennett, R., *The Corrosion of Character: The Personal Consequences of Work in the New Capitalism*. New York: W. W. Norton, 1999.

12 Federici, S., *Revolution at Point Zero: Housework, Reproduction, and Feminist Struggle*. Oakland, CA: PM Press, 2012. This book includes articles from the 1970s that were essential to reconstructing the map of debates on work.

13 Data collected by the Instituto de Estadísticas y Censos, analyzed by Equipo latinoamericano de Economía y género (ELA) (Latin American Team for Economy and Gender). Rodríguez Enríquez, C., *El trabajo de cuidado no remunerado en Argentina: Un análisis desde la evidencia del Módulo de Trabajo no Remunerado. Serie de documentos de trabajo. Políticas públicas y derecho al trabajo.* Buenos Aires: ADC, CIEPP, ELA, 2015.

14 D'Alessandro, M., "Si hay futuro, es feminista: Realidad y utopía hacia la construcción de un feminismo del 99%," *Economíafeminita*, 2017, https://economiafeminita.com/si-hay-futuro-es-feminista-realidad-y-utopia-hacia-la-construccion-de-un-feminismo-del-99/. "According to the data from the International Labour Organization, in Latin America alone, more than 18 million persons work in domestic service, of whom 93 percent are women; 77 percent of the workers are hired informally and earn half of the average salary in these economies."

15 According to 2017 data from the Argentine Labor Ministry, women occupy only 18 percent of union positions (counting secretaries and sub-secretaries), and, of them, 74 percent do so in areas of equality, gender or social services. (I'd like to thank Ileana Arduino, careful reader of statistics, for this information.) *Las mujeres en el mundo del trabajo*, https://www.argentina.gob.ar/sites/default/files/informe_ctio_documentodetrabajo.pdf.

16 The Argentine government pushed a labor reform that made hiring conditions more flexible. One of the arguments used in presenting it was that it was necessary to achieve gender equality.

17 *Especial 8M #Paro Internacional Feminista*, https://economiafeminita.com/especial-8m-paro-de-mujeres/.

18 *Las mujeres en el mundo del trabajo*.

19 Butler, J., *Precarious Life: The Powers of Mourning and Violence*. London: Verso, 2004.

20 "#DesendeudadasNosQueremos," *Ni una menos*, 2 June 2017, www.niunamenos.org.ar/manifiestos/desendeudadasnosqueremos/.

21 Ibid.

22 Sorel, G., *Reflections on Violence*, trans. T. E. Hume. Abingdon: Routledge, 2018.

23 Documentary footage from 1986 included in the 2017 film *The Intense Now* by Joao Moreira Salles.

24 On 3 October 2016, Polish women held a day of protests, known as Black Monday, against the attempt to modify legislation on abortion, criminalizing it. Activists called for a strike, to leave work in order to attend the mobilization.

25 Benjamin, W., *Selected Writings*, Vol. 1: *1913–1926*, ed. M. Bullock and M. W. Jennings. Cambridge, MA: Belknap Press, 1996, p. 246. The article "A Critique of Violence" was published in 1921.

26 Blanqui, A., *Eternity by the Stars*. New York: Contra Mundum Press, [1872] 2013.

27 Rancière, J., "The Radical Gap: A Preface to Auguste Blanqui, *Eternity by the Stars*," *Radical Philosophy*, no. 185, May–June 2014, pp. 19–25.

28 The image of enslaved ancestors is present in "Theses on the Philosophy of History" (1942). There, Benjamin contrasts this image to that of liberated ancestors. He maintains that referring to the struggle of the working class in the future tense erased the memory that fed hate and willingness to sacrifice. In the feminist strikes both images are present. In the debate on abortion, Luciana Peker called the event "the daughters' revolution." The descendants are not the object of the present struggles but the healing of that historic rift. Benjamin, *Illuminations*, ed. H. Arendt, trans. H. Zohn. New York: Schocken Books, [1968] 2011, pp. 253–64.

29 This revived the memory of the train that Leon Trotsky organized in 1918, when the Soviet Revolution was at risk against the reaction of the White Russians. Trotsky traveled the frontlines of the war by train with a group of enthusiastic Bolsheviks, giving speeches at each stop, optimistic revolutionary rallies, calls to heavy combat.

30 The Larkin Plan was presented as a rationalization and modernization of transportation in Argentina, led by the US engineer and general Thomas Larkin, with the support of the World Bank. It consisted, fundamentally, in the replacement of rail transport with automobiles. Between 1958 and 1960, ten multinational car companies were installed. And the railway lines and repair shops were closed.

31 Rozitchner, L., *Vías argentinas: Ensayos sobre el ferrocarril*. Buenos Aires: Milena Caserola, 2010.

32 The scene calls to mind the story "Before the Law" by Franz Kafka: the farm worker hopes and gives his all to survive, until his life is snuffed out. Some of that desperate hope, that implies subjugation to another's hand, is perceived in Weil's narration.

33 Weil, S., "La vie et la grève des ouvrières métallos (sur le tas) (10 juin 1936)," in *La condition ouvrière*. Paris: Gallimard, 1951.

34 "Nos duelen 56," *Somoselmedio.org*, 2018.

35 "Guatemala: acción global por las niñas 'Nos duelen 56,'" www.

guatemalacomunitaria.periodismohumano.com/2017/05/16/
guatemala-accion-global-por-las-ninas-nos-duelen-56/.

36 On 25 March 1911, the Triangle Waist Co. shirt factory in New York caught fire, killing 146 female workers. The majority were young migrants who worked long hours locked inside the factory. "El incendio en la fábrica 'Triangle Shirtwaist' y el Día Internacional de la Mujer: Cien años después," *Organización Internacional del Trabajo*, 8 March 2011, www.ilo.org/global/about-the-ilo/newsroom/news/WCMS_152727/lang--es/index.htm.

37 According to their Facebook page (www.facebook.com/NosDuelen56/), "#NosDuelen56 is a cry for justice through art, journalism, media activism and the various feminisms. It's an exercise of collective memory and of dignity for the 56 girls who were locked up and burned in a Guatemalan government institution on 8 March of this year. Of them, 41 died as the result of this crime of femicide and 15 more were gravely wounded."

38 Sartre, J.-P., *Dirty Hands*, in *No Exit, and Three Other Plays*. New York: Vintage International, 1989.

39 Cecilia Abdo Ferez told me – in conversation – that the Cuernavaca Not One Less collective hangs posters on the streets with a mini bio written in marker pen of the dead or forcibly disappeared women, without images, to counterbalance the media's tendency to use violent and bloody images, turning news hours into horror shows.

40 Dopazo, M., "Rezábamos, para que mi papá se muriera," *La poderosa*, 10 January 2018, www.laposerosa.org.ar/2018/01/rezabamos-para-que-mi-papa-se-muriera/.

41 Mabel Belucci, in *Historia de una desobediencia*, writes a genealogy of the feminist struggles through the lens of disobedience. In particular she narrates the formidable transversality of the national campaign for legal, safe and free abortions.

42 Franklin, B., in Fisher G., *The American Instructor, or, Young Man's Best Companion*. Philadelphia: B. Franklin and D. Hall, 1748.

43 De Amicis, E., *The Heart of a Boy, Cuore: The Journal of an Italian Schoolboy*. Chicago, Rand McNally, 1912.

44 Maupassant, G., *The Necklace, and Other Stories: Maupassant for Modern Times*, trans. S. Smith. New York: Liverlight, 2015.

45 Different moments of the debates can be read in the compilation edited by Jarbado, M., *Feminismos negros*. Madrid: Traficantes de sueños, 2012.

46 Laura Contrera, during a fat-activism workshop at the National Women's Conference, stated: "We fight against the oppression, the discrimination, and the violation of human rights that we experience for being fat, like all people who deviate from the norms of gender, sex, and the body ... We are here to break those

molds and patterns." Díaz Virzi, S., "Más allá de las modelos XL: Activismo gordo: una reivindicación de la gordura," *Clarín Entremujeres*, 13 October 2017, www.clarin.com/entremujeres/genero/activismo-gordo-reivindicacion-gordura_0_Bko6PF0hW.html. Contrera, l., and Contrera, N. C. (eds), *Cuerpos sin patrones: Resistencias desde las geografías desmesuradas de la carne*. Buenos Aires: Madreselva, 2017.

47 Mark Fisher maintains that it is necessary to politicize mental disorder, calling attention to its presumed normality: "Instead of treating it as incumbent on individuals to resolve their own psychological distress, instead, that is of accepting the vast *privatization of stress* that has taken place over the last thirty years, we need to ask: how has it become so acceptable that so many people, and especially so many young people, are ill?" Fisher, *Capitalist Realism: Is There No Alternative?* Ropley, Hants: O Books, 2009.

48 Foucault, M., "The Politics of Health in the Eighteenth Century," *Power/Knowledge: Selected Interviews and Other Writings, 1972–1977*, trans. C. Gordon. New York: Pantheon Books, 1980.

49 Greer, G., *The Change: Women, Ageing and the Menopause*. London: Bloomsbury, 2018.

50 Fisher, *Capitalist Realism: Is There No Alternative?*

51 Virno, P. *Déjà Vu and the End of History*. London: Verso, 2015.

52 Ibid.

53 Bergson, H., *Matter and Memory*, trans. N. M. Paul and W. S. Plamer. New York: Zone Books, 1990.

54 Virno, *Déjà Vu and the End of History*.

Chapter 4 Power, Representation and Bodies

1 The first Marcha das vadias (Slutwalk) took place in Sao Paulo, on 4 June 2011 and was later repeated across several Brazilian cities. In Argentina it was carried out under the name Marcha de las putas. It is meant to challenge sexist justifications for rape: www.marchadasvadiascwb.wordpress.com/conheca-a-marcha/porquevadias/.

2 This mobilization was carried out for the first time in 2000, but it was not repeated annually. It involves female farm workers, indigenous women and *quilombolas* (Afro-Brazilian rural communities consisting of residents of escaped slave settlements), joined under the agricultural workers syndicate movement. In 2015 the march was massive, mobilizing 100,000 persons. The denouncement of sexist violence is central to the Marcha das

margaridas agenda: www.contag.org.br/imagens/f24537_contag_
livreto_marcha_2015_210x297_final-1.pdf.

3 In April 2018, in Florianopolis, Brazil, the Fazendo Gênero/
Mundos de Mulheres (Women's Worlds Congress) was held,
joining the Fazendo Gênero academic conference with an assembly
of women's social movements. In November, in Montevideo,
Uruguay, a session of the EFLAC (Encuentro Feminista de América
Latina y el Caribe; Feminist Conference of Latin America and
the Caribbean) took place. In December, in Cali, Colombia, the
ELLA (Encuentro Latinoamericano de Mujeres; Latin American
Conference of Women) was held. Each of these conferences
had been held before, but attendance in all instances increased
exponentially as organization for 8 March of the following year
took place.

4   Each year, in a chosen location, the organizing commission is held,
     integrating women and organizations from the provinces. Local schools
     host workshops and offer free accommodation to the participants (an
     achievement attributed to the ENM [National Women's Conference]
     no. VII in Neuquén). Defining the names and details of the official
     workshops, the means of financing, the location of the conference's
     opening and closing events, and the route of its final march are some of
     the items debated by the different unions and organizations of women,
     students and politicians that will work together over the year to come.
     Their distinct conceptions on the reach that these conferences should
     have reflect the various concerns of the women's movement. (Bajar,
     S., "Encuentros Nacionales de Mujeres: un recorrido por una experi-
     encia única en el mundo," *Izquierda diario*, 26 September 2016, www.
     laizquierdadiario.com/Encuentros-Nacionales-de-Mujeres-un-recorrido-
     por-una-experiencia-unica-en-el-mundo)

In 2019, the 34th ENM changed its name to Encuentro Plurinacional
de Mujeres, Lesbianas, Trans, Travestis y No Binaries (Plurinational
Conference of Women, Lesbians, Trans, Travestis and Non-Binaries).

5 The 2013 Encuentro Nacional de Mujeres took place in San Juan.
There were fifty-eight workshops, and number fifty-eight was called
Trans Women. The content was described as

     Transgender, transsexual, *travesti*: body, identities and sexuality. Gender
     identity law: the situation in each province, compliance, obstacles and
     possible solutions. Health: current situation and possible responses to
     ITS and HIV/AIDS. Hormone therapy: access to hormone therapy and
     possible effects. Functioning and use of trans-friendly clinics in the
     provinces that include them. Transphobia: challenges for finding work,
     transphobia in education, health, etcetera. Laws and treaties that support
     achievement and enjoyment of our human rights, the current situation
     of contravention codes in each province. Forms of organization and

resistance. The continuity or not of this workshop in the ENM agenda. (www.28encuentronacionaldemujeres.es.tl/TALLERES.htm)

6 "Because our desire is not to achieve respectability but to demolish the hierarchies that structure the identities of individuals who identify as black, sluts, Palestinians, revolutionaries, indigenous, fat, incarcerated, junkies, exhibitionists, *piqueteras*, slum dwellers, women and *travestis*, though we might not all have the ability to birth children, we do have the courage necessary to give birth to another history." Berkins, L., "Travestis: una identidad política," *VIII Jornadas Nacionales de Historia de las Mujeres/III Congreso Iberoamericano de Estudios de Género Diferencia Desigualdad. Construirnos en la diversidad*, 2006, https://hemisphericinstitute. org/en/emisferica-42/4-2-review-essays/lohana-berkins.html.
7 Dillon, M., "8M Todos los mundos," *Las 12, Página 12*, 16 March 2018, www.pagina12.com.ar/101573-todos-los-mundos.
8 Cross, C., and Partenio, F., "Mujeres y participación: Las organizaciones piqueteras y las relaciones de género," *VI Jornadas de Sociología*, Facultad de Ciencias Sociales, Universidad de Buenos Aires, 2004, http://cdsa.aacademica.org/000-045/215.pdf.
9 Ramos Mejía, J. M., *Las multitudes argentinas*. Buenos Aires: Guillermo Kraft, 1952.
10 Le Bon, G., *The Crowd: A Study of the Popular Mind*. Auckland: Floating Press, 2009.
11 Freud, S., *Group Psychology and the Analysis of the Ego*. New York: Bantam Books, 1965.
12 González, H., and Rinesi, E. (eds), *Las multitudes argentinas*. Buenos Aires: IDEP, 1996.
13 Hardt, M., and Negri, A., *Multitude: War and Democracy in the Age of Empire*. New York: Penguin Books, 2004.
14 Verbitsky, H., *La educación presidencial: De la derrota de los setenta al desguace del Estado*. Buenos Aires: Puntosur, 1990.
15 All my writing is dated: in the first week of August of 2018, firefighters mobilized to demand funding, there was an evangelical march against the legalization of abortion, a group demanded justice for the death of Santiago Maldonado, street artists protested the prohibition of art in public spaces, and a group of autonomous neighborhood organizations marched in favor of the legalization of abortion.
16 The first lines of the book published by Not One Less read: "On 3 June 2015, thousands of people from different corners of Argentina took to the streets, mobilized under the message Not One Less. Twenty-three days earlier, a group of journalists had spread the call to march on Twitter. 'No more femicide' was the call: every thirty hours a woman is murdered just for being a woman." Rodríguez, P., *#NiUnaMenos*. Buenos Aires: Planeta, 2015.

17 The stage was separated from the crowd by a kind of fence where the relatives of the victims of femicide stood. The document was read by three well-known people in the cultural and media world: the actress Erica Rivas, the actor Juan Minujín and the illustrator Maitena Burundarena.

18 Virno, P., *A Grammar of the Multitude: For an Analysis of Contemporary Forms of Life*. Cambridge, MA: Semiotext(e), 2003.

19 www.clarin.com/ediciones-anteriores/masiva-marcha-reclamar-seguridad-reforma-politica (NB: URL no longer active).

20 "Manifiestos: 3 de junio 2015," www.niunamenos.org.ar/manifiestos/3-de-junio-2015/.

21 The people who attended the meetings to organize the first 3 June event came, mainly, from the world of journalism or literature. Some were established feminist journalists, such as Marta Dillon or Mariana Carabajal. Others held visible positions in the mainstream media, such as Florencia Etchevez or Valeria Sampedro. Many were self-employed and came from diverse political backgrounds. The author held positions in line with the government party at the time and was director of the Museum of the Book and Language of the National Library of Argentina.

22 "Carta orgánica," *Ni una menos*, 3 June 2017, www.niunamenos. org.ar/quienes-somos/carta-organica/.

23 Document created for the 8 March assembly, "Documento completo del Paro Internacional de mujeres, lesbianas, travestis y trans #8M en Argentina," www.latfem.org/documento-de-la-asamblea8m-de-argentina-paro-internacional-de-mujeres-lesbianas-travestis-y-trans/. All the quotations that follow come from this text.

24 In 2018, one of the main issues publicly debated in Argentina was the legalization of abortion. Massive demonstrations were held. Voices rose up to denounce the supposed distraction of feminism from issues of greater social relevance, such as external debt or the restriction of labor rights. Various collectives responded with actions that showed the important link between the causes. On 31 July, the Not One Less collective, the National Campaign for the Right to Abortion and female subway workers carried out a joint action on all the subway lines, with participation from dozens of other groups, strengthening the link between female labor unionists and independent activists. Basualdo, V., "La tierra tiembla: 'Operación araña' y la rebelión feminista desde las bases," *El cohete a la luna*, 5 August 2018, www.elcohetealaluna.com/la-tierra-tiembla.

25 Badiou, A., *The True Life*, trans. S. Spitzer. Cambridge: Polity, 2017.

26 Fraser, N., "How Feminism Became Capitalism's Handmaiden – and How to Reclaim It," *The Guardian*, 14 October 2013, www.

theguardian.com/commentisfree/2013/oct/14/feminism-capitalist-handmaiden-neoliberal.
27 Mariátegui, J. C., *Seven Interpretative Essays on Peruvian Reality*. Austin: University of Texas Press, 1971; and *La escena contemporánea*. Lima: Amauta, 1972.
28 Deleuze, G., "Bergson: 1859–1941," *Desert Islands and Other Texts 1953–1974*. Los Angeles: Semiotext(e), 2004, p. 39.
29 López, M. P., *Hacia la vida intensa: Una historia de la sensibilidad vitalista*. Buenos Aires: Eudeba, 2010.
30 Lukács wrote that nationalism required a specific philosophical atmosphere, a corrosion of the trust in reason and understanding, the destruction of faith in progress, a credulous attitude toward irrationality, the myth and the mystic. The philosophy of life took care of creating that very atmosphere. Lukács, G., *The Destruction of Reason*, trans. P. Palmer. Atlantic Highlands, NJ: Humanities Press, 1981.
31 In a lecture in 1978, Foucault defines biopower (or biopolitics) as the mechanism by which fundamental biological traits of the human species could become part of politics, a political strategy, a general tactic for power. Foucault, M., *Security, Territory, Population: Lectures at the Collège de France, 1977–1978*, trans. G. Burchell. New York: Palgrave Macmillan, 2009.
32 In the field of philosophy, the interventions of Gilles Deleuze and his interpretations of the works of the vitalist philosophers are fundamental. Deleuze, G., *Nietzsche and Philosophy*, trans. H. Tomlinson. New York: Columbia University Press, 2006; and *Bergsonism*, trans. H. Tomlinson and B. Habberjam. New York: Zone Books, 1991.
33 Lonzi, C., *Sputiamo su Hegel*. Rome: Editoriale grafica, 1970.
34 Ibid.
35 Butler, J., and Athanasiou, A., *Dispossession: The Performative in the Political*. Cambridge: Polity, 2013.
36 Gago, V., *Neoliberalism from Below: Popular Pragmatics and Baroque Economies*. Durham, NC: Duke University Press, 2017.
37 At the peak of the Not One Less mobilization, as social networks, workplaces and public spaces buzzed with this phrase, other signs and notices began to appear, reading "Not Anyone Less," in an attempt to expand the demand to men as well and, in so doing, limit the specificity and feminist radicalism of the demand. I heard several young women respond with the same argument: we are constantly aware that it's risky for us to walk alone on the street, that we could get raped if there's no one around, that it's a bad idea to be alone with a group of guys, that if it's nighttime you have to let your friends or family know you got home safe. This risk as a permanent

condition is not experienced by males. Women are the ones who have to live with vulnerability and build strategies to deal with it.

38 Schettini, A., "Diarios del odio," *Otra parte*, 20 July 2017, www.revistaotraparte.com/semanal/teatro/diarios-del-odio/.

39 Giorgi, G., "La literatura y el odio: Escrituras públicas y guerras de subjetividad," *Transas: Letras y artes en América Latina*, 2018, www.researchgate.net/publication/324680693_La_literatura_y_el_odio_Escrituras_publicas_y_guerras_de_subjetividad.

40 Oberti, A., *Las revolucionarias: Militancia, vida cotidiana y afectividad en los 70*. Buenos Aires: Edhasa, 2015.

41 Calveiro, P., *Política y/o violencia: Una aproximación a la guerrilla de los años 70*. Buenos Aires: Norma, 2005, p. 97.

42 Moreno, analyzing a work by Héctor Schmucler, says that "the body of the popular activists of the seventies was conceived of as subservient to the political tactics," because the militant left had not contemplated the central questions of the links between people, the connection that each one has with their body, the relationship with nature. Moreno, M., "Prólogo," *Fiestas, baños y exilios: Los gays porteños en la última dictadura*, ed. F. Rapisardi and A. Modarelli. Buenos Aires: Sudamericana, 2001, p. 16.

43 Butler, J., *Notes Toward a Performative Theory of Assembly*. Cambridge, MA: Harvard University Press, 2015.

44 Rodrigues, C., "A Revolução Será Feminista," *Le Monde diplomatique Brasil*, 126, January 2018, www.diplomatique.org.br/edicao/edicao-126/.

45 González, H., "La mitad de un echarpe o un canto inconcluso," *Fin de siglo*, no. 3, September 1987.

46 The proletariat "appears in the first instance as the pure *object* of societal events." Lukács, *History and Class Consciousness Studies in Marxist Dialect*, trans. R. Livingstone. Cambridge, MA: MIT Press, 1984.

47 Laclau, E., *On Populist Reason*. London: Verso, 2005.

48 Federici, S., *Caliban and the Witch: Women, the Body and Primitive Accumulation*. Brooklyn, NY: Autonomedia, 2004.

49 Lesbian, Gay, Bisexual, Transgender, Queer, Intersex, Asexual.

50 A chant sung by the Frente de Mujeres (Women's front) of the Universidad Nacional de General Sarmiento, on 8 March 2018, responded to the use of these terms: "The Roman Catholic Apostolic Church / wants to get between our sheets. / We say no way, / we're all whores, lesbians and *travestis*."

51 Judith Butler, in an article published in *Folha de São Paulo* (21 November 2017), exposes gender construction and its political-democratic consequences. She situates the events as a series of violences against the autonomy of women and non-hegemonic

sexualities: from witch hunts to femicides: www.emergentes.com. ar/judith-butler-escribe-sobre-su-teor%C3%ADa-de-género-y-el-ataque-sufrido-en-brasil-1499e8252e1c. Another narration of these events: Bastos, M., "¿En qué siglo estamos?," *Página 12*, 17 November 2017, www.pagina12.com.ar/76352-en-que-siglo-estamos.

52 For Barthes, the tautology is a procedure of the myth, understood as the erasure of the historicity of social phenomena. Barthes, R., *Mythologies*, trans. A. Lavers. New York: Hill & Wang, 1972.

53 There are no reliable statistics on the multiplication of homelessness, but two immediate effects are known. One was a change in policy by banks, which began to lock spaces reserved for ATM machines so that the homeless could not sleep there. Additionally, a network of social organizations emerged to demand public policy solutions from the government.

54 Sexual diversity is not unanimously accepted. Noted cases of institutional violence exist. Lesbians have been arrested based on accusations that are nothing more than normalizing violence: one of them for killing out of self-defense while being raped; another jailed for kissing her partner in a train station. Added to this is the social violence systematically directed toward transgender persons and *travestis*. In June 2018, the first trial for travesticide was held for the murder of Diana Sacayan. In the first months of that year four *travestis* were murdered.

55 Sala is a controversial figure, even among leftist groups, because of the ways in which she built the Tupac Amaru organization, using authoritarian tactics. For more reading on Sala and her organization, see Dujovne Ortíz, A., *Milagro*. Buenos Aires: La Marea, 2018; Gaona, M., *Experiencia popular, ciudad e identidad en el noroeste argentino: La organización social Tupac Amaru de San Salvador de Jujuy*. Oxford: Peter Lang, 2017; Gómez Alcorta, E., "Justicia," *Presa: Un decálogo del caso Milagro Sala*, ed. D. Taitán. La Plata: EME, 2017.

56 Dora Barrancos writes:

> Without doubt the Tupac organization did much more than the Jujuy government during that time. [Milagro's] insolent defiance is measured in the degree to which she is vilified for the lack of honesty in her administration of the resources she helped distribute among indigenous peoples living in abject poverty. Governor Morales summed up his rage toward Milagro and the collective project she produced with the damning exclamation "They stole everything." This belies the fact that some players were left out of the construction business and that Tupac became a redistributive agency. (Barrancos, D., "Una defensa de Milagro Sala: Esa india," *Anfibia*, 2017, www.revistaanfibia.com/ensayo/esa-india/)

57   The abuse of judicial power for political ends is nothing new in our country, or in any other place in the world. Nevertheless, its use as a tool to destroy a political opponent has become, in recent times, a commonplace practice that extends from the judge's chambers of Comodoro Py to the dilapidated courthouses of Jujuy ... The expansion of the Jujuy Supreme Court of Justice from five to nine justices – and the appointment of two radically conservative judges to occupy those positions – and the creation of a new Public Prosecutor's Office, together with the appointment of an attorney general, all in less than a week after Morales took power, as well as the accusation of failure to fulfill functionary duties directed at the public prosecutor who did not initially charge Milagro, solidified the base of a judicial power adept in political control. (Gómez Alcorta, "Justicia," pp. 67–8.)

58 Ibid., p. 63.
59 Butler, J., *Gender Trouble: Feminism and the Subversion of Identity*. New York: Routledge, 1990.
60 Beauvoir, S. de, *The Second Sex*. New York: Knopf, 1953.
61 Federici, *Caliban and the Witch*, p. 152.
62 Abdo Ferez, C., and Rodríguez Rial, G., "Estas hembras que nos estropean todo el infinito," *Apuntes feministas sobre el lazo social, a partir del Ni una menos*, forthcoming.
63 Merleau-Ponty, M., *Phenomenology of Perception*. London: Routledge, 1974.
64 Merleau-Ponty, M., *The Visible and the Invisible*. Evanston, IL: Northwestern University Press, 1968.
65 In his last book he uses the term *flesh*: "We must not think the flesh starting from substances, from body and spirit – for then it would be the union of contradictories – but we must think it, as we said, as an element, as the concrete emblem of a general manner of being." Ibid., p. 147.
66 Theodor Adorno, in *Minima Moralia: Reflections on a Damaged Life* (trans. E. F. N. Jephcott. London: Verso Books, 2005, p. 63), debated what is seen as extortion of decreed happiness: "there is a straight line of development between the gospel of happiness and the construction of camps of extermination."
67 I allude to Spivak's classic question: "Can the subaltern speak?," which allows us to recall that the subaltern is always a relational category and not identitary, that the voice is not given, that this place of enunciation is problematic and functions as a rewriting. Spivak, G. C., *Can the Subaltern Speak?* Basingstoke: Macmillan, 1988.
68 An example of the multiple dimensions put into play: in 2017 a small collective emerged called Las nietas de Judith (Granddaughters of Judith) dedicated to gathering resources – food, clothes, school supplies – to support food kitchens in the area of San Miguel. The

Catholic Church has a strong influence in this region, and these types of charities were traditionally led by Christian activists. The members of Las nietas de Judith define themselves as feminists. Interviewed by a member of the group, they explain: we are the granddaughters of the witches that they couldn't burn (citing a chant repeated at the women's marches), and Judith is for Butler who taught us that gender is not something natural.

69 "The common as improper." Espósito, R., *Communitas: The Origin and Destiny of Community*, trans. T. Campbell. Stanford, CA: Stanford University Press, 2009.

70 Belucci, M., *Historia de una desobediencia*. Buenos Aires: Capital Intelectual, 2014; Carbajal, M., *El aborto en debate: Apuntes para una discusión pendiente*. Buenos Aires: Paidos, 2009.

71 Bilbao, B., Cuerpos y poder: Análisis de las experiencias y representaciones mediáticas de los feminismos situados en el presente argentino Buenos Aires (2003–2012), PhD dissertation, Universidad Nacional de Quilmes, 2018.

72 "Carta orgánica," *Ni una menos*.

73 Silvina Pascucci points to the presence of women in the organization and the defense against police repression and anarchist activism in the conflict. There were strikes in 750 *conventillos* and around 140,000 people participated. Pascucci, S., "La huelga de inquilinos de 1907," *Diario Crítica de la Argentina*, 17 August 2009, www.carteleradehistoria2.wordpress.com/2009/08/17/la-huelga-de-inqulinos-de-conventillos-de-1907-por-silvina-pascucci/. Bellucci, M., and Camusso, C., "La huelga de inquilinos de 1907: El papel de las mujeres anarquistas," *Cuadernos CICSO*, no. 58, 1987.

74 Lemebel, P., "Presagio dorado para un Santiago otoñal," *De perlas y cicatrices*. Santiago de Chile: Eslasandra Ediciones, 2013, p. 295.

75 Arguedas, J. M., *Los ríos profundos*. Lima: Estruendo mudo, 1958.

76 Certeau, M. de, Giard, L., and Mayol, P., *The Practice of Everyday Life*, Vol. 2: *Living and Cooking*. Minneapolis: University of Minnesota Press, 1998.

77 In the assemblies held to organize the international women's strikes in Buenos Aires – in 2017 and 2018 – some of the issues resolved were the shared document to be read, the list of people who would speak on stage – who would be visible – and the order in which the organizations would march. Later, conflicts emerged: misunderstandings over what had been decided, routines for occupying the street that went against what had been agreed upon. Nevertheless, the constructive power of the assemblies is undeniable.

78 The assembly held in the tent set up by workers who had been made redundant by PepsiCo. occurred on 26 July 2017. Bajar,

S., "Asamblea #NiUnaMenos por PepsiCo: 'Algo muy grande que está por nacer,'" *La izquierda diario*, 27 July 2017, www. laizquierdadiario.com/Asamblea-NiUnaMenos-por-PepsiCo-Algo-muy-grande-que-esta-por-nacer.

79 On 24 September 2017 an assembly was held among a handful of feminist organizations in Patagonia, demanding the appearance of Santiago Maldonado, alive (his body appeared a month later, on 17 October). Dillon, M., "Asamblea Ni Una Menos," *Página 12*, 25 September 2017, www.pagina12.com. ar/64978-asamblea-ni-una-menos.

80 On 8 December 2017 a group of feminist organizations mobilized in Jujuy to demand release of the members of Tupac Amaru held as political prisoners and convened an assembly called Jallalla (www.tiempoar.com.ar/nota/miles-de-mujeres-agitaron-las-calles-de-jujuy-por-la-libertad-de-milagro-sala).

81 Dilma Rousseff led Brazil between 2011 and 2016, when she was unseated by an institutional coup. In Chile, Michelle Bachelet governed from 2006 to 2010 and, in a second term, from 2014 to 2018. Cristina Fernández de Kirchner was president of Argentina for two consecutive terms between 2007 and 2015 (www.pagina12. com.ar/diario/suplementos/las12/13-10228-2015-12-16.html).

82 Camila Vallejo in Chile (born 1988) and Manuela D'Avila in Brazil (born 1981) emerged from student activism to become well-known members of parliament in their countries. In Peru, Verónika Mendoza (1980) lost by a hair.

83 The government of Dilma Rousseff was harshly criticized. Her predecessor, Lula da Silva, had built a program for distribution of resources inscribed in a development strategy that benefited everyone. Rousseff, from the same party, aimed to combat the financial crisis by adding business leaders to her cabinet and was challenged by a large popular movement. Nevertheless, the reasons for her impeachment seem to belong to the Latin American tradition of coups, which starts off claiming that the problem is corruption or guilt for some crime and ends up appealing to traditional values of family and military life. The evangelical bench of parliament, made up of leaders of the conservative restoration, was central to the coup. Dominzain, J. M., and González, D., "La caída'," *Anfibia*, 2018, www.revistaanfibia.com/cronica/la-caida/; de Gainza, M., and Peres, I., "Pelea entre blancos," *Anfibia*, 2018, www.revistaan-fibia.com/ensayo/pelea-entre-blancos/.

84 In 2009 the Integral Law to Prevent, Sanction and Eradicate Violence against Women was passed. A year later the Marriage Equality Law passed (opening the institution of marriage to include people of the same sex). In 2012 the Gender Identity Law was

passed. Years earlier, the Sexual Health and Reproduction Law and the Integral Sexual Education Law were passed. These laws constitute a legal repertoire that emerged from the demands of the movements for diversity and feminism, which found an unusual receptivity in those years.

85 The Ministry for Women, Racial Equality and Human Rights was eliminated by the government of Michel Temer as soon as he took power.

86 The Hambre Cero (Zero Hunger) program was put in place by Lula da Silva's government in 2003. According to official figures, 3 million persons were able to rise out of poverty as a result of its implementation (www.fao.org/3/a-i3023s.pdf).

87 The Asignación Universal por Hijo (AUH; Universal Assistance per Child) program was created in 2009 by the Argentine government. It provides social security assistance to children under eighteen whose parents earn less than the minimum living wage or who are unemployed or work in the informal economy. In 2017, more than 4 million beneficiaries received the subsidy. For information on the reach and limitations of the program, see www.unicef.org/argentina/informes/análisis-y-propuestas-de-mejora-para-ampliar-la-asignación-universal-por-hijo.

88 The Ellas Hacen (Women Do) program was created in 2013 and targeted women in vulnerable situations. In order to qualify, the woman had to be a head of household, unemployed, live in a slum, and have children under the age of eighteen and/or with disabilities who were enrolled in the AUH. Among the program's objectives were educational initiatives that would allow the beneficiaries to earn a high-school diploma: training and the acquisition of cooperative tools with a gendered perspective.

89 Margarita Barrientos, social activist of indigenous origin, became central to the right wing's communication and publicity campaign. She is presented as a non-political activist who merely hands out food. President Mauricio Macri visits the Los piletones food kitchen every Christmas and has done so since his time as mayor of the city of Buenos Aires. In the media treatment of the issue, Barrientos is presented as the antithesis of Milagro Sala, as a non-confrontational leader who merely provides social assistance.

90 The governor of the province of Buenos Aires, María Eugenia Vidal, constructed her public image around traditional family values, with explicit public statements against the rights of women. In the debate over the legalization of abortion, she declared herself in favor of maintaining penalization. In her campaign publicity, she is repeatedly portrayed in domestic scenes: buying groceries at the supermarket or toys for her children.

91 *Yegua* (nag, female horse) is used in the Argentine variety of Spanish as a derogatory term for a woman.

92 For example, in 2012, the magazine *Noticias* ran the headline "Cristina's pleasure": "El goce de Cristina," *Perfil.com*, 7 September 2012, http://noticias.perfil.com/2012/09/07/el-goce-de cristina. In 2015, the same magazine published as its cover art an illustration of the president being burned at the stake: "El pacto para que Cristina no vuelva nunca más," *Perfil.com*, 15 December 2015, http://noticias.perfil.com/2015/12/17/ el-pacto-para-que-cristina-no-vuelva-nunca-mas/.

93 The Gender Equality Law had already received partial parliamentary approval, but it was not on the agenda for the last session of the Deputies Chambre in 2017. The consensus among female deputies of all the blocks of parliament forced its incorporation into the agenda, and it was approved by an ample majority.

94 Castellanos Llanos, G., "Los estilos de género y la tiranía de los binarismos: De por qué necesitamos el concepto de géneroleceto," *Aljaba*, 20 December 2016, www.scielo.org.ar/scielo. php?script=sci_arttext&pid=S1669-57042016000100006.

95 Arendt, H., *The Human Condition*. Chicago: University of Chicago Press, 1958.

96 Butler, *Notes Toward a Performative Theory of Assembly*.

97 In the town of Moreno, in the province of Buenos Aires, in 2013, a state maternity clinic was created with humanized birthing practices. Women in labor may decide their birthing position and the moment they will be separated from their child. At the same clinic safe abortions are carried out, with pills. The institution is called Estela de Carlotto, in homage to the president of the Grandmothers of the Plaza de Mayo. It is an example of the modes in which feminists may offer ideas and strategies for use in public institutions. The directors who had been fundamental to the development of this maternity clinic and its installation among the women who lived in the area were replaced in 2017 (www. anccom.sociales.uba.ar/2016/11/22/mujeres-respetadas/; NB: URL no longer active).

98 Gilly, A., *The Mexican Revolution*. New York: New Press, 2006.

Chapter 5 Modes of Appearing

1 The International Feminist Collective is a network of organizations from different countries that defines itself as

a coalition of movements, networks, collectives, persons and organizations that promotes campaigns and strengthens actions of the feminist struggle around the world. As the Zapatista women said in their call to protest on 8 March: rage, rebelliousness and respect nourish forms of autonomy, non-submission and revolt in different parts of the world. We say that desire moves us: it's a desire to join as sisters in the active search for dignity for everyone and for our territories, in defense of life and Mother Earth against capitalist violence. We are driven by the desire for revolution. (www.facebook.com/nosotrasparamos/)

2 Spivak, G., *Can the Subaltern Speak? Reflections on the History of an Idea*, ed. R. C. Morris. New York: Columbia University Press, 2010.
3 The manifesto "Nosotras proponemos" (We propose), a feminist intervention in the artistic field, names and at the same time attempts to invoke these problems – for example, "gay misogyny" (www.nosotrasproponemos.org/nosotras/).
4 Abdo Ferez, C., "¿Cómo evidenciar políticamente la(s) violencia(s)? ¿En qué política? (Para un spinocismo feminista)," *Figuras del discurso III*, 2018, p. 7.

5   Magenta shines again and is a celebration of itself. It is a pure color, even without being a primary one; an unsaturated color that cannot be reproduced on a single wavelength. ... Together we collectively appropriate girlie-pink and we turn it into something dangerous, disruptive. Threatening the patriarchy, insolent and autonomous. The color that was conceived of as normalizing, classifying toys and genders, calming to feminine moods and indicator of softness, appears now, by collective action, as shrill, irreverent, and disruptive. Barbie meets Chuckie. ("El arco y el iris," *Lobo suelto*, 2018; www.lobosuelto.com/?p=20525)

6 Wittig, M., *The Straight Mind and Other Essays*. Boston: Beacon Press, 2002.
7 "We have all gathered together, women, lesbians, trans, and feminized bodies of the world to propagate the virus of non-submission." "Manifiesto: La marea no se detiene: #NosotrasParamos," *Ni una menos*, 21 August 2018, www.niunamenos.org.ar/manifiestos/la-marea-no-se-detienenosotrasparamos/.
8 Gramsci, A., *Prison Notebooks*, Vol. II, ed. And trans. J. A. Buttigieg. New York: Columbia University Press, 1996.
9 Lauría, D., "Latinoamericano," *Untref*, 2017, www.untref.edu.ar/diccionario/agregar.php.
10 Heller, A., *Sociología de la vida cotidiana*. Barcelona: Península, 1977.
11 "We had to wait until the twenty-third edition (in 2014) of the Dictionary before they eliminated meanings such as 'weak, unstable' associated with 'feminine,' and for acceptance of terms adapted from

the social reality such as 'presidenta.' But the Dictionary continues to harbor sexist definitions, such as the well-known case of 'hysteria' – 'more common in women than in men,' as the dictionary reads still today, against all medical criteria." Remacha, B., "La curiosa misoginia de la RAE," *El diario*, 5 April 2016, www.eldiario.es/cultura/RAE-institucion-tradicionalmente-misogina_0_502200361.html. Bazán, J., "Real Academia Española: mujeres 'fáciles', 'sexo débil' y el abecé del machismo," *La izquierda diario*, 30 January 2018, www.laizquierdadiario.com/Real-Academia-Espanola-mujeres-faciles-sexo-debil-y-el-abece-del-machismo.

12 González, H., "Ni una menos: reinvención de lo político," *Nuestras voces*, 4 February 2017, www.nuestrasvoces.com.ar/a-vos-te-creo/una-menos-reinvencion-la-politica/.

13 Burneo Salazar, C., "El lenguaje inclusivo es un peligro y una posibilidad," *Letras libres*, 7 August 2018, www.letraslibres.com/espana-mexico/cultura/el-lenguaje-inclusivo-es-un-peligro-y-una-posibilidad.

14 "Manifiesto 1," *Ni una menos*, 3 June 2015, www.niunamenos.org.ar/manifiestos/3-de-junio-2015/.

15 "Manifiesto 4," *Ni una menos*, 19 October 2016, www.niuna-menos.org.ar/manifiestos/nosotras-paramos/.

16 "Manifiesto 8M 2018," *Ni una menos*, 9 March 2018, www.niuna-menos.org.ar/manifiestos/8m-2018/.

17 "Manifiesto 4," *Ni una menos*, 19 October 2016.

18 "Manifiesto: La marea no se detiene. #NosotrasParamos," *Ni una menos*, 21 August 2018.

19 Rita Segato analyzes, in the context of the debate over the femicide of Micaela García, the complexities of this appropriation: www.paginajudicial.com/rita-segato-"el-garantismo"-y-el-sentido-comun-los-jueces (NB: URL no longer active). The position of Not One Less was to say no to the punitive demogogy and support of misogyny.

20 In 2018, the G-20 summit was held in Argentina. The women who organized the W-20 were a female deputy – in a government that had cut funding to public education and retirement – and a female leader of agribusiness who was involved in a dispute with rural economies. They declared the objective of the forum to be the economic support and empowerment of women and the taking on of financial responsibilities by women in popular sectors, displacing issues related to the effective reproduction of life and autonomy for all women: www.infobae.com/sociedad/2017/12/11/se-lanza-el-women-20-la-agenda-de-crecimiento-inclusivo-y-el-desarrollo-equitativo-del-g20/.

21 For a journalistic analysis of the "commodity feminist," see "La

sororidad está de moda: El feminismo pop de Chanel," *La marea*, 9 April 2015, www.lamarea.com/2015/04/09/la-sororidad-esta-de-moda-el-feminismo-pop-de-chanel/.

22 Volóshinov, V., *Marxism and the Philosophy of Language*. Cambridge, MA: Harvard University Press, 1986. While this book was published by Volóshinov, it is attributed to his mentor Mikhail Bakhtin. The book's Spanish translator states that the issue of authorship is still unresolved.

23 This YouTube video shows the ad campaign for the perfume Purple, plastered across subway platforms near the university: "Campaña en Subte: United Colors of Benetton," *Grupo Vía*, 2017, www. youtube.com/watch?v=0tdyf0aAV18. Steps away was the morgue where the autopsy of the murdered activist was being carried out: www.pagina12.com.ar/73241-una-intervencion-por-santiago.

24 The action was called "United Killers of Benetton," *Anred*, 1 November 2017, www.anred.org/?p=69828.

25 Rey, S., "Fuera, indio," *Anfibia*, 2017, www.revistaanfibia.com/cronica/fuera-indio/.

26 "Cómo operan los trolls que atacan a la familia de Santiago Maldonado," *La vaca*, 11 October 2017, www.lavaca.org/notas/como-operan-los-trolls-que-atacan-a-la-familia-de-santiago-mal-donado/.

27 "Santiago Maldonado," *Ni una menos*, 1 September 2017, www.niunamenos.org.ar/noticia-abajo-home/santiago-maldonado/.

28 Reguillo, R., *Paisajes insurrectos: Jóvenes, redes y revueltas en el otoño civilizatorio*. Barcelona: Ediciones NED, 2017.

29 The *Latfem* portal (www.latfem.org), the journals *Virginia Bolten* (www.virginiabolten.com.ar), *Diario digital femenino* (www.diariofemenino.com.ar), *Oleada* (www.oleada.com.ar), the radio Futurock, with explicitly feminist programming, were added to existing publications such as the fundamental supplement "Las 12" of the newspaper *Página 12*. They also expanded and consolidated the networks of female journalists: Periodistas de Argentina en Red por una Comunicación No Sexista (Female Journalists of Argentina in Network for Non-Sexist Communication) and Red Internacional de Periodistas con Visión de Género (International Network of Female Journalists with a Gender Perspective).

30 Aubenas, F., and Benasayag, M., *La fabrication de l'information: Les journalistes et l'idéologie de la communication*. Paris: La Découverte, 1999.

31 The Occupy Wall Street movement emerged in 2011 as tens of thousands of people took to the streets against submission to an economy driven by corporate finance. Lawrence, J., "The international roots of the 99% and the 'politics of anyone,'" *IC: Revista*

científica de información y comunicación, http://institucional.us.es/
revistas/comunicacion/10/8-68-2-PB.pdf.

32 The Nuit Debout movement began as the occupation of the Place de la
République in Paris on 31 March 2016 in order to challenge the reform
of labor laws. It spread to many cities, as a horizontal movement
without leaders. Pulgar Pinaud, C., "Nuit Debout: occupation des
places, convergence des luttes et droit à la ville en France," *Citego.
org*, 2016, www.citego.org/bdf_fiche-document-1099_fr.html.

33 On 26 September 2014, a conflict with graduate students in Iguala,
Mexico, ended with six dead, two seriously wounded and forty-
three disappeared. The students had been intercepted on their
way to a demonstration. Levels of political violence and crimes
related to drug trafficking are very high in Mexico, so that violence
is now conceived as normal. This was broken by the case of the
students, which awakened a campaign of demands for transparency
concerning what had happened. González Rodríguez, S., *Los 43
de Iguala, México: Verdad y reto de los estudiantes desaparecidos.*
Barcelona: Anagrama, 2015.

34 After the first #3J, the feminist tide has not ceased to grow, and each
one of the subsequent calls to march exploded on social media: the
#7N march in Spain; #24A march in Mexico were accompanied
by a virtual action in which almost 100,000 women participated
by posting the hashtag #MiPrimerAcoso [My first harassment]; the
#1J march in Brazil was based in the influential #PrimeiroAssédio
and #EstuproNaoECulpaDaVitima movements; the #3J 2016 in
Argentina. On 13 August of that year "Not One Less Peru" was
created. On 3 October in Poland there was a strike against the
criminalization of abortion. On 19 October 2016 the first women's
strike in Argentina occurred. On #26N in Italy "Non Una Di Meno"
was held. In 2017 the Women's March inaugurated the Trump era
on 21 January and the #8M International Women's Strike was held
in more than 50 countries around the world. (Alcaraz, M., "Ni Una
Menos: politizar el uso de las tecnologías," *GenderIT.org*, 2017,
www.genderit.org/es/feminist-talk/edicion-especial-ni-una-menos-
politizar-el-uso-de-las-tecnolog).

35 "At what point did the Not One Less march become a political
action? They forgot to defend the most important thing – women,"
said Diego Poggi, social network columnist with the station TN,
which led the criticism of the massive and diverse feminist march
as if politics would sully its tide of messages. Peker, L., "El runrún
que deja la ola Ni Una Menos," *Página 12*, 5 June 2017, www.
pagina12.com.ar/42213-el-runrun-que-deja-la-ola-ni-una-menos.
Systematic campaigns with this message appear on the Not One
Less Facebook page.

36 A mainstream journalist in a hegemonic media outlet – Jorge Lanata, in the newspaper *Clarín* – maintains that the movement takes advantage of women by first presenting fair demands (femicide is intolerable) only to then link them to unjust political demands (such as the release of political prisoners): www.clarin.com/opinion/causa-convocante-cortocircuitos_0_By0d46uM-.html.

37 See, for example, the coverage of the first international women's strike, on 8 March 2017, in the newspaper with the largest readership: www.clarin.com/sociedad/incidentes-frente-catedral-marcha-dia-mujer_0_ByiWIMCql.html. The photos chosen and the sequence of events narrated omitted the careful construction of the mobilization, its massive turnout, the process that made it posible.

38 With the exception of the *Buenos Aires Herald*, the press silenced the crimes of state-sponsored terrorism, in some cases even allowing intelligence services to dictate how the news would be reported. Blaustein, E., *Decíamos Ayer: La prensa argentina bajo el Proceso*. Buenos Aires: Ediciones Colihue, 1998.

39 Verbitsky, H., *Rodolfo Walsh y la prensa clandestina*. Buenos Aires: Ediciones La urraca, 1985.

40 For example, one city councilwoman used the expressions "The message has been contaminated," "They are the ones who politicized it – it has nothing to do with gender violence or the IMF or the payment of debt. They corrupted everything, they don't play clean, they don't represent me." A before and after were marked. An initial moment in which the struggle was limited to legitimate demands and a later moment in which these demands were supposedly manipulated: "Buzzini cuestionó la 'politización' de la marcha 'Ni una menos,'" *La auténtica defensa*, 2018 (www.laautenticadefensa.net/149915). Some of the mothers of the victims of femicide opposed the use of the slogan Not One Less for the legalization of abortion. One of them stated: "Chiara was fourteen, she was pregnant, and the Not One Less was started for her. In that first Not One Less march I felt like I belonged, because it wasn't political or sectorial or religious, and because everyone participated: women, men and children." They recorded a video that went viral and was rebroadcast by media outlets as part of the strategy to condemn the misappropriation of the movement: (www.infobae.com/sociedad/2018/06/03/madres-del-ni-una-menos-piden-que-no-se-relacione-la-marcha-a-la-ley-del-aborto-es-una-contradiccion/).

41 Not only in the media discourse. The current government constructs dichotomous messages, which counter the spontaneous mobilizations (carried out in defense of government policies) and those involving participants who have been bussed in, motivated by the handing out of food (*choripan*). Castilla, E., "Colectivos y choripanes: La

radicalización gorila del discurso de Cambiemos," *La izquierda diario*, 2 April 2017, www.laizquierdadiario.com/Colectivos-y-choripanes-la-radicalizacion-gorila-del-discurso-de-Cambiemos. The image of the bus paid for by a social or political organization to transport protesters from locations far from the site of the demonstration is held up as proof that these persons have not mobilized of their own will. In the mobilizations of the sectors that support conservative policies, it is often said "I came here by my own means."

42 Himitian, E., "Ni Una Menos: Un reclamo masivo que se fracturó," *La nación*, 4 June 2018, www.lanacion.com.ar/2140888-ni-una-menos-un-reclamo-masivo-que-se-fracturo.

43 Borelli, J., "Operaciones 3.0: Cómo trabaja el ejército de trolls que busca incidir en la opinión pública," *Tiempo argentino*, 2 January 2018, www.tiempoar.com.ar/nota/operaciones-30-como-trabaja-el-ejercito-de-trolls-que-busca-incidir-en-la-opinion-publica.

44 Vollenweider, C., "Movimiento de mujeres y agenda política en Argentina," *Celag.org*, 10 June 2018, www.celag.org/movimiento-mujeres-agenda-politica-argentina/.

45 The governor of the province of Buenos Aires appeals to the phrase "Not one less" as she simultaneously vetoes protocol for non-punishable abortion and declares herself to be against the legalization of abortion. She takes a scalpel to the phrase, isolating it from the context in which the feminist mobilizations created it. "Dura carta del colectivo Ni Una Menos a Vidal por dejar 'desamparadas a las bonaerenses,'" *Políticargentina.com*, 28 October 2016, www.politicargentina.com/notas/201610/17435-dura-carta-del-colectivo-ni-una-menos-a-vidal-por-dejar-desamparadas-a-las-bonaerenses.html.

46 Adorno, T., *The Jargon of Authenticity*, trans. K. Tarnowski and F. Will. Evanston, IL: Northwestern University Press, 1973.

47 Berger, J., *Confabulations*. New York: Penguin Random House, 2016.

48 "Carta orgánica," *Ni una menos*, 3 June 2017, www.niunamenos.org.ar/quienes-somos/carta-organica/.

49 Marcela Lagarde analyzes the construction of this statement as historical maceration: "Countless women have been building for at least two centuries our gender identity, the mark of our specific human condition. To bestow the word woman with a history up to now silenced and belittled by misogyny, we have resignified it and made it necessary to all comprehensive discourse." "El castellano, una lengua de caballeros," *Mujeres en red*, www.nodo50.org/mujeresred/marcela_lagarde-elcastellano.html.

50 Virno, P., *A Grammar of the Multitude: For an Analysis of Contemporary Forms of Life*. Cambridge, MA: Semiotext(e), 2003.

51 Benjamin, W., "The Work of Art in the Age of Mechanical Reproduction," *Illuminations*, ed. H. Arendt, trans. H. Zohn. New York: Schocken Books, [1968] 2011, pp. 217–51.

52 MAFIA is a collective of independent photographers that emerged in 2012: www.somosmafia.com/wp/quienes-somos/. They are also key to the production of images that are shared internationally. See their interesting portfolio of 8 March images, called "Poderosas," which compiles images from different countries: www.somosmafia. com/wp/portfolio/genero/poderosas/.

53 Emergentes is a communication collective, established in 2015. It develops collaborative coverage and has a special section dedicated to feminism: www.emergentes.com.ar/feminismos/home.

54 "Ni una menos: A un mes del 3 de junio," *Página 12*, 3 July 2015, www.pagina12.com.ar/diario/suplementos/las12/13-9876-2015-07-07.html.

55 This is the main political square in the country. Surrounded by the government headquarters, the cathedral, the cabildo, where the process of independence began, and the Ministry of the Economy, it is the point where demands and conflicts merge. Lerman, G., *La plaza política: Irrupciones, vacíos y regresos en Plaza de mayo*. Buenos Aires: Colihue, 2005.

56 The mobilizations of 24 March are articulated, each year, with new meanings, renew the conflicts and struggles of each specific moment. In recent years, there has also been a zone of feminist reinterpretation. Korol, C., "Un 24 de marzo internacionalista y feminista," *Marcha*, 24 March 2018, www.marcha.org.ar/un-24-de-marzo-internacionalista-feminista-hasta-la-libertad-siempre/.

57 Amati, M., Díaz, S., and Jait, A., "Memoria, ritual y performance en las conmemoraciones nacionales del 'pasado reciente' en Argentina: El 24 de marzo y el 2 de abril," *Academia*, 2013, www.academia. edu/10624165/Memoria_ritual_y_performance_en_las_conmemoraciones_nacionales_del_pasado_reciente_en_Argentina_el_24_de_marzo_y_el_2_de_abril.

58 The Argentine Pride marches began in 1992 and occur on the first Saturday of November. Different to the majority of mobilizations, the marches don't end in the Plaza de Mayo but start from there and march to Congress. Attendance and street presence has increased annually (www.marchadelorgullo.org.ar).

59 DaMatta, R., *Carnivals, Rouges, and Heroes: An Interpretation of the Brazilian Dilemma*. Notre Dame, IN: Notre Dame Press, 1991.

60 Bakhtin, M., *Rabelais and His World*, trans. H. Iswolsky. Bloomington: Indiana University Press, 2009.

61 Many activists, as part of the mobilization ritual, expose their breasts or their torso for at least some parts of the march.

62 "Yuta" is a colloquial term for the police. It originates from lunfardo. The phrase "Ni yuta ni tuya" could translate as "Not a cop and not yours" and speaks against both police repression and machista possessiveness.

63 James, D., and Wolfson, L., "17 y 18 de octubre de 1945: El peronismo, la protesta de masas y la clase obrera Argentina," *Desarrollo económico*, 27/107 (1987), pp. 445–61.

64 DaMatta, *Carnivals, Rouges, and Heroes.*

65 Ibid.

66 These are annual meetings of exchange, reflection and mobilization. The first was held in 1986 and attracted a thousand women. In recent years the number of attendees has exceeded 60,000. The organizing commission explains: "The modality of the National Women's Conference is like nothing else anywhere in the world, and that allows us each year to include thousands more: it is self-summoning, horizontal, federal, self-financed, plural and profoundly democratic" (www.encuentrodemujeres.com.ar/historia-del-encuentro/).

67 *Colectivo Varones Antipatriarcales*, www.colectivovaronesantipatriarcales.blogspot.com.

68 "Arte Urgente: encuentro de activistas y colectivos artísticos en el Espacio Memoria," 10 September 2017, http://correos.espaciomemoria.gov.ar/noticia.php?not_ID=1064&barra=noticias &titulo=noticia.

69 The artists who promoted the initiative were Rodolfo Aguerreberry, Julio Flores and Guillermo Kexel.

70 Longoni, A., and Bruzzone, G. (eds), *El siluetazo*. Buenos Aires: Adriana Hidalgo, 2008, p. 8.

71 In 2001 there occurred a double crisis in Argentina, both political and financial. In December of that year, a series of economic measures included the retention of personal savings held in banks. The measure was called, colloquially, the *corralito*, as if there were a "little fence" that kept people from accessing their money. The economic crisis was profound, evident in the levels of unemployment and poverty, but reached a tipping point for financial reasons. This gave way to a popular revolt, which ignored martial law, on 19 and 20 of December, days which saw lootings, assemblies, mobilizations, neighborhood meals. And this continued over the months that followed.

72 Grupo de Arte Callejero: www.grupodeartecallejero.wordpress. com.

73 "*Invasion* was carried out in December 2001, hours before the popular rebellion on 19 December and the fall of the government of President Fernando De la Rua. The action consisted of throwing 10,000 toy soldiers tied to parachutes from a building in the city

center, the dolls floating to the ground at the entrances of financial institutions and surprising pedestrians." "G.A.C. – Grupo de Arte Callejero," 1997, www.cvaa.com.ar/03biografias/grupo_arte_callejero.php.

74 After the president's speech announcing martial law, a protest began in residential sectors, and people marched toward the National Congress to shouts of "Stick your martial law up your bum."

75 The Etcétera group carried out several interventions in 2001 connected to human rights and the defense of the right to civil protest: www.cvaa.com.ar/03biografias/etcetera_grupo.php. In 2003 the Mujers Publicas collective was formed, which defined itself as a feminist group of visual activism. They continue to carry out powerful interventions: www.mujerespublicas.com.ar. Eduardo Molinari reconstructs a complex and mobile map of collectives. To GAC and Etcétera, he adds Escombros, Cero Barrado, Cimarrón, ABTE, Mondongo and others considered bizarre: "People who do whatever they want, without any pre-established formula." Molinari, E., "Arte y política a la luz del sol," *El siluetazo*, ed. Longoni and Bruzzone.

76 See www.mujeresdeartestomar.org.

77 See www.facebook.com/Aúlla-350703305115437/.

78 See www.augelasmariposas.wordpress.com/manifiesto.

79 This collective carries out actions in Rosario on dates important to the feminist struggle (8 March, 3 June, 25 November). It does not speak out publicly and maintains a provisional name.

80 The collective doesn't have its own webpage, but some videos of its interventions have been posted: see www.vimeo.com/165040677/.

81 See www.resquiciocolectivo.wixsite.com/website.

82 Mujeres de Artes Tomar defines itself as a "collective of artists that proposes artistic actions to celebrate life, trying to link collective and personal transformation."

83 See www.nosotrasproponemos.org. One of the main promoters of the movement is the art critic and curator Andrea Giunta. The manifesto received more than 2,700 signatures before the signing period was closed.

84 Around 8 March, a series of interventions were carried out in art museums in Buenos Aires, Entre Ríos, Neuquén, Santa Fe, Salta, San Luis, Córdoba, La Rioja, Mendoza, Santiago del Estero, Tucumán and Misiones to highlight the lack of works by female artists on display (www.nosotrasproponemos.org/8m2018-acciones/).

85 See www.pagina12.com.ar/98547-y-ahora-que-estamos-juntas.

86 The names (Mothers of Plaza de Mayo, Grandmothers of Plaza de Mayo, HIJOS [Children]) indicate family relationships, but the movement is not limited to people with personal connections. The

Mothers made an early and marked effort to welcome all supporters into the organization. HIJOS (established in the mid-1990s), in addition to demanding policies linked to memory, truth and justice, aimed to recover the revolutionary tradition of their parents' generation. Diana Taylor makes an interesting analysis of the differences between the public interventions of the different groups. Taylor, D. "'You Are Here': The DNA of Performance," *Drama Review*, 46/1 (2002), pp. 149–69.

87 Fuentes, M., "Performance, política y protesta," in *What Is Performance Studies?*, ed. D. Taylor and M. Steuernagel. Durham, NC: Duke University Press, 2015 (https://scalar.usc.edu/nehvectors/wips/performance-poltica-y-protesta).

88 For 8 March 2017, the percussion group of the state workers' syndicate (ATE) changed the lyrics to the popular song "Despacito" by Luis Fonzi, a song that was very popular at the time. The recordings went viral. The version was known as "the Not One Less song" (https://noticias.perfil.com/2017/05/30/niunamenos-ya-tiene-su-version-de-despacito/).

89 Taylor, D., and Fuentes, M., *Estudios avanzados de performance*. México: Fondo de Cultura Económica, 2011, p. 19.

90 Bergson, H., *Matter and Memory*, trans. N. M. Paul and W. S. Plamer. New York: Zone Books, 1990.

91 Treibel, G., "Arte es libertad," *Página 12*, 10 March 2018, www.pagina12.com.ar/100507-arte-es-libertad.

92 At the same time, the entertainment and marketing industries attempted to translate the force of feminist invention into a commercial resource. The Nike campaign "Juntas imparables" (Together unstoppable) appropriates marching, rebellion and celebration as advertising elements (www.elmostrador.cl/noticias/multimedia/2018/09/07/juntas-imparables-la-campana-de-nike-que-se-cuadra-con-el-movimiento-feminista-en-america-latina/).

Provisional Epilogue

1 The national campaign for the right to abortion was launched in 2005 and presented its plan for legalization before the National Congress eight times. The plan was reviewed by parliament for the first time in 2018. *Campaña Nacional por el Derecho al Aborto Legal Seguro y Gratuito*: www.abortolegal.com.ar.

2 In this interview, Ofelia Fernández, activist in the high-school students' movement, clearly explains this strand of activism and its aims: www.youtube.com/watch?v=6Isni9a7w6E.

3 The occupations began in mid-April 2018 and extended to

thirty-two establishments. They demanded non-sexist education and an end to abuses against women. See www.latercera.com/tendencias/noticia/feminismo-chileno-vive-revolucion-mas-importante-40-anos/172111/.

4 See www.theclinic.cl/2018/05/14/usted-vino-dar-una-prueba-oral-la-ordenen-alumnas-derecho-la-uc-firman-carta-supuesto-machismo/.

5 Davis, A., *Freedom Is a Constant Struggle: Ferguson, Palestine, and the Foundations of a Movement*. Chicago: Haymarket Books, 2016.

Index